The Coming of
NEO
Feudalism

A WARNING TO THE GLOBAL MIDDLE CLASS

JOEL KOTKIN

Encounter
BOOKS

New York • London

First American edition published in 2020 by Encounter Books,
an activity of Encounter for Culture and Education, Inc.,
a nonprofit, tax-exempt corporation.
Encounter Books website address: www.encounterbooks.com

Manufactured in the United States and printed on
acid-free paper. The paper used in this publication meets
the minimum requirements of ANSI/NISO Z39.48-1992
(R 1997) (*Permanence of Paper*).

FIRST AMERICAN EDITION

LIBRARY OF CONGRESS CATALOGING-IN-PUBLICATION DATA

Names: Kotkin, Joel, author.
Title: The coming of neo-feudalism : a warning
to the global middle class / by Joel Kotkin.
Description: First American edition. | New York : Encounter Books, [2020]
Includes bibliographical references and index.
Identifiers: LCCN 2019044952 (print) | LCCN 2019044953 (ebook)
ISBN 9781641770941 (cloth) | ISBN 9781641770958 (ebook)
Subjects: LCSH: Social classes—History—21st century.
Distribution (Economic theory)—History—21st century.
Social history—21st century.
Classification: LCC HT609 .K68 2020 (print) | LCC HT609 (ebook)
DDC 305.509/05—dc23
LC record available at https://lccn.loc.gov/2019044952
LC ebook record available at https://lccn.loc.gov/2019044953

To Mandy, who means everything to me

CONTENTS

PREFACE

This is a book neither of the right nor of the left. It is an attempt to diagnose trends that are leading to a more hierarchical and more stagnant society. It also stands as a warning to the global middle class. Although this die may be cast, I hope the book will stir discussion and spark action to halt the current trajectory toward neo-feudalism across much of the world.

As a lifetime Democrat, now Independent, I do not see this as an ideological or partisan issue. I believe that the vast majority of people, conservative as well as progressive, do not look forward to a future defined by class immobility and immense concentrations of both wealth and power. This is a global phenomenon that includes not just the United States but also the United Kingdom, Australia, Canada, most of continental Europe, and the rapidly advancing countries of East Asia.

Reporting from the ground—particularly in the United States, Australia, the UK, Singapore, India, and China—have done much to shape this book. But I have taken inspiration also from thinking about what the great analysts of the past—Alexis de Tocqueville, Karl Marx, Max Weber, Daniel Bell, Taichi Sakaiya, Alvin Toffler—would have made of the current situation.

The future that appears on the horizon is not one that I desire for any country, or for my own children. This book is meant to rally those who cherish the independence, freedom, and possibilities for upward mobility that have been the hallmarks of liberal democracy over the past few centuries.

PART I

How Feudalism Came Back

History never repeats itself. Man always does.

—Voltaire

CHAPTER 1

The Feudal Revival

Feudalism is making a comeback, long after it was believed to have been deposited into the historical dustbin. Of course it will look different this time around: we won't see knights in shining armor, or vassals doing homage to their lords, or a powerful Catholic Church enforcing the reigning orthodoxy. What we are seeing is a new form of aristocracy developing in the United States and beyond, as wealth in our postindustrial economy tends to be ever more concentrated in fewer hands. Societies are becoming more stratified, with decreasing chances of upward mobility for most of the population. A class of thought leaders and opinion makers, which I call the "clerisy," provide intellectual support for the emerging hierarchy. As avenues for upward mobility are diminishing, the model of liberal capitalism is losing appeal around the globe, and new doctrines are arising in its place, including ones that lend support to a kind of neo-feudalism.

Historically, feudalism was hardly a monolithic system, and it lasted much longer in some places than others. But certain salient features can be seen in feudal structures across medieval Europe: a strongly hierarchical ordering of society, a web of personal obligations tying subordinates to superiors, the persistence of closed classes or "castes," and a permanent serflike status for the vast majority of the population.[1] The few dominated the many as by natural right. Feudal governance was far more decentralized than either the Roman Empire that preceded it or the nation-states that followed, and it depended more on personal relationships than does liberal capitalism or statist socialism. But in the feudal era a static ideal of an ordered society, supported by a mandatory orthodoxy, prevailed over dynamism and mobility, in a condition of economic and demographic stagnation.

The clearest parallel in our own time is the concentration of wealth in fewer hands, following upon an era of robust social mobility. In the second half of the twentieth century, growing prosperity was widely shared in the developed world, with an expanding middle class and an upwardly mobile working class—something seen in many developing countries as well. Today, the benefits of economic growth in most countries are going mainly to the wealthiest segment of the population. One widely cited estimate suggests that the share of global wealth held by the top 0.1 percent of the global population increased from 7 percent in 1978 to 22 percent in 2012.[2] A recent British parliamentary study indicates that this global trend will continue: by 2030, the top 1 percent is expected to control two-thirds of the world's wealth.[3]

This wealth tends to be handed down from one generation to the next, creating something akin to a closed aristocracy. It may not have a legally privileged status or political power by right of inheritance, but its wealth can buy influence with government and over the culture. Thus we see an oligarchy emerging in supposedly democratic countries, with a neo-feudal aristocracy grafted onto a powerful central state.

As in the Middle Ages, the power and privilege of this oligarchy are supported by an influential cognitive elite, or what I call the clerisy. The term was coined by Samuel Taylor Coleridge, who envisioned a group of secular intellectuals guiding society with their knowledge, as the cultural role of the church waned. Today's clerisy are the people who dominate the global web of cultural creators, academia, the media, and even much of what remains of traditional religious institutions. They share many beliefs with the oligarchs—on globalism and the environment, for example—and spread them around to the wider population as a secular orthodoxy. But like the medieval clergy, they sometimes act as a check on the power of economic elites.

The clerisy and the oligarchy correspond to the medieval clergy and nobility—or the First Estate and Second Estate, as they came to be known in France. Beneath them are the vastly larger group corresponding to the "commoners" in the feudal era, or the Third Estate: those who were neither anointed nor ennobled. Today's Third Estate, which I call the "yeomanry," has two distinct parts. There is a property-owning middle class, analogous to the old English yeomanry but with the same spirit of independence transported into an urban or suburban context. Historically the yeomanry played a critical part in overturning the feudal order—but today their counterparts are being squeezed beneath the oligarchy. Second, there is a working class who are becoming more like medieval serfs, with diminishing chances of owning significant assets or improving their lot except with government transfers.

Although the two groups that constitute the Third Estate are falling behind, they can still pose a challenge to the oligarchs and the clerisy, as they are no longer quiescent in the face of globalism and technological obsolescence. We are seeing what one sociologist describes as "the defection of the working class" from a traditional allegiance to the political left, along with a simultaneous rejection of global capitalism and its cosmopolitan value structure.[4] Though the challenge to the oligarchy tends to come from the populist right, there are other forces that could attack from another direction, particularly younger workers and the less affluent portions of the clerisy, who together might form what one conservative writer has described as "a zombie army of anti-capitalists."[5] Even as a new feudalism appears to be setting in, it is stirring up counterforces that promise turbulent times.

History Also Regresses

History does not always move forward, to a more advanced or enlightened condition. The collapse of classical civilization is a case in point. That civilization had its cruel and unjust aspects, including the extensive use of slaves, but it also engendered cultural, civic, and economic dynamism that spread from the Near East to Spain, North Africa, and Britain. It developed a body of philosophy, law, and institutional forms that laid the basis of modern liberalism. But as classical civilization unraveled— from a combination of internal dysfunction and external pressure—its territories devolved into political disorder, cultural decline, and economic and demographic stagnation.

While we can put a date to the end of the Roman Empire in the West, the process of cultural decline extended over centuries. The backward trajectory is clear by the sixth or seventh century, in the demise of learning, the rise of religious fanaticism, the decline of cities and the collapse of trade, and Malthusian stagnation: Europe's population in the year 1000 was about the same as it had been a millennium earlier.[6] The formerly vibrant urban middle orders had faded away, and the class of landowning peasants shrank as agricultural land was consolidated into huge estates. Class relations became more rigidly hierarchical, with a hereditary nobility and powerful clerics at the top. These ruling classes often competed and fought among themselves, but they were distinctly privileged in comparison with most of the population, who would endure life as landless serfs. The ideal vision of society was static, and the aim was not to find new fields to plow, not to innovate or grow, but instead to maintain an equilibrium within a largely fixed system.[7]

In the second millennium, markets and towns began to grow again, craft guilds formed, philosophy and learning quickened. The Third Estate was rising: both rural smallholders and a prospering, literate bourgeoisie in the growing cities. With prosperity came a bigger public voice, and the Catholic Church and the nobility gradually lost power as a consequence. A system based on free markets, liberal values, and a belief in progress evolved in Europe and spread to North America and Oceania.

Like all social structures, the liberal order brought its own injustices. Most shamefully, slavery was revived and extended to newly colonized territories. In addition, the industrial revolution replaced cottage industries with factories and created an impoverished urban proletariat living at the very edge of subsistence. But during the twentieth century, especially after the Second World War, life became measurably better even for most of the working class, and the middle orders continued to grow in prosperity and numbers. Some government action came into play—for example, subsidizing homeownership, building new infrastructure, and permitting labor unions. Linking such policies to the engines of economic growth promoted a mass movement to affluence, the premier achievement of liberal capitalism.

Although liberal capitalism has generated many social, political, and environmental challenges, it has freed hundreds of millions from the widespread servility, entrenched cruelty, and capricious regimes that have dominated most of history. The material conditions of life have improved dramatically, not only in Europe and America but throughout much of the world. In the five hundred years up to around 1700, economic output per capita was flat, which means that a person of median income in 1700 was no better off, economically speaking, than the average person in 1200. By the mid-1800s, particularly in the West, economic output had increased markedly; the growth accelerated after 1940 and spread to the rest of the world.[8]

Bending the "Arc of History"

Liberal capitalism first fueled Western dominance, and then the economic rise of other countries as well. The economic boom that followed the end of the Second World War and extended to large parts of the world with the collapse of Communism nurtured confidence about the global future. The key to increasing prosperity appeared to be in our hands. Optimistic notions about an "arc of history" bending inexorably to greater prosperity and social justice were embraced on both right and left—for example, by President George W. Bush and by President Barack Obama.[9]

Beginning in the 1970s, the arc started bending backward in the regions that gave birth to capitalism and modern democracy—Europe, Australia, and North America. Upward mobility for the middle and working classes began to stall, while the fortunes of the upper classes rose dramatically. Economies kept growing, but most of the benefits were harvested by the very rich—the top 1 percent and especially the top 0.1 percent—while the middle classes lost ground.[10]

In 1945–1973, the top 1 percent in America captured just 4.9 percent of total U.S. income growth, but in the following two decades the richest 1 percent gobbled up the majority of U.S. growth.[11] The combined wealth of the richest four hundred Americans now exceeds the total wealth of 185 million of their fellow citizens.[12] In European countries, with their socialistic welfare policies, the upper middle class pays very high taxes while the wealthiest find ways to hide their income sufficiently to maintain and even increase their dominance. Surprisingly, in progressive-oriented countries such as Finland, stock ownership is considerably more concentrated among the very richest people than in the United States.

The trend is not only a Western one. In avowedly socialist China, for example, the top 1 percent of the population hold about one-third of the country's wealth, and roughly 1,300 individuals hold about 20 percent.

Since 1978, China's Gini coefficient, which measures inequality of wealth distribution, has tripled.[13] Globally, the ultra-rich are an emergent aristocracy. Fewer than one hundred billionaires together now own as much as half of the world's assets, the same proportion owned by around four hundred people a little more than five years ago.[14]

The concentration of wealth is also clear in property ownership. In the United States, the proportion of land owned by the one hundred largest private landowners grew by nearly 50 percent between 2007 and 2017, according to the *Land Report*. In 2007, this group owned a total of 27 million acres of land, equivalent to the area of Maine and New Hampshire combined; a decade later, the one hundred largest landowners held 40.2 million acres, more than the entire area of New England.[15] In much of the American West, billionaires have created vast estates that many fear will make the rest of the local population land-poor.[16]

Landownership in Europe too is becoming more concentrated in fewer hands. In Great Britain, where land prices have risen dramatically over the past decade, less than 1 percent of the population owns half of all the land. On the continent, farmland is being consolidated into larger holdings, while urban real estate has been falling into the hands of a small number of corporate owners and the mega-wealthy.[17]

In the United States, long seen as the great land of opportunity, the chance of middle-class earners moving up to the top rungs of the earnings ladder has dropped by approximately 20 percent since the early 1980s.[18] Across the thirty-six wealthier countries of the Organization for Economic Cooperation and Development, the richest citizens have taken an ever greater share of national GDP, and the middle class has become smaller. Much of the global middle class is heavily in debt, mainly because of high housing costs, and "looks increasingly like a boat in rocky waters," suggests the OECD.[19] Rates of homeownership are stagnant or plummeting in the high-income world, including the United States, Canada, and Australia.[20]

Globalization of the economy has served the interests of the upper classes but not the rest. For example, the shift of production to China alone has cost well over a half million manufacturing jobs from Great Britain, once an industrial powerhouse, and an estimated 3.4 million jobs from the United States.[21] Economists may point to better aggregate growth and lower prices for consumers, but most people do not live in "the aggregate." They live in their individual reality, which in many cases has gotten bleaker even as the economy overall has improved.

In a world growing more bifurcated, elite communities are surrounded by urban poor and by small towns that are fading and becoming destitute. Globalization "has revived the citadels of medieval France," writes Christophe Guilluy, a leftist geographer.[22] Like the castle towns of Japan or the walled cities of medieval Italy, a few choice locales are enclaves of privilege, while the less appealing places are inhabited by the newly servile classes.[23]

The New Power Nexus

Just as the clerical elite shared power with the nobility in the feudal era, a nexus between the clerisy and the oligarchy lies at the core of neo-feudalism. These two classes often attend the same schools and live in similar neighborhoods in cities such as New York, San Francisco, or London. On the whole, they share a common worldview and are allies on most issues, though there are occasional conflicts, as there were between the medieval nobility and clergy. Certainly, they hold similar views on globalism, cosmopolitanism, the value of credentials, and the authority of experts.

This power nexus is enabled by technologies that once were widely seen as holding great promise for grassroots democracy and decision making, but have become tools for surveillance and a consolidation of power. Even as blogs proliferate, giving the appearance of information democracy, a small group of companies—mostly based on the West Coast of the United States—exercise tightening control over the flow of information and the shape of the culture. Our new overlords do not wear chain mail or top hats, but instead direct our future in jeans and hoodies.[24] These technocratic elites are the twenty-first-century realization of what Daniel Bell prophetically labeled "a new priesthood of power" based on scientific expertise.[25]

The future of politics, in the high-income countries at least, will revolve around the ability of the dominant estates to secure the submission of the Third Estate. As in the Middle Ages, this requires imposing an orthodoxy that can normalize and justify a rigid class structure. The power of the nobility in the feudal order was justified through the agencies of religion and custom, blessed by the church. The modern clerisy often claim science as the basis of their doctrines and tout academic credentials as the key to status and authority. They seek to replace the bourgeois values of self-determination, family, community, and nation with "progressive" ideas about globalism, environmental sustainability, redefined gender roles, and the authority of experts. These values are inculcated through the clerisy's dominance over the institutions of higher learning and media, aided by the oligarchy's control of information technology and the channels of culture.

Losing Faith in Liberal Democracy

One consequence of the current economic trends is growing pessimism throughout the high-income world. Half of all Europeans believe that future generations will suffer worse economic conditions than they did, according to the Pew Research Center. In France, the pessimistic view predominates by seven to one. A pessimistic trend is also marked in the usually more upbeat societies of Australia (64 percent), Canada (67 percent), and the United States (57 percent). Overall, Pew found that 56 percent of residents in advanced economies believe their children will do worse than they did.[26]

Pessimism is also growing in East Asia, which has been the economic dynamo of the current era. In Japan, a full three-quarters of those polled expect things to be worse for the next generation, and that expectation also predominates in such successful countries as Taiwan, Singapore, and South Korea.[27] Many young people in China have reason for pessimism: in 2017, eight million college graduates entered the job market to find they could only earn salaries that they might have gotten by going to work in a factory straight out of high school.[28]

Another sign of pessimism is declining birth rates, particularly in the high-income countries. In Europe as well as Japan, and even in the once relatively fecund United States, fertility rates are nearing historic lows, even though young women state a wish to have more children.[29] This demographic stagnation, another throwback to the Middle Ages, has various explanations, including women's high levels of participation in the workforce and a desire for more leisure time. Other reasons are economic, including a shortage of affordable family housing. Liberal capitalism in its heyday built large stretches of affordable housing for the upwardly mobile middle and working classes, but the new feudalism is creating a world where fewer and fewer people can afford to own homes.[30]

A trend of diminishing expectations has weakened support for liberal capitalism even in solidly democratic countries, particularly among younger people.[31] Far more than older generations, they are losing faith in democracy, not only in the United States but also in Sweden, Australia, Great Britain, the Netherlands, and New Zealand. People born in the 1970s and 1980s are less strongly opposed to such undemocratic assertions of power as a military coup than are those born in the 1930s, 1940s, and 1950s.[32]

Today there is a turning away from democratic liberalism around the world. Authoritarian leaders are consolidating power in countries that previously appeared to be on a liberalizing path—Xi Jinping in China, Vladimir Putin in Russia, Recep Tayyip Erdogan in Turkey. In more democratic countries, we can see a new longing for a strongman—such as the bombastic and often crude Donald Trump, as well as equivalents in Europe, some of them more functionally authoritarian. Many people who are losing faith in the prospects of liberty look for a paternalistic protector instead. Authoritarian leaders often rise by evoking the imagined glories of the past and stoking resentments both old and new. At the end of the Cold War, the world seemed to be traveling on a natural "arc" to a more democratic future, but today's new world order has instead become a promising springtime for dictators.[33]

Peasant Rebellions

The feudal order did not go unchallenged in the Middle Ages: periodically there were peasant uprisings, sometimes led by religious dissidents. Could we see a kind of uprising from within the Third Estate today? The modern yeomanry can still mount a resistance, but the expanding "serf" class, without property or a stake in the system, might prove far more dangerous to the dominant orders.

Like the revolutionaries of 1789, many in today's Third Estate are disgusted by the hauteur and hypocrisy of the upper classes. In prerevolutionary times, French aristocrats and top clerics preached Christian charity while indulging in gluttony, sexual adventurism, and lavish spending. Today, many in the struggling middle and working classes see the well-to-do displaying their environmental piety by paying "green" indulgences through carbon credits and other virtue-signaling devices, while these "enlightened" policies impose extraordinarily high energy and housing costs on the less well off.[34] Alienated elements of the middle and working classes are responding with what might be likened to a modern peasants' rebellion. It can be seen in a series of angry votes and protests against the policies championed by the clerisy and oligarchy—on climate change, global trade, and migration. This anger was expressed in the election of President Trump, in the support for Brexit, and in the rise of populist parties across Europe.[35]

Perhaps nowhere is the rebellion more evident than in France: a clear majority of French people regard globalization as a threat, while most executives, many trained at elite schools, see it as an "opportunity."[36] In an echo of 1789, the so-called *gilets jaunes* (yellow vests) demonstrated against higher gas taxes in the winter of 2018–19. The protests began in small towns, but then moved into the Parisian suburbs.[37]

In the United States, restiveness among the Third Estate has prompted discussion among the oligarchs and the clerisy about expanding the scope of the welfare state, with subsidies and direct cash payments for the masses, in the hope of staving off rebellion by those who no longer see a possibility of improving their own lot. But will that be enough?[38]

Is a Feudal Future Inevitable?

The return to feudalism is not necessarily inexorable. To change the course we are on, we first need to understand and acknowledge what is happening. We possess the advantages brought by centuries of liberal capitalism and free intellectual inquiry; we have knowledge of the past feudal era, and of what democratic capitalism achieved. We do not have to be like the proverbial frog slowly boiling, unaware of its fate.

Reversing the slide into a neo-feudal order will require the development of a new political paradigm. The current "progressive" approach to "social justice," with its attachment to a powerful central government, will only strengthen the clerisy by vesting more authority in the "expert" class. On the other hand, the devotees of market fundamentalism, refusing to acknowledge the dangers of oligarchic power and the harm being done to the middle and working classes, might further a political trajectory that threatens the viability of capitalism itself. Some prominent business executives now recognize the problem and seek ways to remedy it, but there is much less awareness or concern among market ideologues on the right.[39]

A new perspective is needed, but it can emerge only when the reality of an emergent neo-feudalism is widely acknowledged and its dangers understood. There is still time to challenge this threat to liberal values. "A man may be led by fate," wrote the great Soviet novelist Vasily Grossman, "but he can refuse to follow."[40] The future course of history is never inevitable if we retain the will to shape it.

CHAPTER 2

The Enduring Allure
of Feudalism

Modern thinking tends to cast the Middle Ages as a benighted and backward time, although some historians regard that common perception as exaggerated and unfair. By the same token, feudalism is widely seen as a retrograde form of social and political organization, but it developed for a reason, to fill pressing needs of the time. As Roman governance dissolved, it left a power vacuum. Slowly, a new elite grew, and a new system of power relations that would last in some form for a millennium or more in some places.[1] Its persistence suggests that some version of feudalism could still have an appeal in modern times.

Feudalism in the Middle Ages varied from one place to another, but everywhere it centered on a distinct social hierarchy, the submission of inferiors to superiors, and restricted mobility for the lower classes—the vast majority of the population. Property was mostly consolidated into large manors. The urban middle classes dwindled as towns declined, and the independent peasantry mostly descended into serfdom. Large landowners took on public functions—justice, taxation, military—and offered protection to their dependent workers against the threat of marauders. In exchange, peasants surrendered the right to own land and the freedom to move off the estate their forebears had worked.[2] The laborers who were the key to economic production lived a constrained existence, in semibondage to a landowner. Most remained close to home; 80 percent of Europe's population never went more than twenty miles from their place of birth.[3]

Above them, the nobility had their own form of subordination. The most powerful nobles received homage from lesser nobles, who became their vassals and were invested with a fief (*feodum*), a piece of land, which over time became hereditary. The vassal could lease parts of the fief to his dependents, both noble and common. A vassal pledged allegiance to his lord and usually was obligated to provide military service.[4] Loyalty to one's immediate lord was the central organizing principle of society. "I will love what thou lovest; I will hate what thou hatest," ran an Anglo-Saxon oath of commendation.[5]

Feudalism favored inheritors of the largest estates and the greatest nobles, who constructed castles to enhance and display their power. The system provided a measure of order and security in the chaos left behind by the breakdown of imperial or royal administration. For the most part, people were expected to stay in their hereditary station of life. No matter how capable an individual might be, the stigma of low birth was difficult if not impossible to shake off.

The prevailing model of society consisted of three kinds of people: "those who prayed, those who fought and those who labored."[6] As monarchies grew stronger, John of Salisbury, writing in 1180, portrayed an ideal political order in this organic image: "The King corresponds to the head, the clergy to heart and soul, the nobility to arms, the peasants to the feet."[7]

For the peasants who labored in the fields, and even for the warrior nobility, literacy was considered unnecessary, and it had become mostly a monopoly of the clergy. The Catholic Church had considerable control over what was deemed correct thinking on religious and moral questions, and it claimed a universal authority—although its reach into the homes of the masses was limited, and many pagan and folk beliefs persisted through the centuries. Still, the church's teachings helped maintain the hierarchical order of feudal society.

In medieval Christian doctrine, the world we grasp with our senses is ephemeral, while the spiritual world is more real, and union with God is the supreme end. St. Augustine's view of the secular world as inherently hostile to the City of God took hold widely; man's relationship to God was all-important. Between the sixth and tenth centuries, 26,000 lives of saints were written, but little new in the way of historical or scientific works. Everything—philosophy, painting, literature, politics—was built around a spiritual ideal, and the great buildings of the age represented the "Bible in stone."[8] The emphasis on a future life over the present world diminished the passionate commitment to the *res publica* and family that had shaped classical civilization. Commerce was regarded as essentially immoral, and wealth derived primarily from inherited agricultural estates worked by serfs.[9]

Christianity advanced a doctrine of *spiritual* equality among all people, but the conditions of life in this world were seen as much less important than the life to come. By urging the lower classes to accept their place in this world in exchange for the promise of something better in the hereafter, the church may have been simply reflecting the common understanding of earthly reality, and religious organizations were the most likely source of succor, both material and spiritual, for the ubiquitous poor. But while high-ranking clerics often enjoyed their comfortable status as essentially a branch of the aristocracy, the medieval church's teaching did not encourage the hope of general uplift for the masses.

Making the Case for Feudalism

In the medieval worldview, society was held together by bonds of mutual obligation. At the top, there were bonds within the clergy and the nobility, and bonds between the two, in a kind of mutual aid society. Then there were the obligations of common people to their superiors. Finally, the church provided a floor, a kind of early welfare state for the poor.[10] Individualism was rejected in favor of the nobler concept of an interdependent commonwealth in a spiritually unified Christendom, but with strongly local social structures and loyalties. Even today, some regard this model of society as superior to the liberal capitalist form.[11]

The ideal of an interdependent, ordered society gained new currency in the nineteenth century, partly as a reaction to the social upheaval and physical pollution of the early industrial revolution. Many in the Romantic movement saw much to admire in medieval civilization, as shown in the writings of John Keats, Thomas Carlyle, Matthew Arnold, and Anthony Trollope, and later in Oscar Wilde, D. H. Lawrence, Stefan George, and Thomas Mann. These writers attacked what they saw as the "bourgeois philistinism and social leveling" inherent in capitalist societies. Many of them saw "stupidity" in the middle class, and believed that artists and writers could best address the needs of the proletariat.[12]

Karl Marx and Friedrich Engels conceded that the medieval guilds and localized markets as well as custom had provided artisans and peasants with a modicum of security, which had largely been lost under the pressure of the capitalist market system.[13] Engels even suggested that the Saxon serf in the twelfth century was no worse off than the workers of his own time, who could no longer count on custom and tradition to protect them.[14]

Some enlightened capitalists and aristocrats in the mid-nineteenth century supported steps to offer what Marx called a "proletarian alms bag" to keep the masses from both destitution and rebellion.[15] Similarly, some progressively inclined billionaires today have embraced the ideas of guaranteed minimum income, housing subsidies, and other transfer payments to keep the potentially restive masses from destitution or rebellion.

In the later nineteenth century, some British conservatives advocated something like a "capitalist feudalism," where relations between employer and worker would regain the mutuality believed to have existed in pre-industrial times.[16] Alternatively, a concept of "feudal socialism" would became known, in less provocative terms, as Tory Democracy.[17]

In Russia, where a liberal system never truly emerged, romantics like Tolstoy, as well as right-wing Slavophiles and social revolutionaries, rejected the liberal capitalism of the West and instead evoked a return to the *mir*, a form of community ownership left over from the days of serfdom. "Light and salvation will come from below," wrote Dostoyevsky. The key to social reform would be the *muzhik*, the devout, ill-educated, impoverished peasant—not the sophisticated, Europeanized intellectuals and rising capitalists of the big cities.[18]

Many powerful right-wing movements of the early twentieth century—National Socialism, Fascism, and their imitators elsewhere—also expressed a nostalgia for the Middle Ages. The Italian poet and futurist Gabriele D'Annunzio epoused a "socialist romanticism" that helped lay the foundations of the Fascist corporate state.[19] In France, the leaders of Action Française sought to bring about a "counter-Renaissance" and reimpose the hierarchical corporative structure of the *ancien régime*.[20] In England, Fascist sympathizers like Oswald Mosley lamented the passing of "Merrie old England," swept away by the competitive reality of ethnically mixed modern cities. Even today, some on the European far right see in the Middle Ages an affirmation of traditional Christian values, and find inspiration in the Crusader response to assaults from Islamic aggression.[22]

Contemporary Neo-medievalism

In ways that few could have expected three decades ago, a reaction against liberal ideals has been gaining force in many countries. After the fall of the Soviet Union, Russia has found inspiration in its czarist past, a time of vigorous imperial expansion. Perhaps more remarkably, the Russian Orthodox Church, which was marginalized and often persecuted by the Soviet authorities, has gained moral authority under Vladimir Putin. The Russian regime has even harked back to the period of Mongol domination as a way of tying the state to Central and East Asia.[23]

China's Communist leaders, while officially genuflecting to Maoist ideology, are finding something of value in folk religion and even Confucianism—so reviled by the founders of the People's Republic. It turns out that old virtues like honesty, filial obedience, and respect for hierarchy have their uses in the modern age.[24] Singapore's long-time premier, Lee Kwan Yew, has urged the Chinese regime to adopt Confucianism as a defining feature of Asian capitalism.[25]

Even in the West, the values that drove the development of the modern world—such as confidence in progress and the benefits of economic growth for the general well-being—have come under challenge. In the 1960s, the environmental movement expressed a growing, and understandable, concern over the devastation of the natural world by the modern industrial economy. An ideal of low or even negative economic and demographic growth was popularized by E. F. Schumacher, with his "small is beautiful" philosophy, which would prove particularly consequential in California in the 1970s.[26]

As in the nineteenth-century reactions against industrialization, environmental concerns raise nostalgia for a bygone age. Like a medieval millenarian, Prince Charles of Britain asserts that we are running out of time to save the world. Charles has emerged as perhaps the premier "feudal critic of capitalism," as one socialist publication put it. He views free-market capitalism as a scourge upon the earth, and promotes a new kind of noblesse oblige centered on concern for the natural world and for social harmony.[27]

Environmentalism has even led to a revival of the notion of poverty as a virtue. In the Middle Ages, poverty was regarded as the inescapable condition of life for most people, while monks adopted voluntary poverty as beneficial to spiritual growth; today, poverty sometimes appears to be considered good for the environment. Even the swelling slums of the developing world have been viewed as something to celebrate more than a cause for alarm, in large part because of the slum-dwellers' low consumption of energy and other resources. Michael Kimmelman, an urbanist writing for the *New York Times*, called slums "not just a blight but a potential template for organic urbanism."[28]

Many intellectuals, architects, and planners have promoted values reminiscent of the medieval past as being in better harmony with human nature.[29] Some conservative thinkers, such as the late Roger Scruton, have been critical of the disorderly modern urban world and especially of the suburban culture created by liberal capitalism. Scruton favored a return to a geography of densely populated cities surrounded by a protected countryside, without the middle landscape of suburbs—the places where the property-owning middle classes overwhelmingly live today. Likewise, some leading architects, including Britain's Richard Rogers, seek a return to something like the medieval city with its public market squares, which they consider a more livable alternative to the modern suburban sprawl.[30]

Such backward-looking ideas have been offered as remedies for the weaknesses and failings of modern society. But they might also provide a rationale to discourage upward mobility for the many and to concentrate property in fewer hands.

CHAPTER 3

The Rise and Decline of Liberal Capitalism

iberal capitalism weakened and dissolved the feudal order, allowing a robust middle class to rise. More efficient agricultural practices brought growth into the static economies that had mostly benefited rentiers and inheritors, gradually lifting small property owners such as the English yeomanry. Commercial growth empowered the innovative, aggressive, risk-taking entrepreneurs. New technology, expanding trade, new ideas, and developing institutions transformed feudal society beyond recognition. Where class privilege remained in place over a shifting base, particularly in France, the Third Estate rose up in a violent assault on the last vestiges of feudalism.[1]

The entrepreneurs who chipped away at the feudal order did not generally come from the nobility, who in some cases were prohibited or socially discouraged from engaging in commerce.[2] Aristocratic elites did sometimes give valuable funding and sponsorship to entrepreneurs, many of whom were from groups that had long been persecuted, including itinerant workers and dissenting Protestants, as well as Jews.[3] These commercial risk takers played a major part in creating our modern world, as their technological improvements, opening of trade routes, and building of cities ushered in an era of unprecedented economic growth.[4]

Liberal capitalism laid the basis for Western economic hegemony. In the year 1000, the gross product of China and of India each easily exceeded that of all western Europe combined, and the same was true of the Islamic empire. China remained ahead of Europe in technology until around 1450, according to Joseph Needham. For example, Chinese junks were the world's most advanced ships in the thirteenth and fourteenth centuries, spreading the Middle Kingdom's influence throughout Southeast Asia and beyond. As late as the seventeenth century, India and China were not only more populous than Europe but enjoyed an industrial infrastructure that was equal, at the very least.[5]

The rise of liberal capitalism first in Europe and then in North America dramatically altered the picture. From 1500 to 1913, Europe's share of global GDP rose from 17.8 to 33 percent, while China's share dropped from 25 to 8 percent. By 1913, Western Europe's per capita GDP was roughly seven times that of China or India, while the per capita GDP of the United States surpassed that of these large and venerable nations by a factor of nine.[6] In the later twentieth century, the benefits of liberal capitalism spread to East Asia as well, fueling the success of Japan and South Korea, Taiwan, and Hong Kong.

China Challenges the Liberal Model

The recent ascent of China presents a serious challenge to liberal capitalism as the model for the global future. China's share of the world's economic output has grown dramatically, from 4 percent in 1990 to a projected 21 percent in 2022.[7] Even if this progress slows due to demographic, environmental, and other factors, Chinese is likely to reshape much of the world's economic future with its model of state-directed capitalism, or "socialism with Chinese characteristics."

China's rise is occurring outside the realm of normative Western capitalist values. Unlike Japan in the late twentieth century, China never accepted the primary lodestars of liberal civilization, such as individual political and property rights. Instead, it has developed an alternative to liberal capitalism, and its principles are not only being inculcated in its own population but also being exported to universities and governments around the world.[8]

China's new model of capitalism has profoundly antiliberal aspects, including a distinct sense of social hierarchy, an autocratic central state, an enforced ideology and thought control. Despite a formal adherence to Marxist and Maoist egalitarianism, China today is nurturing a stratified class order, as powerful business elites and their allies in the government construct a system of permanent caste privilege.[9] The state employs ever more intrusive technology to impose strict censorship, with few protections of privacy.[10] "If the U.S. has long sought to make the world safe for democracy," suggests one analyst, "China's leaders crave a world that is safe for authoritarianism."[11]

China's blending of capitalism with authoritarianism is emerging as a persuasive model for economic development. The Chinese model is spreading its influence around East Asia and farther afield, not only in Central Asia but also in South America, parts of Europe, and especially Africa, where there are now an estimated one million Chinese residents. Many people in these countries take inspiration not from the example of New York or London or even Tokyo, but instead from the "Beijing consensus."[12] Most residents of India, the world's largest democracy, believe that China will replace the United States as the world's dominant country within twenty years. At the same time, India's political leadership is adopting illiberal views and policies, including ethnic nationalism, suppression of free speech, and Hindu dogmatism expressed in public policy.[13]

Back to Stagnation

As China's power has waxed, the economies in most advanced countries have stagnated. After a period of rapid expansion, economic growth in the large advanced countries, with the occasional exception of the United States, has slowed to a rate no more than half that of a generation ago.[14] Gains in productivity in the last decade were barely half those in the previous decade and barely one-fourth the average increases between 1920 and 1970. The economist Robert Gordon notes that the newest wave of technology, while dramatically changing how we communicate and get information, has done very little to improve the material conditions of life, particularly in housing and transportation.[15]

The slowdown of population growth, especially in high-income countries, is another aspect of societal stagnation. In Europe, low birth rates have been common for almost a half century now. Europe's population is on track to fall from 738 million to roughly 482 million by 2100. Retirees in a shrunken Germany will then outnumber children under the age of fifteen by a ratio of four to one.[16]

The demographic decline in East Asia has been, if anything, more dramatic. Over the past few decades, fertility has dropped precipitously in China, Taiwan, South Korea, Hong Kong, and Singapore, all with birth rates now well below replacement level.[17] Perhaps the most extreme case is Japan, where the decline had started by the 1960s. If the current trend continues, the island nation's population will drop from 127 million to under 80 million by 2065, according to Japan's National Institute of Population and Social Security Research.[18]

The Chinese population is projected to start declining too. By 2050, China is expected to have 60 million fewer people under age fifteen, a loss approximately the size of Italy's total population. At the same time, China will have nearly 190 million more people who are age 65 and over, approximately equal to the population of Pakistan, the world's fourth most populous country. The ratio of retirees to working people in China is expected to have more than tripled by then, which would be one of the most rapid demographic shifts in history.[19]

The global demographic trend will reshape economies and societies going forward. Today a majority of the world's people live in countries with fertility rates well below replacement level.[20] This number will grow to 75 percent by 2050, according to the United Nations; many societies, including some in the developing world, can expect a rapidly aging population and a precipitous decline in workforce numbers.[21] Overall world population growth could all but end by 2040, says Wolfgang Lutz, and be in decline by 2060.[22]

Shrinking populations in advanced countries will threaten economic growth by limiting the size of the labor force, and will undermine the fiscal viability of the welfare state.[23] This is one reason for the receptiveness of Western governments to high levels of immigration from poorer countries, which continue to produce offspring more prodigiously than wealthier countries. Between now and 2050, half of all global population growth is expected to take place in Africa.[24] A widening demographic imbalance between the poorer and wealthier countries could cause more disruption in both spheres, and lead to a reprise of the mass migrations that did much to undermine the ancient empires of Europe and Asia.[25] Social conflict resulting from high levels of immigration from poorer countries is already a prominent feature of Western politics and seems likely to fester in the coming decades.[26]

The Technology Gap

Technological advances once fueled growing prosperity for the many. Today, automation and the use of artificial intelligence promise to accelerate social divisions both between and within countries. Although it is not clear that these technologies will result in fewer jobs overall, some sectors are especially threatened, notably manufacturing, transportation, and retail—sectors that historically provided steady blue-collar employment. But jobs in those sectors may be even more threatened by regulatory changes, largely justified on environmental grounds, that restrict growth in tangible industries.[27]

What is more likely than mass unemployment in the Western world is a continuing decline of the middle class, as many are forced to subsist in the so-called "gig economy." Between 2005 and 2014, the percentage of families with flat or decreasing real incomes rose to over 60 percent in the twenty-five most advanced economies.[28]

A technologically driven society tends to show a widening gap between the "elect" who are highly gifted in science and tech, and the many who are not. Today it takes only a small cadre of coders, financial experts, and marketing mavens to build a billion-dollar business, without much required in the way of blue-collar workers or even middle managers. In the long run, we could see something of the stark future depicted in *The Time Machine* by H. G. Wells. "We are turning into two races," writes Richard Fernandez: "Eloi who play video games and Morlocks who program them."[29]

In the face of these social challenges, the intellectual classes in the higher-income countries—in the universities, the media, and the arts—almost universally seek to deconstruct the values that guided their countries' ascent and provided the foundation for widespread prosperity. Instead of concerning themselves with addressing the consequences of economic stagnation—more poverty, social immobility, class conflict—many in the clerisy and even the oligarchy promote the ideal of "sustainability" over broad-based economic growth.[30] Just as the medieval clergy preached against materialism, leading figures in today's academia and the media, and even some among the corporate elite, look askance at the very idea of a dynamic economy, a spirit of innovation, and a commitment to improving everyday life. Some even suggest that progress is a myth.[31] In this way, the clerisy reinforce the pessimistic notion that upward mobility is a relic of the past, and that our primary tasks now are to redress social grievances and protect the environment, rather than seek ways to spread wealth and opportunity.[32]

The new feudalism won't feature intrepid knights in armor or fortified castles, or raise soaring cathedrals filled with liturgical chants. Instead it will boast dazzling new technology, and be wrapped in a creed of globalism and environmental piety. Yet for all its modernity, the coming age looks set to replace liberal dynamism and intellectual pluralism with an orthodoxy that puts a premium on stasis and accepts social hierarchy as the natural order of things.

PART II

The Oligarchs

When there is a general change in conditions, it is as if
the entire creation had changed, and the whole world altered.

—Ibn Khaldun (14th century)

CHAPTER 4

High-Tech Feudalism

echnological innovation has long been connected with the growth of capitalist economies. The capitalist revolution of the Early Modern period had far-reaching consequences, disrupting old rhythms of life, as Fernand Braudel explained.[1] But capitalism and new technology together laid the basis for a broadly shared improvement in material well-being and for social mobility. By the same token, the recent tech revolution was once widely seen as not only transformative but generally beneficial. Some have envisioned a new civilization with great opportunities for human development and societal improvement. Yet today we see diminishing social mobility and little real material progress for most people, as economic power is increasingly dominated by fewer companies, particularly in the finance and technology sectors.[2] Our future is coming to look like the "high-tech middle age" that the Japanese futurist Taichi Sakaiya predicted more than three decades ago.[3]

The pioneers of the modern tech industry were once celebrated as exemplars of capitalist competition, illustrating what Joseph Schumpeter called the "creative destruction" that breaks up monopolies and allows others to rise from below. But today's tech leaders increasingly resemble an exclusive ruling class, controlling a few exceptionally powerful companies, and like aristocracies everywhere they are often resistant to any dispersion of their power. As they conquer ever more of the precious digital real estate, they are building a more stratified economic and social order, with widening class divisions, not only in the United States but around the world.[4]

The Birth of the New Oligarchy

California's Santa Clara Valley seems an unlikely incubator for neo-feudalism. Half a century ago, it was just beginning to change from an agricultural region into a vast middle-class suburb. Wealthy people from San Francisco bought elegant estates in the South Bay and created an elite horse country alongside the farms, but most of the growth took the form of modest tracts inhabited by the middle and working classes, including many veterans. "The more people who saw the nicest place in the world to live with their own eyes, and realized it was no more expensive than back home," observes one Bay Area native, "the more they concluded 'I want to live here, too.'"[5]

By the 1950s and 1960s, these pleasant surroundings were attracting skilled but decidedly middle-class technicians and engineers, including Lee DeForest, inventor of the vacuum tube. An emerging tech economy was supercharged by massive defense and space contracts. UC Berkeley, the nation's premier public university, was located not far to the north. Closer by was Stanford, which excelled in the physical sciences and established the Stanford Research Park in 1951. Stanford graduates had already founded Hewlett-Packard in 1939, and an engineering professor who became provost of the university, Frederick Terman, nurtured tech companies in the area.[6]

In the ensuing decades, the Bay Area, including San Francisco, became the world's leading technology hub. This rapid technological growth resulted in a consolidation of wealth and power in a handful of companies. A relatively small cadre of engineers, data scientists, and marketers—a tiny sliver of humanity—began reshaping the world's economy, and its culture as well.[7]

In the Middle Ages, the power of the nobility rested on the control of land and the right to bear arms; the power of today's ascendant tech aristocracy comes mainly from exploiting "natural monopolies" in web-based business. The winners of the digital land grab are a few companies located mostly in Silicon Valley and in the Puget Sound region. Having seized the strategic digital territory, they are eclipsing and replacing the old industrial economy.[8]

By 2018, four tech firms—Apple, Amazon, Google, and Facebook—had a combined net worth amounting to nearly one-quarter of the S&P 500 Top 50, and equal to the GDP of France.[9] Seven of the world's ten most valuable companies are in this sector.[10] The tech giants have also generated huge individual fortunes: eight of the twenty richest people on the planet acquired their wealth in the tech industry.[11] Nine of the thirteen richest people under age 40 are in the tech industry, and all live in California.[12] Only China, home to nine of the world's twenty largest tech firms, presents any kind of challenge to California's tech aristocracy.[13]

From Garages to Gargantua

Silicon Valley was once a center of grassroots innovation where tech companies were started in suburban garages, as epitomized by the remarkable story of Apple.[14] Now the historic startup culture has been strangled by the largest companies with their fantastic resources. Many startups are soon acquired by established firms, rather than having a chance to grow large themselves.[15]

Antitrust actions in the United States have fallen by 61 percent since the early 1980s, leaving the tech oligarchy with almost unlimited power—under administrations of both parties—to acquire or crush competitors.[16] In recent years, Facebook has swallowed potential competitors such as Instagram, WhatsApp, and Oculus, with little resistance from regulators.[17] Google is among the most voracious in acquisitions, purchasing a new venture every other week in one year, and a total of 240 companies as of January 2020.[18]

Armed with massive war chests and the means to buy the best talent, a small number of companies have achieved monopolistic or duopolistic power over some of the world's most lucrative markets. Google controls nearly 90 percent of search advertising, Facebook almost 80 percent of mobile social traffic, and Amazon nearly 40 percent of the world's cloud business along with 75 percent of U.S. ebook sales. Google and Apple together provide over 95 percent of operating software for mobile devices. Microsoft still accounts for over 80 percent of the software that runs personal computers around the world.[19]

As a result, the once buoyant grassroots tech economy now suffers a seriously degraded condition. The entrepreneur not embraced by the big venture firms lives largely at the sufferance of the tech overlords.[20] One online publisher uses a *Star Trek* analogy to describe his firm's status with Google: "It's a bit like being assimilated by the Borg. You get cool new powers. But having been assimilated, if your implants were ever removed, you'd certainly die. That basically captures our relationship to Google."[21]

The rush into artificial intelligence is likely to strengthen the dominant position of those firms that already have enormous reservoirs of both money and talent. A few firms will probably join the oligarchy over time, and some familiar ones may go out of existence or be acquired by others. But the top firms tend to exist as properties of a small number of financiers and technologists who operate within a narrow, self-referential universe.[22]

This concentration of technological power portends a far less democratic future.[23] With their huge cash reserves, the tech oligarchs have plans to dominate older industries like entertainment, finance, education, and retail, as well as industries of the future: autonomous cars, drones, space exploration, and most critically artificial intelligence. Firms like Google, Amazon, and Apple have invested billions to gain post position in both traditional and emerging industries.[24]

Izabella Kaminska, a technology analyst, compares the giant tech firms to the Soviet planners who operated Gosplan, the economic planning agency that allocated state resources across the USSR.[25] Some may consider it preferable to cede such power to private capital rather than party hacks, but it still amounts to a great deal of power in a few hands, with little accountability.[26]

The China Syndrome

China, with its lack of legal restraints, may prove to be the cutting edge of a new technocratic despotism. Its tech sector is second only to that of the United States and increasingly sees itself as Silicon Valley's successor. In certain sectors, including ecommerce and mobile payments, China has already established a powerful lead.[27] Much of China's technology boom results from massive investments by both state-sponsored and private firms in leading-edge technologies. In 2016 this investment was greater than that of Japan, Germany, and South Korea combined, and it produced ten times as many new graduates in engineering, technology, science, and medicine as the United States.[28]

China has spawned its own plutocratic elite, too: the number of Chinese billionaires in 2017 was just behind the number of billionaires in the United States, and growing much faster.[29] Since 2000, many billionaires from tech and other sectors have entered the Communist Party in a seamless manner that Mao Tse-tung would never have countenanced.[30] China thus has two intertwined elites—one political, the other economic. The rise of a technocratic elite might be said to fit neatly into the Marxist notion of "scientific socialism," mobilizing scientists, technicians, and engineers for the common good.[31] But it has demolished the basic egalitarian ethos of socialism. Marx envisioned the working class rising up against the bourgeoisie, but did not anticipate that technically skilled people could become yet another class, with their own capabilities and worldview. The merger of a wealthy tech elite with the political ruling class has created an aristocracy of intellect that replicates the historical role of the Mandarin class in Chinese culture and governance.[32]

Perhaps the most disturbing part of China's technological growth is in the government's use of artificial intelligence to regulate society and public opinion. Sophisticated algorithms are employed to control everything from legal proceedings to permission for marriage.[33] The Communist Party is putting artificial intelligence to work monitoring businesses, in part to make sure their activities are congruent with Party priorities.[34] The regime also uses facial recognition technology and "social credit" scoring, which includes everything from credit worthiness and work performance to political reliability. Surveillance of citizens is sometimes done with the unconscionable connivance of major American tech firms, some of which are also experimenting with bringing similar tools to the private marketplace.[35]

In the future, the Chinese use of surveillance technology could be a model for other countries seeking to employ technology to regulate the lives of citizens. In fact, this kind of surveillance capacity is already being sold to other countries, particularly in Africa, as a tool for regimes to control their populations and spy on political opponents.

"Clean Rich" or High-Tech Monopolists?

To a remarkable extent, the tech elites have presented themselves as dynamic, entrepreneurial outsiders who want to make the world better.

In the early days of the tech revolution, some imagined an almost utopian, communitarian society on the horizon. The California author Stewart Brand, writing in *Rolling Stone* in 1972, predicted that when computers became widely available, we would all become "computer bums, all more empowered as individuals and as co-operators." It would be a new era of enhanced "spontaneous creation and of human interaction."[36] The "early digital idealists" envisioned a "sharing" web that functioned "free from the constraints of the commercial order."[37]

Instead, a technocratic economy is engendering a new kind of hierarchy, favoring highly skilled technicians and engineers. Their dominance will grow as technology plays an ever greater role in the economy, while the value of labor further declines. Americans, long enamored of the entrepreneurial spirit and technological progress, have been slow to see the tech oligarchy as a threat.[38] Leftist historians, alert to the dangers of aristocracy, have tended to focus their ire on financial companies that may be large and powerful but aren't nearly as wealthy or as influential in shaping the economy as the tech sector, which seeks to capture virtually every other industry, including finance.[39]

At the Occupy Wall Street protests in 2011, anticapitalist demonstrators held moments of silence and prayer for the memory of Steve Jobs, a particularly aggressive capitalist.[40] Some people still see Bill Gates, a clear monopolist, as one of the "meritorious entrepreneurs," notes Thomas Piketty.[41] One progressive writer, David Callahan, portrays the tech oligarchs, along with their allies in the financial sector, as a kind of "benign plutocracy" in contrast to those who built their fortunes on resource extraction, manufacturing, and material consumption.[42]

Yet America's tech titans have attained oligopolistic sway over markets comparable to that of moguls like John Rockefeller, Andrew Carnegie, or Cornelius Vanderbilt.[43] They may wear baseball caps rather than top hats, but their economic and cultural power is vast, and likely to become far more so.

CHAPTER 5

The Belief System of the New Oligarchy

n important ways, the tech moguls are quite different from both the industrialists of the late nineteenth century and the managerial elite of the twentieth. They are neither ambitious parvenus nor carefully bred products of the corporate organization. It is not raw ambition or managerial acumen but technical talent that has defined them and made them fabulously wealthy and influential.

As a group, they are far less diverse than the tinkerers and artisans who propelled the industrial revolution. Most come from the upper end of the middle class. Many have at least one parent, sometimes two, with a scientific background. They generally went to elite colleges (although not all of them graduated). Some were technical prodigies even in high school. Not for them the tedium of a newspaper route or a part-time job in a pizza joint or the mail room. The tech elites, wrote one observer, are typically "long on brilliance, but short on hardship."[1]

Despite their sheltered origins, the tech oligarchs tend to regard themselves as more enlightened and progressive than their industrial-era predecessors. In the 1970s and 1980s, the image they projected was the latest incarnation of the American hippie, a kind of "high-tech bandit" having "more in common with artists than with the inhabitants of the corridors of corporate power."[2] The early tech executives—such as those running Hewlett-Packard and Intel—also tended to be paternalistic in their management practices and to consider themselves more forward-thinking than the corporate managers of an earlier time.[3]

The Meritocratic Ideology

The people running today's IT firms do not see middle managers—much less assembly-line workers or skilled artisans—as peers. Their worldview is aligned with the upper echelon of the educated workforce. High numbers of science PhDs are found in their ranks, including CEOs, and a survey of forty-five tech executives found that the vast majority had degrees from elite universities in engineering, computer science, or business. Some of those with no degrees were dropouts from elite institutions.[4] "Software is an IQ business," said Bill Gates, himself a Harvard dropout. "Microsoft must win the IQ war, or we won't have a future."[5]

The tech oligarchs are creating something similar to what Aldous Huxley called "a scientific caste system."[6] It is unlike the industrial era, when corporations depended on people with a wide range of skills: managers and marketers, engineers and technicians, warehouse workers and salespeople. These jobs were often unionized, at least in the manufacturing and energy sectors, so that upper management was compelled at least to consider diverse views on how the business should operate. In contrast, tech firms are rarely unionized, and none of the largest internet-based firms are.[7]

Crucially, the tech giants employ relatively few people in proportion to their revenues. IT firms like Google and Facebook generate up to three hundred times the market value per employee as the likes of GM, Home Depot, and Kroger.[8] (Only the energy sector, whose wealth is based on natural resources, is higher.) In addition, IT companies and the specialized contractors that service them depend heavily on thousands of lower-paid foreign workers, some of whom are close to being indentured servants.[9]

What Do Today's Oligarchs Want?

The tech oligarchs have not produced a coherent political manifesto laying out their vision for the future. Yet it's clear that the IT elite—in firms such as Amazon, Google, Facebook, Apple, and Microsoft—share some ideas that add up to a common agenda.

In the developing technocratic worldview, there's little place for upward mobility, except within the charmed circle at the top. The middle and working classes are expected to become marginal. While the oligarchs might speak of a commitment to building what Mark Zuckerberg calls "meaningful community," they rarely mention upward mobility.[10] Having interviewed 147 digital company founders, Gregory Ferenstein notes that they generally don't expect their workers or consumers to achieve more independence by starting their own companies or even owning houses. Most, Ferenstein adds, believe that an "increasingly greater share of economic wealth will be generated by a smaller slice of very talented or original people. Everyone else will come to subsist on some combination of part-time entrepreneurial 'gig work' and government aid."[11]

Ferenstein says that many tech titans, in contrast to business leaders of the past, favor a radically expanded welfare state.[12] Mark Zuckerberg, Elon Musk, Travis Kalanick (former head of Uber), and Sam Altman (founder of Y Combinator) all favor a guaranteed annual income, in part to allay fears of insurrection by a vulnerable and struggling workforce. Yet unlike the "Penthouse Bolsheviks" of the 1930s, they have no intention of allowing their own fortunes to be squeezed. Instead, the middle class would likely foot much of the bill for guaranteed wages, health care, free college, and housing assistance, along with subsidies for gig workers, who do not receive benefits from their employers.[13]

This model could best be described as oligarchical socialism. The redistribution of resources would meet the material needs of the working class and the declining middle class, but it would not promote upward mobility or threaten the dominance of the oligarchs. This represents a sea change from the old industrial economy. Rather than acquiring property and gaining a modicum of self-sufficiency, workers can now expect a serflike future of rented apartments and frozen prospects.[14] Unable to grow into property-owning adults, they will depend on subsidies to meet their basic needs.

Thomas Piketty observed that the tech oligarchs, like some nineteenth-century industrialists, expect the growing influence of technically gifted people to "destroy artificial inequalities" while "highlighting natural inequalities."[15] But the new tech aristocracy also regard themselves as intrinsically more deserving of their wealth and power than the old managerial elites or the grubby corporate speculators.[16] They believe that they are not just creating value, but building a better world.

While earlier technologies were disruptive of established ways, their purpose was generally to allow people to do things more cheaply and efficiently, to boost productivity and make life easier. Technology was "a traditional action made effective," as the sociologist Marcel Mauss described it. On the whole, it was evolutionary, not revolutionary.[17] But for many in the new elite, technology represents far more than efficiency or convenience. It is both the beginning and the end, the material equivalent of a spiritual journey to nirvana.

Google's vision for the future is characterized by "immersive computing," in which the real and virtual worlds blend together.[18] Tech leaders like Ray Kurzweil, longtime head of engineering at Google, speak about creating a "posthuman" future, dominated by artificial intelligence and controlled by computers and those who program them. They look forward to having the capacity to reverse aging and to download their consciousness into computers. This vision rests on a faith in—or an obsession with—technological determinism, in which new technology is our evolutionary successor.[19] But is this what most people want the future to be?

The Cultural Revolution

What the tech oligarchs are already doing to control the culture should raise alarm. The IT revolution once appeared to be launching a more democratic era in communications, with the "de-massified media" that Alvin Toffler optimistically predicted. But what looked like a more diverse and open media world, where anyone could be a reporter or reach an audience, is turning into one where a very few companies control the information pipelines.[20] Nearly two-thirds of U.S. adults now get their news through Facebook or Google.[21] Millennials in both the United States and the UK are almost three times as likely to get their information from these platforms as from print, television, or radio.[22]

The power of the tech oligarchy has grown at a time when print publishing and the firms that have dominated it are experiencing a secular and probably irreversible decline. Between 2001 and 2017, the publishing industry (books, newspapers, magazines) lost 290,000 jobs—a decrease of 40 percent. Any newspaper or magazine today will have an online presence, but with Facebook and Google dominating the growth in online advertising, it's exceedingly difficult for new or smaller publications to survive. While Google alone made $4.7 billion from news publishers in 2018, the industry continues to shrink.[23] "When you look at what's evolved, and the amount of revenue that's going to the Googles and Facebooks of the world," says Alan Fisco, president of the *Seattle Times*, "we are getting the crumbs off the table."[24]

Even as they devastate the old media, the oligarchs also have the means to purchase some of its most venerable survivors. Since 2010, tech moguls and their relatives have bought the *New Republic*, the *Washington Post*, the *Atlantic*, and the long-distressed *Time* magazine, purchased for $190 million.[25] In China, the estimable *South China Morning Post* was taken over by Alibaba, one of the country's largest online retailers.[26] Owning publications appeals to the vanity of tech oligarchs, giving them enhanced entree to literary and journalistic circles.[27] The publications acquired in this way get an extra edge: they can enjoy the luxury of producing content without worrying much about money.[28]

There are often ritual denials that the new owners of these publications will influence content, but this is in total contradiction with experience. When the equally rapacious moguls of the early twentieth century, like the McCormicks of Chicago or William Randolph Hearst, bought newspapers, they pushed an agenda of imperial expansion, anti-unionism, and resistance to those who would threaten their fortunes.[29] Today's mass media already tend to favor the oligarchy's progressive views—on gender, race, and environmental issues, for example, but with reservations about the concentration of power.[30] Financial dependency is likely to encourage more support for the interests of the tech industry.

News is only one area of the culture being seized by the tech oligarchy. Amazon has achieved enormous influence over the book industry; it is by far the largest seller of books, accounting for upwards of 50 percent of all paper sales and 90 percent of ebook sales, and it possesses the ability to allow knockoffs of published titles.[31] Even well-established publishers like Hachette and Macmillan have found themselves held hostage if they don't adhere to Amazon's requests.[32]

The entertainment industry is also being swallowed up by the tech giants. YouTube, acquired by Google in 2006, has become determinative in the music industry, although artists often do not get the compensation they traditionally received. Music streaming and music videos have become yet another way that firms like Google gain access to ever more personal data, which they can sell to advertisers.[33] Much the same is occurring in video broadly. Netflix, a company financed by Silicon Valley venture firms, is now estimated to be worth more than any of the film studios, and along with Amazon it produces much of the award-winning television programming. In 2018, Netflix spent more on programming than any of the major studios. Netflix and Amazon each have well over 100 million subscribers, far beyond the clientele achieved by the established cable firms.[34]

Not satisfied with controlling information pipelines, the tech oligarchs have been moving to shape content as well. Controllers like those at Facebook and Twitter seek to "curate" content on their sites, or even eliminate views they find objectionable, which tend to be conservative views, according to former employees.[35] Algorithms intended to screen out "hate groups" often spread a wider net, notes one observer, since the programmers have trouble distinguishing between "hate groups" and those who might simply express views that conflict with the dominant culture of Silicon Valley.[36] That managers of social media platforms aim to control content is not merely the perception of conservatives. Over 70 percent of Americans believe that social media platforms "censor political views," according to a recent Pew study.[37] With their quasi-monopoly status, Facebook and Google don't have to worry about competing with anyone, as the tech entrepreneur Peter Thiel observes, so they can indulge their own prejudices to a greater extent than the businesses that might be concerned about alienating customers.[38]

With their tightening control over media content, the tech elite are now situated to exert a cultural predominance that is unprecedented in the modern era.[39] It recalls the cultural influence of the Catholic Church in the Middle Ages, but with more advanced technology.

The Right of Surveillance

The medieval church may have exercised enormous sway over what people believed to be true and proper, but it had nothing like today's tools for monitoring private actions and thoughts. The new technology that allows such erasure of privacy has become central to generating tech wealth: personal data is the raw material of the digital age. Jack Ma, the founder of Alibaba, sees the exploitation of personal data as the "electricity of the 21st century."[40]

Alibaba and other "super platforms" like Facebook, Google, and WeChat operate largely as gatekeepers for those who wish to navigate the digital economy, which means they control access to a considerable part of the overall economy.[41] This position gives them enormous power to collect personal information on users. When Google and Facebook and other gatekeepers do this collecting, "our behaviour is transformed into a product," writes one observer.[42] This data now accounts for up to 20 percent of Europe's GDP, and as it becomes more important, we become like serfs living under what the French analyst Gaspard Koenig describes as "digital feudalism."[43] Our daily lives no longer belong to us alone but are relentlessly commodified. This is, of course, the natural goal of all the major tech firms, and as Jaron Lanier suggests, it all serves to "percolate creepiness and inspire justified paranoias."[44]

Surveillance might go on with little warning to customers. Facebook already admits to having patented technology that would enable snooping on their users by remotely turning on a smartphone's microphone to start recording, although they deny using it.[45] In 2018, Amazon's in-home device Alexa was found to be eavesdropping on people's conversations.[46] Once exposed, such intrusions are often ended, at least temporarily, but there is reason to believe that privacy ranks low in tech company priorities.[47] Google's former executive chairman, Eric Schmidt, once told CNBC: "If you have something that you don't want anyone to know, maybe you shouldn't be doing it in the first place."[48]

The prospect of life under surveillance by technocratic oligarchs is a terrifying one. "If ExxonMobil attempted to insert itself into every element of our lives like this," writes Ellie Mae O'Hagan in the *Guardian*, "there might be a concerted grassroots movement to curb its influence."[49] Irrespective of personal politics, we must begin to recognize the threats to our freedom posed by today's "benign plutocracy."

CHAPTER 6

Feudalism in California, Harbinger of the Future

erhaps the best way to picture the future contours of high-tech feudalism is to examine the present conditions in its fountainhead, California. Many progressives see the Golden State, and especially Silicon Valley, as the harbinger of a better, greener, more egalitarian future.[1] Yet the reality could not be more different. Rather than a model of upward mobility, California is a place now dominated by a small class of exceedingly wealthy and well-connected people, resembling the nobility of the Middle Ages or the elites of the Gilded Age.

California has changed dramatically from the opportunity-rich environment that lured so many millions to the state. From the beginning, California promised much, wrote Kevin Starr, the premier chronicler of the state's history: "While yet barely a name on the map, it entered American awareness as a symbol of renewal. It was a final frontier: of geography and of expectation."[2] Since its entrance to the Union in the mid-nineteenth century, the Golden State was known as a place where ambitious outsiders from diverse backgrounds could prosper and realize their dreams. But today more Californians feel the state is headed in the wrong direction than the right, according to a recent poll by the Public Policy Institute of California, and the proportion reaches above 55 percent in the inland areas.[3] Voters dislike the state legislature even more than they dislike President Trump.[4] Consumer confidence hit a three-year low in 2019, even as some other states, such as Texas and Michigan, saw small upswings.[5] There is also anger over the growing problem of homelessness.[6]

Number One in Wealth, and in Poverty

Social stratification rather than upward mobility now characterizes the social order of California. The state has one of the nation's highest Gini ratios—which measures the inequality of wealth distribution between the richest and poorest residents—and the disparity is growing faster than in almost any other state outside the Northeast, according to James Galbraith, a liberal economist.[7] The gap between middle and upper wages has become the widest in the nation, and while midrange wages are around the same as those in the rest of the nation, they buy less because of much higher taxes as well as energy and housing costs.[8] California's level of inequality is greater than that of Mexico, and closer to that of Central American countries like Guatemala and Honduras than to what is common in developed counties like Canada and Norway.[9]

With adjustment for cost of living, California now has the highest overall poverty rate in the United States, according to the Census Bureau.[10] Fully one-third of welfare recipients in the nation live in California, which is home to barely 12 percent of the total population.[11] A United Way study in 2017 showed that close to one-third of the state's families are barely able to pay their bills.[12] Today, eight million Californians live in poverty, including two million children.[13] Research by the Public Policy Institute found that 45.8 percent of California's children live close to the poverty level, often in substandard housing.[14]

Conditions are especially tough for Hispanics and African Americans, who constitute 45 percent of the state's population. Almost one-third of the state's Hispanics and one-fifth of African Americans hang on the edge of poverty, notes the United Way. Based on cost-of-living estimation tools from the Census Bureau, 28 percent of African Americans in the state live in poverty, compared with 22 percent nationally.[15] Fully one-third of Hispanics, the state's largest ethnic group, are below the poverty line, compared with 21 percent outside the state.[16] Over two-thirds of noncitizen Latinos, including the undocumented, live at or below the poverty line.[17]

The state's vast interior, home to roughly one in three of its residents, suffers the highest poverty rates in the nation.[18] Los Angeles, by far the state's largest metropolitan area, has among the highest poverty rates for major U.S. metros.[19] In parts of Los Angeles, the growing homeless encampments have spawned medieval diseases such as typhus. There are even indications of a comeback for bubonic plague, the signature scourge of the Middle Ages.[20]

As the tech sector and the Bay Area have come to dominate the state's economy over the past fifteen years, conditions have worsened for many if not most Californians. In the past, the state's economic diversity—from agriculture and home building to aerospace and entertainment—provided the means to succeed for a diverse population. The Great Recession hit California more profoundly than the rest of the country, and subsequently the state's income growth has been remarkably concentrated in the tech-heavy Bay Area. Across the state, almost two-thirds of job growth in 2015–16 was in minimum-wage or near-minimum-wage jobs, according to the state's Business Roundtable.[21] Since 2010, according to calculations by Marshall Toplansky of Chapman University, 80 percent of all jobs created in the state have paid under the median income, and half of these under $40,000, a poverty wage in a high-cost state. This is a higher proportion of lower-wage jobs than most other states have shown.[22]

The Hidden Reality of Silicon Valley

The Bay Area of California, heartland of the tech boom and site of one of the most rapid accumulations of wealth in human history, has created not mass affluence but an emergent dystopia. The website CityLab has described the Bay Area as "a region of segregated innovation," where the upper class waxes, the middle class wanes, and the lower class lives in poverty that is becoming unshakeable.[23]

Among the nation's large cities, inequality grew most rapidly over the last decade in San Francisco, reports the Brookings Institution.[24] The California Budget Center named the city first in the state for economic inequality.[25] It is a city of enormous wealth that is plagued by mass homelessness and rife with petty crime, while the middle-class family heads toward extinction. San Francisco lost 31,000 homeowning families over the past decade.[26]

Silicon Valley to the south, once an exemplar of suburban egali-tarianism, has also become much more stratified. As recently as the 1980s, the San Jose area boasted one of the country's most egalitarian economies. Jobs in manufacturing, assembly, transportation, and cus-tomer support allowed people with a wide range of skills to attain the California dream: many factory workers as well as middle managers could achieve homeownership and a comfortable retirement. The 1980s, write Manuel Pastor and Chris Brenner, were "good times for growth and equity in Silicon Valley."[27] But as the Valley has ascended to global preeminence in technology, class divisions have grown ever starker. By 2015, some 76,000 millionaires and billionaires lived in Santa Clara and San Mateo counties, but hundreds of thousands of people were struggling to feed their families and pay their monthly bills. Nearly 30 percent of Silicon Valley's residents rely on public or private financial assistance.[28]

During the boom of the last decade, cost-adjusted wages dropped for middle-class workers, Latinos, and African Americans in Silicon Valley.[29] One reason is the shift of employment away from manufacturing and into software: over the past two decades, the Bay Area has lost around 160,000 manufacturing jobs. The IT industry has greatly expanded, but the newer software companies need fewer workers than other kinds of businesses, including the more traditional tech firms. Their revenues per employee are two to three times those of Intel, for example.[30] They also often employ large numbers of noncitizens on temporary visas, who now constitute upwards of 40 percent of the tech workforce in Silicon Valley.[31] Meanwhile, the numbers of black and Latino employees in the tech industry have been declining.[32]

Employment in the software industry is by no means always lucrative. Left behind are workers in the vast service sector, many of whom work for contractors. Security guards earn around $25,000 annually.[33] Many lower and even midlevel workers at firms such as Google live in mobile home parks, while others sleep in their cars. The Valley has some of the nation's largest homeless encampments.[34]

Once a beacon of middle-class aspiration, Silicon Valley has become "fragmented and divided," note Pastor and Brenner, "with the high-tech community largely isolated from the broader region and particularly those parts of the region that are less fortunate."[35]

Feudalism with Better Marketing

In *Wired* magazine, Antonio García Martínez describes the contemporary Silicon Valley as "feudalism with better marketing." He sees a clear elite of venture capitalists and company founders. Below them are the skilled professionals, well paid but living ordinary middle-class lives, given the high prices and heavy taxes. Below them lies the vast population of gig workers, whom García Martínez compares to sharecroppers in the South. At the bottom, there is an untouchable class of homeless, drug addicts, and criminals.[36]

García Martínez depicts a society that is "highly stratified, with little social mobility." High prices make it all but impossible for most to own homes. Workers in the gig economy have little chance to improve their lot, as they struggle to pay their rent, or are forced to sleep in their cars or on friends' couches, or commute great distances in to work.[37] Roughly half of California's gig workers struggle with poverty.[38] For the "untouchables" below them, the prospects are even grimmer.

This regressive social evolution troubles many on both left and right. There are growing calls for regulation of the tech empire, for more antitrust action, or even for nationalization of the tech giants, not only in the United States but also in Canada and Europe.[39] In recent years, some once favorable progressives have labeled the tech oligarchs as just the latest purveyors of "predatory capitalism" and a mounting threat to democracy.[40]

Ultimately, few stand to benefit from the rise of the tech oligarchy. Almost half a century ago, Daniel Bell predicted in his landmark work, *The Coming of Post-Industrial Society*, that technology would enable those who control it to fulfill "a social alchemist's dream: the dream of ordering mass society."[41] Allowing a small number of technologists and financiers to dominate a huge portion of the economy and the information pipelines, and to monetize every aspect of human behavior, seems incompatible with democratic self-determination.[42]

Stanley Bing's novel *Immortal Life* portrays a society in the near future that is ruled by tech oligarchs. A chaotic government has essentially been replaced by a cabal of superannuated tech moguls who control 97 percent of sales in all market sectors—retail, entertainment, agriculture, and so on—through "one huge, interconnected skein of interests."[43] Democratic government hasn't just been constrained; it has been made superfluous. The overlords implant devices into human brains, and plan to dominate the world by controlling the central cloud that all humanity is plugged into. The novel's subtitle calls the story "soon to be true," and it may not be awfully far from the mark.

What we must ask ourselves is whether we want the hierarchical, socially stagnant, centrally programmed future that the oligarchs have in mind for us. Given what their vision appears to be, and what we already see in California, resisting them represents the great imperative of our time.

PART III

The Clerisy

A thoroughly scientific dictatorship will never be overthrown.

—Aldous Huxley, *Brave New World*

CHAPTER 7

The New Legitimizers

With populist movements and parties gaining influence not only in North America but in Europe and Latin America as well, many have been predicting a new era of authoritarianism, such as portrayed by George Orwell in *1984* or by Margaret Atwood in *The Handmaid's Tale*.[1] But the more likely model for future tyranny is Aldous Huxley's *Brave New World*, where the masters are not hoary Stalinoids or fanatical fundamentalists, but gentle, rational executives known as World Controllers.

The Controllers preside over a World State composed of five biologically engineered social castes, from Alphas at the top to Epsilons at the bottom. Alphas take for granted their preeminence and their right to the labor of lower castes. People no longer have children, since humans are developed in vats. Families have been abolished, except in a few distant "savage reservations." Citizens of the World State live in amenity-rich dormitories and enjoy pleasurable pharmaceuticals and unconstrained sex without commitment or consequences. This family-free life is similar to how Mark Zuckerberg described his ideal Facebook employees: "We may not own a car. We may not have a family. Simplicity in life is what allows you to focus on what's important."[2]

Huxley's scenario eerily resembles what today's oligarchs favor: a society conditioned by technology and ruled by an elite with superior intelligence. The power of the Controllers in *Brave New World* resides mostly in their ability to mold cultural values: like those at the top of today's clerisy they suppress unacceptable ideas not by brute force but by characterizing them as deplorable, risible, absurd, or even pornographic. Because their pronouncements are accepted as authoritative, they can run a thought-dictatorship far more subtle, and efficient, than that of Mussolini, Hitler, or Stalin.[3]

In the Middle Ages, the teachings of the Catholic Church on social and cultural values were generally seen as having great moral authority. The medieval clergy preached a value system heavily influenced by St. Augustine, who had sought to replace the values of classical society— materialism, egotism, beauty, ambition—with chastity, self-sacrifice, and otherworldliness.[4] As Pitirim Sorokin wrote, the clerical class turned the "sensate culture" of classical civilization into an "ideational" one centered on spiritual concerns.[5]

When the cultural role of the clergy diminished in the modern era, their part was gradually taken up by what Samuel Taylor Coleridge termed a "clerisy" of intellectuals. Religious clerics would remain part of this class, though on the whole it grew more secular over time. Today's clerisy includes university professors, scientists, public intellectuals, and heads of charitable foundations.[6] Such people have more or less replaced the clergy as what the great German sociologist Max Weber called "the new legitimizers."[7]

The Ideal of a Cognitive Elite

The concept of a governing class whose superior cognitive ability makes them rightful leaders goes back at least to ancient Greece, when Plato proposed a society run by the brightest and most talented—a vision that Marx described as "an Athenian idealization of the Egyptian caste system." Later utopian literature, such as Thomas More's *Utopia* in the sixteenth century, depicts enlightened people constructing a just and prosperous society, but with strict limits on freedom for the masses.[8]

At the beginning of the twentieth century, H. G. Wells envisioned an "emergent class of capable men" who could take upon themselves the responsibility of "controlling and restricting very greatly" the "non-functional masses." Wells predicted that this new elite would replace democracy with "a higher organism," which he called "the New Republic."[9]

The New Deal era brought considerable support for placing more decision-making power in the hands of university professors and other specialists, and even some well-credentialed journalists. During the Second World War and the Cold War, the idea of relying more on scientists, engineers, and other intellectuals in matters of public policy gained strength.[10] The sociologist C. Wright Mills advocated the creation of a ruling cognitive elite, asking, "Who else but intellectuals are capable of discerning the role in history of explicit history-making decisions?"[11]

As economic competition from Germany, Japan, and other countries grew in the 1970s, some American policy intellectuals argued for establishing a powerful cadre of planners to bring rational order to the "untidy competitive marketplace," which they saw as weakening the American economy.[12] Today, people such as the journalist Thomas Friedman and the former Obama budget adviser Peter Orszag have called for granting more power to credentialed "experts" in Washington, Brussels, or Geneva, in the belief that our societal problems are too complex for elected representatives to address.[13]

Today's "Knowledge Class"

Half a century ago, Daniel Bell recognized an emerging "knowledge class," composed of people whose status rested on educational attainment and access to knowledge in a postindustrial society.[14] Theoretically it represented a meritocracy, but this class has become mostly hereditary, as well-educated people, particularly from elite colleges, marry each other and aim to perpetuate their status. Between 1960 and 2005, the share of men with university degrees who married women with university degrees nearly doubled, from 25 percent to 48 percent.[15] As Bell observed, parents of high status in a meritocracy will use their advantages to improve their children's prospects, and in this way, "after one generation a meritocracy simply becomes an enclaved class."[16]

Michael Lind uses "professional and graduate degrees" as a way of measuring what he calls the "managerial overclass," which includes "private and public bureaucrats who run large national and global corporations" as well as directors of nonprofits and university professors. He estimates the "overclass" to be some 15 percent of the American population.[17] Charles Murray defines a "new upper class" more narrowly, as the most successful 5 percent in managerial positions, the professions, and the media, and he estimates it at roughly 2.4 million people out of a country of over 320 million.[18] (By comparison, the First Estate in France was around 1 percent of the population on the eve of the revolution.)[19] In France today, Christophe Guilluy identifies a "privileged stratum" of people who gain from globalization, or at least are not harmed by it, and who operate from an assumption of "moral superiority" that justifies their privilege.[20]

What I designate as the clerisy is a group far larger and broader than the oligarchy. It spans a growing section of the workforce that is mostly employed outside of material production—as teachers, consultants, lawyers, government workers, and medical providers.[21] These professions are largely insulated from the risks of the marketplace. They also make up an increasing proportion of the workforce in the high-income countries: many of the fastest-growing occupations since 2010 have been in the arts, personal care, and health care, usually tied to nonprofits or the state. Meanwhile, those in private-sector middle-class jobs—small-business owners, workers in basic industries and construction—have seen their share of the job market shrink.[22]

The picture is similar in Europe. In France, well over a million lower-skilled industry jobs have disappeared in the past quarter century, while the numbers of technical jobs have increased markedly in both the public and private realms.[23] Those who work for state industries, universities, and other clerisy-oriented sectors enjoy far better benefits, notably pensions, than those working in the purely private sector.[24]

Many of the people in these growing sectors are well positioned to exert a disproportionate influence on public attitudes, and on policy as well—that is, to act as cultural "legitimizers."

"Engineers of the Soul"

The clerical estate in the Middle Ages could mold cultural attitudes through its power over education and the written word. In modern times, this role is often played by what Stalin famously recognized as "engineers of the soul"—journalists, novelists, filmmakers, actors, and artists.[25]

Writers and other creative people are often portrayed as being resistant to authority and tolerant of differing viewpoints, but history often reveals them to be no more willing to oppose orthodoxy than anyone else. Many of Russia's most brilliant minds endorsed or assisted the Bolshevik efforts to remake the culture, and were often rewarded with comfortable lives while the masses struggled to survive. The new ruling elites helped themselves to the property and possessions of the old aristocracy.[26]

In Germany, right-wing intellectuals such as Oswald Spengler, Carl Schmidt, and Edgar Jung helped plow the ideological field ahead of the Nazis.[27] Many prominent creative people welcomed the Führer as a fellow artist—albeit one who had failed miserably as such in Vienna—and avidly assisted Hitler's efforts to "cleanse" German culture of foreign contamination. In the first months of the regime, "testimonials of loyalty rained down upon it unrequested," writes the historian Frederic Spotts. Some of those testimonials were self-serving, he suggests, since Nazi policies were hostile to leftist intellectuals and artists, as well as gays and Jews.[28]

Whether on the left or the right, totalitarianism "represents the twentieth-century version of traditional religiosity with its own dogmas, priesthood and inquisitions," notes the historian Klaus Fischer.[29] The priests of totalitarianism have often been academics or artists or intellectuals—representatives of a modern clerisy.

Toward a New Orthodoxy

In the decades following the Second World War, a healthy debate about culture and society took place in the United States—albeit within limits— between conservatives and liberals, and even Marxists. In contrast to the brazen propaganda of the Soviet and Fascist regimes, the U.S. news media embraced an ideal, though not always followed in practice, of impartiality and respect for the validity of numerous viewpoints.

Today the news media are increasingly inclined to promote a single orthodoxy.[30] One reason for this is a change in the composition of the journalistic profession: working-class reporters, many with ties to local communities, have been replaced by a more cosmopolitan breed with college degrees, typically in journalism. These reporters tilt overwhelmingly to the progressive side of politics; by 2018, barely 7 percent of U.S. reporters identified as Republicans, and some 97 percent of all political donations from journalists went to Democrats.[31] Similar patterns are found in other Western countries too. In France, as two-thirds of journalists favor the socialist left, and sometimes spend considerable effort in apologizing for anything that might offend certain designated victim groups.[32] The political tilt in journalism has been intensified by a geographical concentration of media in fewer centers—especially in London, New York, and San Francisco.[33]

At the same time, as a 2019 Rand report shows, journalism is steadily moving away from a fact-based model to one dominated by opinion. Usually it is left-leaning opinion that dominates, but a shift toward opinion also appears in the residual media institutions on the right. The Rand study suggests that the result for society is "truth decay."[34]

Entertainment media are also turning into bastions of left-wing orthodoxy. Once divided between conservatives and liberals, Hollywood now tilts heavily to the left, as do its imitators elsewhere. Jonathan Chait, a liberal columnist, reviewed the offerings of major studios and networks, and found "a pervasive, if not total, liberalism."[35] This tilt reflects the political views of the executives: over 99 percent of all political donations by major entertainment executives in 2018 went to Democrats.[36]

There is a conservative branch of the "clerisy" today: some journalists and academics and residents of think tanks. But they have little influence in the dominant mainstream media, the universities, or the wider culture. The real cultural power and influence are in what Thomas Piketty calls the "Brahmin left" rather than the "Merchant right."[37]

The modern clerisy tend to believe themselves more enlightened than the average person—on attitudes about the family, for example—and seek to impose their own standards through the media, the education system, and various arenas of cultural production. Their judgments about such issues as race relations and "white privilege" can be even more unforgiving than traditional religious teaching on homosexuality, divorce, or birth control. People who venture outside the "correct" worldview may be made to feel they have committed a kind of "original sin," for which they can ask forgiveness but will nevertheless remain excommunicated.[38]

Technocratic Authoritarianism

Those who harbor a sense of natural superiority tend to support strong governmental action in line with their personal values and an overconfidence in their own competence, according to research by Slavisa Tasic of the University of Kiev on decision making in government.[39] But the history of unaccountable rule by "experts," or those claiming intellectual superiority, is less than encouraging for liberal democracy.

Mussolini's Fascist ideology is now viewed as reactionary and clownish, but it highlighted the idea of a society governed with scientific principles by a cognitively superior ruling class.[40] Soviet Communism, the sworn enemy of Fascism, followed a similar technocratic course. In the late 1890s, Engels saw technology as the key to achieving the productivity gains that could transform societies without the need for capitalism.[41] Marx believed utterly in the crucial role of technocratic administrators and scientists in society. He even offered to dedicate *Das Kapital* to Charles Darwin.[42] Marx's first successful acolytes, the Bolsheviks, believed that a small, ideologically motivated elite could turn a backward Russia into the most advanced and progressive regime on earth. The Bolsheviks would replace the old aristocracy with their own ideological elite, whom they believed could orchestrate a more egalitarian society. "If 10,000 nobles could rule the whole of Russia," Lenin asked. "why not us?"[43]

At the time of the USSR's collapse, the *nomenklatura* constituted a true elite of 750,000 people. They and their families were a mere 1.5 percent of the population, not far different from the nobility's percentage in fourteenth-century France.[44] While Stalin had hoped they would come from a "special mold," they showed themselves to be "ordinary mortals as fallible as other men." After the fall of the Soviet regime, some members of the *nomenklatura* used their influence to gain control of privatizing industries, emerging as powerful oligarchs.[45]

The most powerful clerisy on earth today is in China. Intellectuals and scholars long played an influential role in Chinese politics and administration—similar to the role once played in the West by clerics when they were by far the most literate element of the population.[46] Traditionally, the Mandarinate followed Confucianism, which celebrates learning not "for the sake of the self" but as a way to cultivate "the communal quality" that could help shape the society, as the Chinese scholar Tu Wei-ming writes.[47]

While Mao Tse-tung was hostile to the old Mandarinate, he placed a high value on technical expertise, with a typically Marxist faith in science. "We shall teach the sun and moon to change places," he predicted, and he needed the brainpower of his nation to do so.[48] Yet the scientific and technical experts either respected or feared the ruling authorities so much that they did not openly confront the insane policies of the Great Leap Forward that led to a famine and killed as many as 36 million people.[49] One witness, the journalist and author Yang Jisheng, writes that the Party cadres viewed the peasants as "expendable." The cadres "became overbearing and vicious in imposing one campaign after another, subjecting disobedient people to beatings, detention and torture."[50]

After Mao, the Chinese government opened itself up to more grassroots input, particularly in the economy, and welcomed some diversity of viewpoints.[51] But as the horrors of the Maoist period receded into the past, entrepreneurial skill became less valued and a higher importance was given to academic credentials. In contemporary China, and indeed throughout East Asia, an elite college degree often determines social status, the ability to earn enough for a decent apartment, and whom one can marry or even date.[52]

Academic credentials are the ticket into the "professional and managerial class" that staffs the most powerful bureaucracies of the Chinese state.[53] According to a recent survey, this highly educated class does not constitute a potential opposition to the Party state, but instead serves as a bulwark of the authoritarian regime. David Goodman suggests that highly educated Chinese would likely oppose any democratizing reform that could allow the less-educated masses to assert their voices. Even the Chinese students who study in the United States and elsewhere in the West support the regime, as it will benefit them when they return.[54]

The modern Mandarinate is helping to direct society and regulate the lives of citizens with the aid of intrusive technology. As we have seen, for example, a "social credit" system is used to award various rights or privileges, such as the right of travel, to those who show proper behavior.[55]

Who Watches the Watchers?

Members of the contemporary clerisy who hold positions of power like to be seen as disinterested actors, making rational choices for the good of society. But they are people with their own prejudices and self-interest. Japan's much-lionized public bureaucracy has been portrayed as a model of selfless, patriotic bureaucracy, dedicated to the public good, but in reality many top bureaucrats move on to high-paying jobs in the very industries they once monitored, under a system known as *amakudari* or "descent from heaven."[56]

In the United States and Europe, elite bureaucrats tend to deny any ideological bias or class interest. But as James Burnham noted, they generally share an ideology of "managerialism," centered on efficiency in producing the results desired by managers themselves. As the managerial class grows in power, it becomes more self-referential. Its members are responsible not to the citizenry, but only to other managers and to those regarded as part of a qualified peer group.[57]

The complexity of problems facing our society—climate change, mass migration, or the effects of technology, for example—may often seem beyond the competency of elected representatives. If higher education made for better people with wiser judgment, it might be tolerable to hand great powers for controlling society to highly educated experts. But as Aldous Huxley observed, scientists and other experts do not own a monopoly on either virtue or political wisdom.[58]

There are clear dangers in ceding too much power to unelected and unaccountable elites who claim moral authority or expertise backed by higher education. Rule by the most educated and highly credentialed people is profoundly illiberal, observes Yascha Mounk, a Harvard progressive.[59] Many elite progressives—the core of the clerisy—might prefer such a model for society, but it would endanger political pluralism, especially when the credentialed elites are overly sure of their own correctness. A survey commissioned by the *Atlantic* notes that the highly educated are now arguably the least politically tolerant group in America.[60]

In coming decades, the clerisy could employ "new intellectual technology" as a means of "'ordering' the mass society," as Daniel Bell predicted.[61] Technology might be employed to reprogram attitudes on everything from the environment to the notion of "unconscious bias" against racial and sexual minorities. Companies like Google as well as college campuses already use technology to monitor and "correct" the thinking of employees.[62] The Chinese government's efforts to monitor thoughts and regulate opinion, sometimes assisted by U.S. tech firms, could prove a harbinger of things to come in Europe, Australia, and North America.[63]

Before we permit the clerisy to have such powers, we may want to consider the old Latin phrase: *Quis custodiet ipsos custodes*—who watches the watchers?

CHAPTER 8

The Control Tower

niversities have long served as gatekeepers for the upper classes, but they are doing less well at what was arguably their greatest twentieth-century triumph: expanding opportunities for the many.[1] The reach of higher education grew dramatically in the last century, and so did the importance of academic credentials for getting good jobs. Elite degrees have become more crucial for access to the most lucrative positions, even as the top schools have grown more socially exclusive.

This is not just an American story. In China, for example, the regime has greatly expanded higher education, especially in technical subjects, in a drive to achieve economic and technological preeminence. The number of college *teachers* in China has risen by one million in the past two decades.[2] But higher education also serves as a key to entrance into the nation's ruling class, and an elite degree is highly prized. By 2012, at least five of the nine members of the Politburo Standing Committee, China's top decision-making body, had children or grandchildren who had studied at elite American universities in a program launched ten years ago by the Communist Party to train the next generation of Mandarins.[3]

Looking at the question globally, David Rothkopf, author of *Superclass: The Global Power Elite and the World They Are Making*, compiled a list of more than six thousand members of what he calls the global "superclass": leaders of corporations, banks and investment firms, governments, the military, the media, and religious groups. From this list,

Rothkopf and his colleagues drew a "globally and sectorally representative sample" of three hundred randomly selected names, and found that nearly three in ten had attended one of twenty elite universities, particularly Stanford, Harvard, and the University of Chicago.[4]

Universities have also been seen as reinforcing the preeminence of what John Sexton, president of New York University, calls the "idea capitals" of the world, such as New York, Boston, London, Paris, and Beijing—all having universities and their graduates as a major part of their economic growth engine.[5]

Forging the New Elite

Perhaps nothing has so defined or enhanced the role of the clerisy in American society as the expansion of universities. Enrollment in colleges and universities in the United States increased threefold between 1910 and 1940.[6] Another great expansion began as the postwar baby boomers were reaching college age. The total number of people enrolled in college in the United States grew from 5 million in 1964 to over 7.6 million in 1970, and then to some 20 million today.[7] The percentage of college graduates in the labor force soared from under 11 percent in 1970 to over 30 percent in 2010—a proportion that has remained about the same since then.[8]

The increase in college attendance is even greater globally. Across the world, the number of enrollments in higher education was expected to grow from 214.1 million in 2015 to 250.7 million by 2020, and may rise to 377.4 million by 2030 and 594.1 million by 2040. Some 40 percent of college students will then be in East Asia and the Pacific, while South and West Asia will be home to more than a quarter of all college students.[9]

Cutting against this democratizing trend in the United States, however, is the soaring cost of a university education: it more than tripled as a proportion of the national median salary between 1963 and 2013.[10] This has made the top universities more socially exclusive, even as they have become more important for success. The elite universities have grown richer both in their endowments and in the academic qualifications of the students they admit, relative to less well-positioned institutions.[11]

Harvard, Princeton, Stanford, and Yale collectively enroll more students from households in the top 1 percent of the income distribution than from households in the bottom 60 percent.[12] Well-to-do families can better afford not only the high tuition costs of elite universities but also the expense of excellent primary and secondary schools. Only 2.2 percent of the nation's students graduate from nonsectarian private high schools, yet these graduates account for 26 percent of students at Harvard and 28 percent at Princeton.[13] High-income parents can also give their children such advantages as museum trips, SAT coaching classes, and unpaid internships. Robert Reich, a lion of the left and a former Harvard professor, characterizes the modern elite universities as being designed mainly "to educate children of the wealthy and upper-middle class."[14]

Today's leading universities are filling the role envisioned by Charles Eliot, who became Harvard's president in 1869: taking the lead in creating an enlightened national ruling class—the Alphas, if you will.[15] A *National Journal* survey of 250 top American public sector decision makers found that 40 percent of them were Ivy League graduates. Only a quarter had earned a graduate degree from a public university.[16]

Top universities have considerable power over access to the best jobs in the private sector. Nitin Nohria, dean of the Harvard Business School, has shown how corporate leaders in the second half of the twentieth century shifted away from reliance on family networks or religious communities in hiring, toward a preference for an MBA or similar credentials from a business school. This change might have had a democratizing effect, but the intense competition for jobs effectively winnows down the pool to graduates of the most select institutions. Those without an elite degree may find a corporate niche, but often as a contractor or in a low-level position that offers little chance of climbing the ladder through hard work and experience.[17]

In Britain likewise, the expansion of higher education was once regarded as a means of breaking down class barriers, but university degrees now accentuate these divisions instead. As the emphasis on academic credentials grew, notes David Goodhart, so did the advantage of the graduates from elite schools, who are mostly upper-class. These schools account for 7 percent of all college graduates, but 50 percent of the nation's print journalists and 70 percent of the senior judiciary.[18]

There are not only class divisions between elite schools and the rest, but even a growing class divide within universities in the United States. Administrators, deans, and tenured faculty live in what one writer compares to a modern form of manorialism, where luxury and leisure come as of right.[19] Yet much of the actual academic work is done by a class that more closely resembles the impoverished parish priests of medieval times. Teaching adjuncts now constitute 70 percent of the U.S. academic workforce—up from 55 percent four decades ago—and one in four of this group lives on some form of public assistance. Some of them actually see their commitment to the academy as akin to a monk's "vow of poverty."[20]

Redefining Knowledge

The historian J. B. Bury, in 1913, described the Middle Ages as a time when "a large field was covered by beliefs which authority claimed to impose as true, and reason was warned off the ground."[21] The relationship between reason and revelation was a challenging question in medieval universities, which all had a liberal arts curriculum in addition to one or more of the advanced professional faculties: law, medicine, and theology. Church authorities wanted to have clergy trained in the defense of orthodox doctrine after heretical movements had arisen, and they were watchful over the teaching of theology in the universities. Theology was the dominant field at Paris, where scholars were licensed to teach by the bishop. The University of Paris became a staunch guardian of orthodoxy, and in the 1300s it held a conclave to affirm the reality of demons that were supposedly infecting society.[22]

At the same time, medieval scholars regularly debated contrary propositions, and tried to reconcile reason with revelation, or the natural philosophy of Aristotle with Christian doctrine. Church authorities attempted to suppress ideas considered heretical, with condemnations and sometimes imprisonment, though in the long run they were not successful.[23] John Wycliff espoused heretical doctrines at the University of Oxford in the fourteenth century, and Jan Hus did likewise at the University of Prague in the early fifteenth century. In other fields, the idea of an expanding body of knowledge gradually began to displace a focus on learning what had already been said by "authorities."

Over the centuries, the university gradually emerged as a beacon of open inquiry and tolerance for different viewpoints. The liberalizing trend was strongest at first in the Netherlands, which in the seventeenth century had more university students than England and attracted many from other countries. In other parts of Europe, professors could still be fired for deviations from orthodoxy, but all in all the university became a leading center for contending opinions, for experimentation, and for the synthesis of disciplines.[24] It was a place for pushing the frontiers of knowledge and for passing down the accumulated wisdom of the past.

Half a century ago, Pitirim Sorokin observed something different appearing in the academic world: "a frantic eagerness to know 'more and more about less and less.'"[25] University professors today seem determined to narrow the field of inquiry, specializing in obscure topics of little interest to anyone outside the university, or even to many inside. The vast majority of academic articles—so crucial for getting tenure—are rarely cited, especially in the social sciences and humanities.[26] Academic life has grown sterile and irrelevant to most people, even as an academic degree has become more important than ever for an individual's prospects.[27]

Repressing Tolerance

Once seen as champions of free thought and inquiry, universities have been reverting to something more like a medieval model in which heretical ideas come under assault. Today the attack is likely to come from inside, rather than from an external oversight body like the Catholic Church. Even so, the zeal for enforcing ideological orthodoxy is reminiscent of the pattern in states such as the Soviet Union,[28] or Nazi Germany, where universities served as a "stronghold" of the regime.[29]

The current mission in universities, and even in lower schools, is "to promote" a particular set of beliefs rather than "to *teach*," notes Austin Williams.[30] Instead of celebrating a diversity of opinion, academia seems to have adopted the notion of "repressive tolerance" developed by the German philosopher Herbert Marcuse, who said that tolerance for different views—that is, views he disapproved of—was really a form of oppression. Although himself an exile from Nazi repression, Marcuse insisted that liberal societies were hardly less oppressive than the Nazi or Soviet systems and no more deserving of support. He asserted that the concept of "liberty" was employed as a "powerful instrument of domination."[31]

Marcuse would likely be pleased that today's universities are achieving levels of unanimity that one might have found in a medieval school of theology or in a Soviet university. In 1990, according to survey data by the Higher Education Research Institute at UCLA, 42 percent of professors identified as "liberal" or "far-left." By 2014, that number had jumped to 60 percent.[32] A few years later, a study of fifty-one top-rated colleges found that the proportion of liberals to conservatives was generally at least 8 to 1, and often as high as 70 to 1. At elite liberal arts schools like Wellesley, Swarthmore, and Williams, the proportion reaches 120 to 1.[33] The skew is particularly acute in fields that most affect public policy and opinion. Well under 10 percent of faculty at leading law schools, such as Harvard, Yale, Stanford, Columbia, and Berkeley—schools that graduate many of the nation's leaders—describe themselves as conservative.[34]

In other countries too, academia is far to the left of the general population. Roughly half of British voters lean to the right, while less than 12 percent of academics do.[35] Similar ratios are common across Europe and in Canada.[36]

This political skewing has the effect of transforming much of academia into something resembling an ideological reeducation camp. For example, prominent schools of journalism, including Columbia's, have moved away from teaching the fundamentals of reporting, to openly advancing a leftist "social justice" agenda.[37] Even some progressives, like the legal scholar Cass Sunstein, recognize that "students are less likely to get a good education, and faculty members are likely to learn less from one another, if there is a prevailing political orthodoxy."[38]

Yet there seems to be little desire among university administrators to counter the slide ever deeper into ideological conformism. Instead, many are promoting it. One college president in Canada, for example, justified efforts to tamp down on "free speech" by saying it was intended to encourage "better speech" and to protect "the humanity of students, faculty and staff."[39] As many as twenty campuses in the United States ask professors to sign a pledge to support the official campus doctrines concerning "diversity" of a superficial kind, which does not mean diversity of opinion. These pledges eerily reprise the "loyalty" pledges that were common during the darkest days of the Cold War.[40]

As a result, universities appear to be nurturing a generation of activists who more resemble Bible-thumping preachers than open-minded intellectuals. The new university-minted activists tend to look for "moral purity" on issues surrounding the doctrine of "intersectionality," said James Lindsay, an atheist philosopher. "They especially tend to demonize heretics or blasphemers or anyone who goes too far outside that dogmatic

structure of belief and threatens it. Those people are often excommunicated."[41] According to recent studies of cognitive behavior, the products
of today's universities are inclined to maintain rigid positions on various
issues, confident of their own superior intelligence and perspicuity, and
to be intolerant of other views. For example, the *Atlantic* found less tolerance for differing opinions in the Boston area, and other places with a
high proportion of university graduates, than in less-educated regions.[42]

An Age of "Mass Amnesia"

Universities can get away with obscurantism and enforced ideological
conformism because of their enormous power over labor markets. They
are no longer primarily about learning, as Jane Jacobs noted, but about
providing the credential needed for a high-paying job.[43] One recent study
of American college students found that more than one-third "did not
demonstrate any significant improvement in learning" in four years of
college.[44] Employers report that recent graduates are short on critical
thinking skills.[45]

Equally worrying is that students in the West are not acquiring
familiarity with their own cultural heritage. Universities no longer take
the care they once did to transmit the genius of the past—with its often
inconvenient lessons—to the next generation. We are in danger of "mass
amnesia," being cut off from knowledge of our own cultural history,
writes Jacobs.[46]

In the early Middle Ages, much of the thought and writing from
the classical era was lost through neglect, as literacy plummeted and the
attention of clerics turned first to theological matters—although what
was preserved from the classical past is thanks to the diligent labors of
the monks who copied and recopied manuscripts.[47] Most peasants and
even many nobles, being illiterate, lacked firsthand knowledge not just
of classical works but even of the Bible. Today's young people are not so
illiterate but are often ignorant of the past.

It's ironic that while we enjoy easier access to information than ever
before, we are falling behind in real knowledge. We are replacing books
with blogs, and essays with tweets. Book reading outside of school or
work has declined markedly among the young in particular. A survey
done in 2014 found slightly over half of American children saying they

liked to read books "for fun," down from 60 percent in 2010.[48] This is not just an American trend. A landmark study by University College London tracked 11,000 children born in 2000 up to age fourteen and found that only one in ten ever did any reading in their space time as teenagers.[49]

Unfortunately, the universities too often are not picking up the slack by offering a curriculum rich in classic literature and history. University policies on curriculum largely ignore writers such as Homer, Confucius, Shakespeare, Milton, Tocqueville, or the founding fathers.[50] Some books are scorned for having been written by dead white males, who as a group are linked to such horrors as slavery, the subjugation of women, and mass poverty. At many U.S. colleges, books written before 1990 are considered "inaccessible" to students.[51]

A decay in the teaching of history and civics may help explain why millennials, despite their higher rates of university education, are far more likely than previous generations to be dismissive of basic constitutional and civil rights. They are also far more likely than their elders to accept limits on freedom of speech, which is a natural result of the political culture on campuses. Some 40 percent of millennials, notes the Pew Research Center, favor suppressing speech deemed offensive to minorities—well above the 27 percent among Gen Xers, 24 percent among baby boomers, and only 12 percent among the oldest cohorts, many of whom remember the Fascist and Communist regimes of the past.[52]

Similarly, European millennials display far less faith in democracy and less objection to autocratic government than previous generations, who lived either under dictatorships or in their aftermath. Young Europeans are almost three times as likely as their elders to believe that democracy is failing.[53]

The expansion of higher education may once have exemplified the promise of liberal civilization to increase opportunity for all. But universities could now be accelerating the decline of liberal culture by graduating students who too often have not learned what brought it into existence.

CHAPTER 9

New Religions

"Religion is a central defining characteristic of civilizations," observed Samuel Huntington.[1] We can see its importance in the evolution of the earliest cities in Mesopotamia and Egypt, India and China. Religion provided a view of the world that helped people cope with disasters and the fear of death, offering hope for immortality.[2] It provided a moral code and a means of social cohesion. As traditional churches have lost influence in the modern era, a space has opened for the growth of new spiritual affiliations to serve similar purposes.

The Catholic Church today is divided and enmeshed in scandal. The formerly dynamic evangelical movement is losing adherents in the developed world. Across the board, America, once considered an exception to the global secularizing trend, is now rapidly "unchurching."[3] The millennial generation in the United States are leaving religious institutions at a rate four times that of their counterparts three decades ago; almost 40 percent of people ages 18–29 have no religious affiliation.[4]

The trend is even more pronounced in Europe, where well over 50 percent of those under age 40 do not identify with any religion. The big loser here is Christianity. In the United Kingdom, there are as many Muslims now attending weekly prayer as Christians attending church. Since 2001, the country has seen the closure of some five hundred churches.[5]

This does not mean that religious belief is disappearing; many people reject organized faiths but maintain some spiritual values.[6] Today, fewer people than ever attend church, but two-thirds of unaffiliated Americans polled by Pew still believe in God or a universal spirit.[7] These individuals may be looking for some new spiritual rock upon which to rest their hopes or their search for meaning.

The Church of "Social Justice"

There are new religious currents emerging within some long-established faith traditions. In Catholicism, Reform Judaism, and various mainline Protestant denominations, orthodox beliefs are being supplemented or even supplanted by what could be called a gospel of social justice activism.[8] This trend reflects the changing character of universities and theological seminaries, where faculties lean heavily to the left. In religion departments of top liberal arts colleges, liberals outnumber conservatives by 70 to 1.[9]

The "woke" members of today's progressive churches are changing religions from within, and the churches most committed to the progressive course are in the most serious decline. Mainstream Protestant denominations have lost five million members in the past decade.[10] The Catholic Church, now under a reforming and politically progressive pope, is losing adherents not only in North America and Europe, where the pope's views are widely applauded, but also in his homeland of Latin America. Today roughly one in four Nicaraguans, one in five Brazilians, and one in seven Venezuelans are former Catholics.[11] In contrast, the more conservative faiths—including some evangelical churches, Orthodox Judaism, and fundamentalist Islam—are still robust, thanks in part to higher birth rates, particularly in the developing world.[12]

Despite the vitality of some denominations, it is entirely possible that the traditional, mainstream religions in the West will be doomed to cultural irrelevance within a few decades. According to Pew, for example, Christianity will be the minority faith across Britain and in some other European countries by 2050.[13]

The Green Faith

As traditional faiths are waning, environmentalism is coming to resemble a faith for the new age. Christianity offered guidance for how one should live and conduct one's personal affairs in a manner pleasing to God, but the green movement seeks to steer people toward a life in better harmony with nature. Environmentalism, says Joel Garreau, has become "the religion of choice for urban atheists."[14]

Like medieval Catholicism, the green faith foresees impending doom caused by human activity.[15] To people in the Middle Ages, wrote Barbara Tuchman, "apocalypse was in the air." The Final Judgement, brought on by human sin, was not only real but imminent. St. Norbert in the twelfth century predicted that the event would come within the lifetime of his contemporaries.[16] Similarly, the environmental movement—whether religious, scientific, or leftist—routinely traces a direct line from human materialism to looming catastrophe.[17]

In his highly influential 1968 book, *The Population Bomb*, Paul Ehrlich claimed that humanity would "breed ourselves to extinction" if birth rates were not severely curtailed. A widely hailed Club of Rome report in 1972 predicted massive shortages of natural resources unless there was a shift to lower birth rates, slower economic growth, less material consumption, and reduced social mobility.[18] Often such pronouncements are accepted uncritically in media, academic, and political circles.[19] Yet these apocalyptic predictions, like those in the Middle Ages, could turn out to be exaggerated or even plain wrong.[20] Contrary to environmentalist dogma from the 1970s, for example, natural resources, including energy and food, did not run out, but became more readily available.[21]

This is not to say that real environmental crises do not need to be confronted, any more than Christianity's critique of human sin and selfishness should be considered irrelevant to our lives. But today as in the past, there is an element of hypocrisy among some of those who tell others to be content with poverty or extol its virtues. In the Middle Ages, most parish priests and their communicants suffered great material hardship, while many bishops lived in luxury, "loaded with gold and clad in purple," as Petrarch put it.[22] Similarly, environmentalists aim to impose austerity on the masses while excusing the excesses of their ultra-rich supporters.[23]

Even as they urge everyone else to cut back on consumption, the "green rich" buy a modern version of indulgences through carbon credits and other virtue-signaling devices.[24] This allows them to save the planet in style. Recently, an estimated 1,500 GHG-spewing private jets were flown to Davos carrying people to a conference to discuss the environmental crisis. Few of the high-profile climate activists seem willing to give up their multiple houses, yachts, or plethora of cars.[25]

Perhaps most disturbing, some in the green movement have become highly dogmatic in their views, often denigrating or even persecuting those who dare dissent in any way. Today, open discussions on the environment and how best to preserve the planet are about as rare as open debate over God's existence would have been in the Catholic Church of the eleventh century.

Some veteran climate scientists—such as Roger Pielke and Judith Curry, or the Greenpeace founder Patrick Moore, or former members of the UN International Panel on Climate Change—have been demonized and marginalized for deviating from what Curry has described as an overly "monolithic" approach to the issue of climate change.[26] Some climate activists even seem ready to take dissenters to court in an effort to ban their ideas by legal means. Not only energy companies but think tanks and dissident scientists have been targeted for criminal prosecution.[27]

These tactics are all too reminiscent of the medieval Inquisition.[28] It is a very poor way to tackle a complex scientific issue, where open inquiry and debate are needed, observes Steve Koonin, President Obama's undersecretary of energy for science.[29]

Transhumanism: The Faith of the New Ruling Class?

Another contender to be the new faith of the oligarchy is "transhumanism," the search for eternal life through technology. "The rise to power of net-based monopolies coincides with a new sort of religion based on becoming immortal," writes Jaron Lanier.[30] Potentially the most radical and far-reaching of the emerging creeds, transhumanism is a distinctly secular approach to achieving the long-cherished religious goal of immortality.[31] The new tech religion treats mortality not as something to be transcended through moral actions, but as a "bug" to be corrected by technology.[32]

Although it sounds a bit like a wacky cult, transhumanism has long exercised a strong fascination for the elites of Silicon Valley. Devotees range from Sergei Brin, Larry Page, and Ray Kurzweil (of Google) to Peter Thiel and Sam Altman (Y Combinator). Kurzweil celebrates new technologies that allow for close monitoring of brain activity.[33] Y Combinator is developing a technology for uploading one's brain and preserving it digitally.[34] The aim is to "develop and promote the realization of a Godhead based on Artificial Intelligence."[35]

In some ways, transhumanism seems natural for those who hold technology above all other values. It dispenses with the physical and emotional realities of belonging to a church. Transhumanism offers a "marketing opportunity for new technology," notes Thomas Metzinger of Gutenberg Research College in Mainz. An immortality app can be offered for sale to the transhumanist customer base.[36]

This new faith represents a major break with traditional religions. Christianity, Judaism, and Islam stressed the essential equality of people (at least among the faithful), and commanded acts of charity and other good deeds toward the less fortunate. These teachings would eventually feed into democratic and egalitarian thinking, particularly in the West.[37] Equality is not something that concerns the transhumanists, though. Yuval Noah Harari sees instead a future where "a small and privileged elite of upgraded humans" gain control of society and use genetic engineering to cement the superior status of their offspring. Their aim will be not to follow God's laws but to become gods themselves, by a kind of directed and accelerated evolution:

> Bioengineering is not going to wait patiently for natural selection to work its magic. Instead, bioengineers will take the old *Sapiens* body, and intentionally rewrite its genetic code, rewire its brain circuits, alter its biochemical balance, and even grow entirely new limbs. They will thereby create new godlings, who might be as diferent from us *Sapiens* as we are different from *Homo erectus*.[38]

Clearly the tech elites' search for immortality does not address issues that affect those still living within nature's limits. Someone needing assistance in a disaster is more likely to look toward a church member than a data scientist for help. Organized faiths at their best serve as powerful instruments of social improvement, with particular concern for the needy. The secular social justice warriors may be passionately committed to their causes, but often it is groups like the Baptists or the Church of Jesus Christ of Latter-Day Saints who come to the rescue faster and more effectively in a crisis.[39]

Religious institutions have long brought together people of disparate backgrounds and economic status, building social bonds between them and serving as unifying transmitters of tradition and cultural identity. In contrast, the new forms of religion seem likely to divide people along political and cognitive lines. Without a physical basis in local communities, they don't encourage the mingling of diverse people, but tend to be self-selecting for those who see themselves as both morally and intellectually superior to the vast majority of the population. They may offer guidance on how to prolong life, but little in the way of moral instruction. A world without traditional religion might still have people with spiritual awareness, but it would be short on the blessings of institutions that have promoted community, sacrifice, and faith for millennia.

PART IV

The Embattled Yeomanry

No bourgeois, no democracy.

—Barrington Moore

CHAPTER 10

The Rise and Decline of Upward Mobility

F ar from the congenial warmth of the Mediterranean shores, the Netherlands sits on the cold and waterlogged fringe of northern Europe. The ancient inhabitants of the region, the Batavi, served Rome as auxiliaries but gave little in the way of tribute. They didn't have much to trade, but they never lost their sense of independence. In the first century they rebelled against Roman imperial taxes, and though eventually defeated, they left an enviable reputation for ferocity.[1] In time, this obscure race, nurtured on a hard-won spit of soggy land, would lead a shift in the balance of world power away from the Mediterranean, China, and the Islamic empire, toward a handful of small countries along the North Sea.

The Low Countries occupied a tiny corner of the continent, short in natural resources, but by the thirteenth century the inhabitants had begun to expand their territory by draining swamps and building dikes. Improvements in agricultural methods led to an early commercialization of the countryside and fueled a wider economic "takeoff." As the economic historian Jan de Vries observed, "capitalism grew out of the soil in Holland."[2] The region was more urbanized than most of Europe, with a sizable population of artisans and prosperous merchants. In the sixteenth century, the northern provinces rejected Catholicism in favor of Calvinism, a creed more congenial to commerce.

After expelling their Spanish Habsburg rulers in the seventeenth century, the United Provinces built the world's most powerful maritime empire, with a fleet larger than all the rest of Europe's put together. Amsterdam's port, where as many as eight thousand ships were docked, bustled with a rich trade in foodstuffs, hemp, hops, and dye plants. The opportunistic Dutch expanded their commercial activity in part by pioneering technological changes decades ahead of their competitors.[3]

But arguably the greatest achievement of the Dutch lay in creating a republic free from aristocratic or clerical domination, as the expulsion of the feudally inclined Spanish overlords empowered the bourgeoisie.[4] The Dutch expanded human rights, including those of religious minorities and women, and cultivated a keen interest in children and the nuclear family. Dutch culture was family-centered, inventive, sober, frugal, and tolerant. A separation of science and philosophy from religion was exemplified in the writings of Baruch Spinoza, among others.[5] Although majority Calvinist, the country boasted large colonies of Catholics, Jews, and other outsiders, including Muslims; roughly a third of Amsterdam's population in 1650 were foreign-born. Some immigrants came as merchants or artisans, but even the poorest, observed one Dutchman in 1692, "cannot die of hunger if he works hard."[6]

As late as the eighteenth century, the Dutch Republic was regarded as a poor country, and the British viewed it as "the indigested vomit of the sea."[7] But the reclaimed land helped raise a substantial class of small landowners at a time when most property in Europe was owned by the aristocracy or the church. The growing ranks of proprietors were the heart of Dutch dynamism, and they set down "the geographical roots of republican liberty," notes the historian Simon Schama.[8]

The Rise of the Yeomanry

The Dutch Republic represents an early and robust growth of economic and social mobility, shaking up the more static, hierarchical order that was typical of the medieval world. A similar process would spread through western Europe and then far beyond.

The middle orders—neither slaves nor elites—had long suffered under heavy taxation and restrictions on their choices. Most peasants, unable to stay on their own farms, had been compelled to place themselves under the protection of a powerful landlord. Reduced to serfdom and bound to labor on a particular estate, they were legally "unfree." This reality for the masses became entrenched during the Middle Ages.[9]

A series of historical developments undermined the basis of the stratified, agrarian order. These include a warming climate, a diminishing threat of invasion, more efficient agricultural practices, a demographic rebound, and the revival of commerce and urban culture, particularly around the Mediterranean and the Baltic.[10] By the thirteenth century, serfdom was waning in much of western Europe. Some manumitted serfs would suffer from the loss of basic protections afforded in the feudal system, but others were able to acquire land for their own farms, or start enterprises in the reinvigorated cities.[11]

Advances in military technology also served to lift the status of commoners. Most people could not afford to buy the armor or maintain the horses used by the medieval warrior nobility, but small landowners and artisans could wield new weapons such as the longbow, and eventually pikes and muskets, and serve as foot soldiers for kings or princes. When a force of common soldiers could defeat heavily armored knights on horseback, it signaled decline for the military dominance of the feudal nobility.[12] Organized citizen forces would become more important in warfare—as in Cromwell's New Model Army, which epitomized a new kind of military organization during the English Civil War.[13] Eventually, the legions of revolutionary France challenged the entrenched aristocracy in the historic heartland of feudalism. In 1792, Goethe watched an army of patriotic French volunteers together with soldiers of the former royal army defeat the vaunted Prussians at Valmy, and remarked: "Here and on this day begins a new era in world history."[14]

At the same time, economic growth led to rising expectations for what the common person could attain in life on earth, something rare in feudal times.[15] For many centuries, or even millennia—despite advances in agriculture and the growth of commerce—average incomes remained nearly the same and material conditions changed little. It was only during the seventeenth century that sustained economic growth appeared to be possible. Average income then began to rise dramatically, first in Britain and the Netherlands.[16]

When the industrial revolution was proceeding apace, Karl Marx declared the rising bourgeoisie to be "the first to show what man's activity can bring about" by exchanging the veneer of religiosity and chivalry with "naked, shameless, direct, brutal exploitation."[17] He saw a new form of oppression on the horizon. Marx's analysis held much truth, as a growing urban proletariat suffered under dismal working conditions and grim prospects. But his prognostication that capitalism would become ever more oligarchic proved to be exaggerated.

Capitalism did not produce the dystopia that Marx predicted, but instead uplifted a large portion of the masses and created a solid middle class (a designation first used in Britain in 1812).[18] A study covering the United Kingdom, the Netherlands, and the United States shows that all three saw a rapid decline in the concentration of wealth from the 1820s up to the 1970s.[19] Never before had so much prosperity and relative economic security been so widely enjoyed.[20] And with more prosperity came a stronger political voice.

The End of Mobility

This remarkable social uplift, the great achievement of liberal capitalism, is now distinctly threatened, and with it the long-term future of democracy. In the last four decades, the wealth gap between the rich and the middle class has grown to levels not seen since the dawn of the industrial era.[21] In many countries, the income gap between the top 1 percent of the population and the remaining 99 percent is at an all-time high.[22]

In the United States, the historic heartland of middle-class aspiration, the chance of midrange earners moving up to the top rungs of the income ladder has declined by approximately 20 percent since the early 1980s.[23] But the diminishing of upward mobility is a global phenomenon. It is also occurring in sub-Saharan Africa and Russia, as well as Latin America and India.[24]

European countries renowned for their robust social welfare provisions are showing the same pattern. Social mobility has declined in over two-thirds of European Union countries, including Sweden.[25] Germany is significantly less equal than its EU peers, with richer households controlling a bigger share of assets than in most other western European states. The bottom 40 percent of German adults hold almost no assets at all; barely 45 percent own homes.[26]

This trend is even more marked in the English-speaking world. In Great Britain, a decline in the numbers of middle-wage jobs has depressed wages at the lower end, and increased unemployment among the young; more broadly, it has brought a halt to social mobility.[27] "We are facing a new set of problems," said Frances O'Grady, general secretary of the once powerful Trades Union Congress. "We have people with degrees doing Mickey Mouse jobs and young people who will have no occupational pension and no house to sell to see them through old age."[28]

In the United States, inequality decreased substantially in the first half of the twentieth century, but has grown dramatically since the 1970s. The wealth differential between middle-income and upper-income households had reached unprecedented levels by 2015.[29] Data from the Census Bureau show that the share of national income going to the middle 60 percent of households has fallen to a record low.[30] Wealth gains in recent decades have gone overwhelmingly to the top 1 percent of households, and especially the top 0.5 percent.[31]

The property-owning middle class has never been monolithic, and today some have benefited from the increasing value of their homes. Those in the upper-middle class who hold elite professional or managerial positions have done well, particularly in the older generation.[32] Overall, the biggest winners from the largely asset-based prosperity following the Great Recession were those with large holdings of property or stocks, rather than Main Street businesses or ordinary homeowners.[33] As one conservative economist put it succinctly in 2018, "The economic legacy of the last decade is excessive corporate consolidation, a massive transfer of wealth to the top 1 percent from the middle class."[34] In the United States, an affluent class of roughly 1.35 million—the top 1 percent—is doing fine, but wealth gains have been especially concentrated among the top 0.1 percent, roughly 150,000 people.[35] Since the mid-1980s, the share of national wealth held by those below the top 10 percent has fallen by 12 percentage points, the same proportion that the top 0.1 percent gained.[36]

The same trends are appearing in East Asia, which in the recent past showed the most dramatic growth in the size and prosperity of the middle class in the world. Since 1990, famously egalitarian Japan has seen not only a declining average standard of living but also a considerable widening of the gap between the wealthy and everyone else.[37] In China, egalitarian socialism may be the prevailing ideology, but the country is now more unequal than most Western nations. Its Gini index—a measure of inequality—has gone from highly egalitarian in 1978 to more stratified than Mexico, Brazil, or Kenya, as well as the United States and virtually all of Europe.[38] The nascent middle class made some progress, but the big gains occurred in the top 1 percent of the population, and particularly in a tiny fraction of that group. The income of the ultra-wealthy expanded by more than twice the national average rate.[39] Middle-class Chinese people now find it difficult to buy property or get ahead.[40]

Discouraging Democracy

The earliest democracies in Athens and Rome rested on an assertive property-owning middle class. Aristotle warned about the dangers of an oligarchy that would control both the economy and the state; in fact, an ever greater consolidation of wealth played a role in undermining Greek democracy and the citizen-led Roman Republic. By the end of the Republic, over 75 percent of all property was owned by roughly 3 percent of the population, while over four-fifths owned no property.[41]

The political economy that would define the Middle Ages had roots in imperial Rome, when small farmers and artisans were being displaced by slaves imported from the far ends of the expanding empire. Occupations and social status came to be determined by heredity. The middle ranks of citizens, whom Gibbon called "the most respectable part of the community," were burdened by debt. A growing portion of the citizenry, unable to feed themselves or find honest work, subsisted on state-sponsored "bread and circuses": in the late Roman Empire, 300,000 Romans held bread tickets.[42] The backbone of the *res publica* had become something of a proletarian mob.

In the feudal era, most people labored in fields they did not own, and most were illiterate. The idea of self-government for the masses would have seemed absurd, even sacrilegious, and was barely even considered.[43] A comeback of democracy depended principally on a property-owning middle class and on respect for commercial enterprise, which was widely viewed as ignoble in the Middle Ages. A growing commercial economy, first in Italy and the Low Countries, would help fuel the growth of an assertive middle class in western Europe. But the same did not happen everywhere even in countries that became wealthy and powerful.

Chinese culture was long defined by the values of the Mandarins, who generally despised the commercial class. In the eleventh century, Hsia Sung portrayed merchants as being infected with greed and love of luxury, and complained that peasants were diverted away from honest agricultural work to seek an "idle living by trade." Such prejudices were reinforced with heavy taxes and regulatory burdens on entrepreneurs, while the central state established monopolies over key commodities such as salt, iron and wine.[44] The social status of entrepreneurs remained low well into the modern era, which clearly impeded China's progress toward an industrial revolution.[45] Chinese entrepreneurship flourished mostly on the imperial periphery, or outside the boundaries of the empire, often in places controlled by European powers.[46]

The Mandarin class and the great landowning families continued to dominate Chinese society, while the strength of family loyalties and obligations left little room for a sense of individual rights. Aristocracy remained commonplace across Asia, at least until the American occupation in Japan and the Communist revolutions in China, Vietnam, and elsewhere.[47] The aristocratic and clerical establishments exercised a strong control over social life. In China, innovative merchants and artisans did not dare challenge the class system, but instead accepted its Mandarin values.[48]

The class hierarchy was, if anything, more oppressive in India, with its strictly defined, closed castes. The Vaishyas, or nonservile commoners, were considered inferior to the priestly (Brahmin) and warrior (Kshatriya) castes, and were subject to imperial confiscations, which discouraged business investment and expansion. One of the authors of India's constitution in the twentieth century, B. R. Ambedkar, who came from the lowest caste, the Dalits, said he feared Brahmin repression of enterprise more than anything that might have come from British colonialists.[49]

Even in parts of Europe and its colonies, the persistence of feudal attitudes slowed the rise of a middle class, and of democracy. Spain conquered much of the world, but nevertheless stagnated both economically and socially under a system that the seventeenth-century economist Martín González de Cellorigo described as one dividing society between "rich who loll at ease, or poor who beg," lacking "people of the middling sort, whom neither wealth [in land] nor poverty prevents from pursuing the rightful kind of business enjoined by natural law."[50]

In the New World, the "customs and values of old Castile" were grafted onto Spanish colonies, suggested Robert D. Crassweller.[51] In Mexico
and Argentina, for example, society was dominated by the Catholic
Church and a well-off leisured class supported by vast numbers of slaves
and semi-slaves.[52] The legacy of this economic and social order would
discourage the growth of democratic institutions over the long term. Even
today, landownership in Latin America is highly concentrated, which
is one reason why the middle class has been so weak and authoritarian
politics so pervasive.[53]

The Development of Western Democracy

In most of western Europe, aristocratic and ecclesiastical domination
of landownership gave way to a more "individualistic" concept of property rights.[54] A substantial class of independent smallholders developed
and began to demand the rudiments of constitutional order and self-
governance.[55] Artisans and merchants practiced an early form of self-
governance within their guilds. It was the ascendant middle class, willing
to challenge the aristocracy and even the clergy, that drove democratic
reform. As the radical social theorist Barrington Moore said a half century ago, "no bourgeois, no democracy."[56]

To be sure, the Western progress toward more democratic governance
did not at first give equal rights to all—far from it. Prosperity came partly
at the expense of indigenous peoples in European colonies, including
those of the Dutch and the British. Belgium's control of the Congo was
particularly heinous, with the use of forced labor from the native residents
to serve a small European minority of crony capitalists and government
administrators.[57] American success was built in part on the destruction
of indigenous cultures and a revival of the abhorrent practice of slavery.
But these democratic countries were not unique in their cruelty; other
colonial expansionists—such as the Russians, the Ch'ing Chinese, and
the Japanese—were typically far from gentle.[58]

Moreover, the places once colonized by Western nations have generally benefited from the legacy of liberal capitalism. The democratic, liberal
spirit thrives, albeit under greater pressure, in both Hong Kong and India,
for example, as well as those places that grew under the influence of the
United States, such as South Korea and Taiwan. Democratic capitalism
brought widely shared prosperity to a large part of the world.

But today a new generation, in the United States and much of the high-income world, faces diminishing prospects of owning land or advancing into a comfortable middle-class life. Instead of a progressive, woke, egalitarian age, we may be entering an era that is more feudal in its economic and social structure.

CHAPTER 11

A Lost Generation?

"Young people do not degenerate; this occurs only after grown men have already become corrupt," wrote Montesquieu in the eighteenth century.[1] Our children may take this statement to heart when they find that their elders are leaving them with a poorer future. Three-quarters of American adults today are not confident that their children will be better off than themselves.[2] A Pew poll in 2017 found that parents are more likely to think their children will be financially worse off than themselves rather than better off.[3]

In the United States, a country built on aspiration, the fading prospects for the new generation are painfully obvious. About 90 percent of those born in 1940 grew up to earn higher incomes than their parents, according to researchers at the Equality of Opportunity Project. The same is true for only 50 percent of those born in the 1980s.[4] Baby boomers enjoyed an era of a rising middle class, but millennials inherit a world in which the middle class is struggling almost everywhere, notes the OECD.[5] According to a recent study by the Federal Reserve Bank of St. Louis, millennials are in danger of becoming a "lost generation" in terms of wealth accumulation.[6]

The generational shift could have a profound effect on our economic, political, and social order. Compared with their parents, young people today are more likely to have a future with no substantial assets or property. A Deloitte study projects that millennials in the United States will hold barely 16 percent of the nation's wealth in 2030, when they will be the largest adult generation by far. Gen Xers, the preceding generation, will hold 31 percent, while boomers, entering their eighties and nineties, will still control 45 percent of the nation's wealth.[7] A recent analysis of Federal Reserve data shows that young Americans with a college degree today earn about the same on average as boomers without a degree did at the same age. While an elite degree opens doors to the upper strata of society, the same is far from true of all college degrees. Upwards of 40 percent of recent college graduates now work in jobs that don't typically require a college degree.[8]

The economic prospects of individuals now depend greatly on their year of birth, with the younger cohorts generally doing worse than earlier generations.[9] It is no surprise that recent college graduates report the highest levels of anxiety in the country, and that Americans in the post-millennial generation, or Generation Z, are the most likely to embrace socialistic views.[10]

The same pattern appears in virtually every advanced country. The Pew Research Center found that poll respondents in France, Britain, Spain, Italy, and Germany are even more pessimistic about the next generation than those in the United States.[11] Pessimism about the next generation is also widespread in important developing countries such as India, South Africa, and Nigeria.[12] Among the most pessimistic countries, however, is Japan, where three-quarters of those polled believe that things will be worse for the next generation.[13]

The Decline of Homeownership

During the mid-twentieth century, homeownership rates in the United States grew rapidly, from 44 percent in 1940 to 63 percent thirty years later.[14] Now the trend is in the opposite direction. According to Census Bureau data, the rate of homeownership among young adults at ages 25–34 was 45.4 percent for Generation X, but dropped to 37 percent for millennials.[15]

Similar trends are seen in other high-income countries. Australia historically has had high rates of homeownership, but the rate among those 25–34 years old dropped from more than 60 percent in 1981 to only 45 percent in 2016. The proportion of owner-occupied housing has dropped by 10 percent in the last 25 years.[16] A trend toward long-term "rentership" has also been found in Ireland.[17]

In the United Kingdom, only a third of millennials own a home, compared with almost two-thirds of baby boomers at the same age. In the 1960s, those born before the Second World War spent 8 percent of their income on housing, but millennials now spend almost a quarter. British millennials today, on average, will need nineteen years to save for a home deposit; it took only three years in the 1980s. A third of millennials, according to projections, will have a lifetime of renting, with less space, poorer conditions, often longer commutes, and more insecurity than the baby boomers experienced.[18] A report in 2018 found twice as many British millennials living in rental housing than their Gen X predecessors. At least one-third of British millennials are likely to remain renters for life.[19]

The trend seems likely to spread to China, which for the last three decades has seen vigorous growth in homeownership. Now, in the face of soaring property prices, many children of the working class and even the middle class will probably not be able to achieve homeowner status. A growing percentage of all apartments are rentals, particularly in the large cities such as Beijing and Shanghai.[20] Most young Chinese people may be destined to pay rent to the landowning class rather than own a piece of the pie themselves.[21]

The New Real Estate Feudalism

Some pundits have suggested that the decline of homeownership is a reflection of changing preferences among younger people. This notion is repeatedly asserted by orthodox elements of the clerisy—urban planners, social pundits, liberal intellectuals. It is echoed by investors who seek to create a "rentership" society where people remain renters for life, enjoying their video games or attending to their houseplants, never knowing the pleasure of having a real garden or backyard of their own.[22] Such a plan could assure a steady profit for the landlord class, but would destroy the dream of ownership for the average person.[23] In reality, most young people in advanced countries tell surveyors that they desire a single-family home, as did their elders.[24]

The problem is policies—notably in California, the United Kingdom, Canada, Australia—regulating land use in ways that elevate the price of real estate beyond the reach of far too many people. In some places there are distinct moves to make single-family homes all but impossible to build. Virtually all regions of the world with the highest home prices have regulations designed to encourage development in the inner urban rings and discourage or even ban construction on the more afford-able periphery.[25] In Australia these rules have raised housing prices by $100,000 or more.[26]

Policies to restrict development, particularly on the urban periphery, are sometimes justified by invoking a lack of developable space. But even in the relatively crowded United Kingdom only 6 percent of the land is urbanized, while barely 3 percent of the United States is urbanized. The figure is 0.2 percent in Canada, and less than 0.3 percent in Australia.[27] We are seeing an artificial shortage of developable space, which generates wealth for current homeowners while making it far harder for younger people to own property.[28]

In places that have high population densities, the situation is even worse. In Hong Kong, where housing prices have tripled in the past decade, some 210,000 middle-class and working-class residents now live in tiny spaces—some described as hardly bigger than a coffin—in illegally subdivided apartments. It is easy to blame a shortage of space, but here too there are policies that control land use for the benefit of local government and powerful speculators.[29]

One critic of these policies, Alice Poon, in *Land and the Ruling Class in Hong Kong*, accurately labels it a "feudalistic" system.[30] Kenneth Tong, a 34-year-old academic researcher living with his parents, compares his generation's predicament to playing a game of monopoly that has been going on for fifty years and all the property is taken. "If you continue to play this game," he says, "the disparity between rich and poor will be wider . . . and more and more people will live in abysmal conditions."[31]

Inheritance Makes a Comeback

In the emerging neo-feudal world, the older generations benefit from rising home values and rental income, as do the well-heeled institutional investors.[32] But their good fortune needs to be weighed against the shrink-ing prospects for a younger generation who face a formidable challenge in boosting their net worth and escaping serf status.[33] Homes today account for roughly two-thirds of the wealth of middle-income Americans, and homeowners have a median net worth roughly eighty times that of renters, according to the Census Bureau.[34]

In this new order, "inherited wealth will make a comeback," writes Thomas Piketty. Inheritance as a share of GDP in France grew from roughly 4 percent in 1950 to 15 percent in 2010. Millennials who received bequests inherited more money than many workers make in a lifetime. The growing importance of inherited assets is even more pronounced in Germany, Britain, and the United States.[35]

In the next generation, inheritance may play a bigger role in the social order than it has since the nineteenth century. The children of property-owning parents are far better situated to own a house eventually (often with parental help) and enter what one writer calls "the funnel of privilege."[36] In America, a country with a national mythology that looks askance at inherited wealth, millennials are three times as likely as boomers to count on inheritance for their retirement. Among the youngest cohort, those ages 18–22, over 60 percent see inheritance as their primary source of sustenance as they age.[37]

Back to Steady-State?

Some people see the diminishing prospects for property ownership as a long-overdue rejection of middle-class materialism. The environmental magazine *Grist* envisioned "a hero generation" that will escape the material trap of suburban living and work that ensnared their parents.[38] This view is popular among the elite clerisy, particularly the green advocates. It also holds appeal for the rentier class—which Piketty calls the "enemy of democracy"—as they would be assured of steady profits by collecting rents while the middle class loses independence.[39]

The younger generations, increasingly destined to be without property of their own, are even losing ownership of their personal data. They hand over large amounts of personal information, often unknowingly, to big tech firms in exchange for free services. Rather than the much-ballyhooed "sharing economy," we are seeing an economy based on mining personal data for the benefit of a few companies. In this way, the middle class will become digital serfs in what Gaspard Koenig calls "digital feudalism."[40]

CHAPTER 12

Culture and Capitalism

C lose ties and common goals shared between a powerful, wealthy class and a priestly or intellectual class have shaped many cultures throughout history, including the feudal era.[1] Today a symbiosis between the economic oligarchy and the clerisy poses the biggest threat to the future of the middle class, as it serves to promote values and advance policies harmful to their well-being.

The link between business and the clerisy in modern times is especially strong in China, where businesses take advantage of their ties to decision makers in government. The Chinese scholar Zhou Xiaohong suggests that these two classes together control most of the country's wealth. After all, nearly 40 percent of private entrepreneurs also belong to the Communist Party.[2]

In the West, entrepreneurs have historically tended to be a force for liberalization and for limiting the power of entrenched aristocracies and clerical elites, since "commerce desires to be free," in the words of the seventeenth-century Dutch economist Peter de la Court.[3] By contrast, leading oligarchs in today's tech and finance sectors are often inclined to support the heavy-handed "progressive" policies embraced by the dominant elements of the clerisy—as long as it doesn't threaten their own fortunes.[4] Thus the real cultural power lies in the "Brahmin left," to use Thomas Piketty's term.[5]

"Post-Economic Goals"

Alvin Toffler predicted almost half a century ago that growing affluence would result in replacing the profit motive with more aesthetic goals, a quest for self-fulfillment, or unbridled hedonism. "Affluence serves as a base from which men begin to strive for post-economic goals," he wrote.[6] The "woke" values of the upper classes are an example of such "post-economic" goals.

Many business leaders—and the vast majority of students at the Harvard Business School—favor what the philosopher John Gray calls "hyper-liberalism," defined as a "mixture of bourgeois careerism with virtue-signaling self-righteousness."[7] A large proportion of top CEOs see it as their responsibility to influence public attitudes and policy, rather than simply meet the needs of shareholders or serve customers. A kind of "corporate vigilantism" has appeal for some business leaders.[8] The notion of social responsibility plays into advertising and CEO pronouncements in firms such as Audi, Gillette, Procter & Gamble, Nike, Apple, and Pepsi.[9] To be sure, this might please some consumers, while alienating many others.

People in occupations like construction, the energy sector, or agriculture tend to favor less intrusive economic and social policies. On the other hand, well-educated managers of major companies and their technical staff are naturally attracted to the idea of a society ruled by professional experts with "enlightened" values—that is, by people much like themselves.[10] This trend among corporate leaders brings the oligarchy closer to the elements of the clerisy—lawyers, academics, the media—that have long looked down on the middle orders. "Rid society of the dictatorship of the middle class," the literary historian Vernon Parrington suggested in the late 1920s, "and the artist and the scientist will erect in America a civilization that may become what civilization was in earlier days, a thing to be respected."[11]

The Green Class Order

The "Brahmin left" and their allies in the oligarchy are in conflict with the yeomanry on environmental issues above all. In 1972, the influential book

Limits to Growth was published with backing from major corporate interests, led by Aurelio Peccei of Fiat. The authors' long-term vision was based on the notion that the planet was running out of resources at a rapid pace. They called for establishing "global equilibrium" through restrictions on growth and "a carefully controlled balance" of population and capital.[12] The goal was to end economic growth in the near future, which would effectively put an end to upward mobility as we have known it.

The understandable concern over climate change today has tightened the alliance between the clerisy and the oligarchs. Nonprofit foundations—depositories for old money, including that of the Fords and the Rockefellers—have become leading advocates of radical climate policies. Many of these policies are directly injurious to the middle class and working class, by inflating energy and housing prices, for example, or by stifling industrial development.[13]

The oligarchs and the clerisy are generally better able to afford the costs of environmental radicalism. The ultra-wealthy are not much worried about high prices, while the clerisy typically are cloistered in institutions—such as academia, the media, or government—that are relatively unharmed by regulatory burdens. They can hector everyone else, writes the progressive author Anand Giridharadas, since they "have continued to hoard the overwhelming share of progress" while "the average American's life has scarcely improved."[14]

The wealthy can demand strict environmental policies to curb climate change because they can afford it—as long as the policies are not so radical as to restrict their ability to live in mansions or fly in private jets. By contrast, bans on fossil fuels would seriously harm an oil rigger, factory employee, or construction worker who drives an old truck to work.[15]

Some environmental zealots, such as the *Guardian*'s environmental reporter George Monbiot, openly hope for a recession as a way to reduce carbon emissions, even if it causes people to lose their jobs and homes. For this reason, James Heartfield, a Marxist historian, says that "green capitalism" represents a new ruse for the upper classes to oppress those below them. The "Brahmin left" essentially employ a concern for global ecology to force the middle and working classes to absorb the costs of centrally imposed scarcity, under the pretext of "human survival."[16]

Literacy and Empowerment

While the middle classes are being squeezed by policies they have had little ability to shape, their future is still largely within their own hands. But that depends on maintaining or recovering the values and habits that gave birth to a strong middle class, including literacy and a commitment to learning.

In the middle of the fifteenth century, literacy rates in Europe were generally quite low—perhaps 5 percent overall in England, though substantially higher in cities and in the more urbanized societies of the Netherlands and Italy. Few women were literate. This changed dramatically after the introduction of the printing press, especially in the cities of northern Europe. By 1650, about half the British population could read. Literacy in the Netherlands soared to about 85 percent by 1750.[17]

A literate populace was better equipped to demand rights and oppose injustice, to understand written charters, and to organize effectively around a common program; indeed, a few literate peasants may have had a leading part in the rebellions of the later Middle Ages. High rates of literacy in colonial America allowed traders and mechanics to spread the revolutionary message against the monarchy and helped them organize their resistance, as Benjamin Franklin noted.[18] In twentieth-century America, a literate culture was widely shared between cultural arbiters and the middle class. Average Americans in the 1950s were purchasing large numbers of classical works and books by contemporary authors such as Ruth Benedict and Saul Bellow. Many enjoyed watching Shakespeare plays on television, with one program attracting a remarkable 50 million viewers.[19]

That common culture is now fraying from both directions. Cultural creators are inclined to gear their products not so much to the tastes of the mass market as to the particular concerns of the clerisy. Television audiences for shows like the Academy Awards have been declining, especially among the young, as prizes rarely go anymore to quality films with broad popularity, such as *West Side Story*, *The Sound of Music*, or even the original *Lord of the Rings*. Instead, award-winning films are chosen primarily for their appeal to insiders.[20] At the same time, Hollywood makes most of its money from cartoonish superhero movies, suited to a postliterate audience.[21]

Reading for enjoyment is in decline among the young today, as we have seen. Despite high rates of college attendance, cognitive skills seem to be weakening too. Many employers in the United States report difficulty finding workers capable of having a serious conversation. Over 60 percent of applicants are found to be lacking in basic social skills.[22] Today's teens are becoming limited in their experiences to what they access on their phones and social media. Rather than opening minds, social media seem to be creating a generation with little ability to communicate in person.[23]

There are growing concerns about the affects of social media on the minds of young people. Sites like Facebook and Instagram have been linked to reduced attention span: research indicates that the average attention span has fallen 50 percent since 2000, mainly due to social media use.[24] Young people are turned into internet "addicts" through marketing tactics reminiscent of the much-denounced attempts of tobacco companies to hook teens on their product with subtle messaging.[25] A former Facebook executive who was vice president for user growth, Chamath Palihapitiya, is now so worried about the influence of social media that he tries to keep his own children from too much exposure—as do some other tech executives. Palihapitiya warned that the social network is "ripping apart the social fabric of how society works."[26]

The Nuclear Family

Along with literacy, another characteristic of a successful bourgeois society historically was greater emphasis on the nuclear family, rather than extended kin groups, as the basic social unit. Motherhood was elevated in the cultural imagination, and a more tender regard was shown for children.

Barbara Tuchman observed that medieval songs, folk tales, and literature often portrayed children being hunted, abandoned, drowned, or lost in the woods—at a time when barely half of children survived to adulthood. Women were cast mostly in the roles of "flirts, bawds and deceiving wives." The only strongly positive image of motherhood, said Tuchman, was that of the Virgin Mother.[27]

Despite the biblical command to be fruitful and multiply, singlehood was highly valued by the Catholic Church. St. Ambrose, the fourth-century bishop of Milan, considered the unmarried to be "as the angels in heaven." During the Middle Ages, large numbers of talented people entered monasteries or convents, and the ideal of celibacy was enjoined upon the whole Catholic priesthood, which further depressed cultural as well as demographic vitality. As many as 15 percent of the population in preindustrial Europe are estimated to have been permanently celibate.[28]

A more dynamic economy in the Early Modern period helped usher in new attitudes toward motherhood, children, and families. In cities like Amsterdam, the development of a prosperous, liberal culture went hand in hand with a growing emphasis on the nuclear family as the fundamental cell of society and a driver of aspirations for social betterment.[29] Simon Schama describes a "Republic of Children" built around the nuclear family. Many travelers to the Netherlands, he writes, "were certainly surprised by the softness with which children were treated." The great paintings of the Dutch Golden Age illuminate this new domesticity. The medieval obsession with the Virgin Mother and the unrealistic cherubim typical of Renaissance painting were replaced with domestic images characterized by "uncompromising earthiness."[30]

This familial focus played a critical role in the rise of democratic institutions. At the time of the American founding, family solidarity was widely considered essential to self-governance. Families provided succor and security, as well as the moral guidance required for living free from overbearing authority. John Adams wrote, "The foundations of national morality must be laid in private families."[31]

Post-Familialism

Family culture is eroding today, especially in high-income countries. What is emerging is a post-familial society, in which marriage and family no longer play a central role. In the United States, the rate of single parenthood has grown from 10 percent in 1960 to over 40 percent today.[32] In Britain, 8 percent of households in 1970 were headed by a single parent; now the rate is over 25 percent. The percentage of children born outside marriage has doubled over the past three decades, to 40 percent.[33]

Post-familial attitudes are, if anything, even more common in continental Europe. By 2000, more than half of births in Sweden were to unmarried women (though most of them cohabiting). The rates in most Western countries are trending the same way.[34]

While childbearing outside of marriage has become more commonplace, birth rates overall have declined: the percentage of American women who are mothers is at its lowest point in over three decades.[35] Among the reasons suggested are the limited prospects for income and affordable housing for those now at the age of family formation. Many people have come to regard children as a luxury, since the costs associated with childrearing, including school and housing, have risen far faster than incomes.[36] This is true not only in the United States, but in virtually all wealthy countries, including those with extensive welfare states.[37]

In East Asia today, a powerful work culture appears to be undermining the long-existing familial culture. "In Singapore, women work an average of 53 hours a week," observes Wolfgang Lutz, a demographer. "Of course, they are not going to have children. They don't have the time."[38] This echoes what Alvin Toffler in 1970 described as a growing immersion in work at the expense of family life. He envisioned a revolution in marriage that would result in a "streamlined family," relying on professional child-raisers. The ideal of long-term marriage would give way, he expected, to more transient relationships and numerous partners at different stages of life.[39]

The old bourgeois emphasis on the importance of family is being replaced in many societies by a preference for single and unattached living. This trend was promoted by the rise of bohemianism in the twentieth century, emphasizing individual empowerment over family obligation. In the United States, more than a quarter of households in 2015 were single-person households. In urban areas like New York City, that figure is estimated at nearly half.[40]

The same pattern can be seen in East Asia, where family attachments were traditionally very strong. In China, nearly 70 percent of adults ages 18–36 are on their own. The growing numbers of single households have been a bonanza for online streaming services that offer a "human connection" to isolated individuals and migrant workers.[41] In Japan, the harbinger of modern Asian demographics, the number of people living alone is expected to reach 40 percent of the whole population by 2040.[42] More and more people are not only living alone but dying alone. There are estimated to be four thousand "lonely deaths" in Japan every week.[43]

An Unmoored Generation

Capitalism and bourgeois culture grew together symbiotically, but the success of capitalism may have sown the seeds of that culture's destruction.[44] Nearly half a century ago, Daniel Bell saw an affluent "new class" rising with values profoundly divergent from the traditional bourgeois norms of self-control, industriousness, and personal responsibility. Instead, it favored a new type of individualism, unmoored from religion and family, which could dissolve the foundations of middle-class culture.[45]

In Japan, traditional values such as hard work, sacrifice, and loyalty are largely rejected by the new generation, the *shinjinrui* or "new race." These younger Japanese, writes one sociologist, are "pioneering a new sort of high quality, low energy, low growth existence."[46] Nearly a third of Japanese in their thirties have never had sex—not a good indicator for family formation.[47]

The yeomanry will need to recover the family values and ambition that once built a thriving middle class, as a defense against falling backward into a more serflike status. More broadly, the future of democracy will depend also on societal values that help elevate people from the lower classes to the middle, from single persons to responsible parents, from propertyless to owners.

PART V

The New Serfs

*One day the property owning class will be overwhelmed
by events far beyond their expectations and quite
outside their comprehension.*

—Friedrich Engels, *The Condition of the
Working Class in England*

CHAPTER 13

Beyond the Ring Road

Pass the fifth ring road outside Beijing and you enter a world very different from the glittering façades of China's modern urban centers. Rather than new high-rises, this district on the periphery consists largely of jerry-rigged buildings and shacks. The streets are dusty, animals lie about in the midday sun, and men line up outside a house known to accommodate the world's oldest profession. It's like a flashback to the China of forty years ago, a poor country where the masses could barely eke out the most basic existence.

Around every major Chinese city, and many smaller ones, lie similar settlements of migrant workers—estimated to number over 280 million—who travel from the impoverished countryside to work on construction sites, bus tables, and perform other tasks that are generally eschewed by the more fortunate Chinese who have urban *hukou*, or residence permits. Unable to claim residency in the city, China's migrants lack access to education and health care. Although they do many of the most dangerous jobs, barely one in four has any form of insurance against injury at work.[1]

China may be the world's factory, but much of the work is done by these unprotected migrants, including children who work at nighttime constructing Amazon's Alexa.[2] Li Sun points out that China's great wealth derives from a "worker-made" economy that would fit a classically Marxist definition of exploitation. Many people work sixty-hour weeks for barely $63 a week in pay. In modern China, former peasants are reprising the role played for millennia by their ancestors who built the wealth of the Middle Kingdom but shared in little of it.[3]

The poverty of rural China is what drives migration to the cities. Around the world, rural areas are typically poorer than cities, but the disparities are usually not so stark as in China. Rural households in America are 4 percent poorer on average than urban households; the difference in China is 63 percent. The much-vaunted Chinese middle class amounts to roughly 12 percent of the population, mostly legal residents of cities, while the 43 percent of the population living in the countryside struggle to subsist.[4] Their road to a better life in the wealthiest urban centers is being blocked, as big cities like Beijing and Shanghai have been declared "full." By 2018 the government was beginning to expel some migrants from big cities, leaving them not only unable to work, but homeless.[5]

The migrants represent just part of a new working class who must fend for themselves without the security promised by the Maoist-era "iron rice bowl." Two-thirds of all Chinese people are either peasants, agricultural laborers, industrial workers, or migrant laborers—all groups unlikely to make it into the middle class by Chinese standards. The vast majority work in the unregulated "informal economy."[6]

Opportunities for the working class to move up are also being restricted by the government's focus on advanced technology sectors and automated production, while a slowing of population growth is reducing the demand for construction workers. Because of the generally poor quality of education in rural areas, migrants typically lack the skills needed to find work in the growing sectors of the economy.[7]

Joe Zhang, writing in the *South China Morning Post*, describes how members of his rural family moved to the city for opportunity, but now the work has dried up:

> Most of my cousins left their farmland about two decades ago for the construction boom in Shenzhen and Zhejiang, and their adult children joined them in recent years. Now their journey back to the village is going to be a painful one.
>
> My cousin Jinghuai is staying put in Shenzhen for now. In 1979, he was almost beaten to death by public security officials for fighting with our village head, and I helped secure his release because I had the unique social status of being the first and only university student from

the commune at the time. Jinghuai dreads moving back to the village, but he will have to if he cannot find another job in Shenzhen soon.[8]

The broad-based upward mobility once seen in the West—and more recently in Korea, Taiwan, and Singapore—may never come to China. Wages in the manufacturing sector are not high enough to lift people into the middle class, writes Nan Chen. "Rather than replicating the middle-class growth of post–World War II America," she observes, "China appears to have skipped that stage altogether and headed straight for a model of extraordinary productivity but disproportionately distributed wealth like the contemporary United States."[9]

The challenges confronting China's migrant workers today are part of a broader global trend of weakening prospects for the working class: diminishing opportunities and declining incomes. Beginning in the 1980s, the industrial labor force globally has received a shrinking share of the gross domestic product pie. In 1975, the labor share was about 64 percent of corporate income, but it dropped to 59 percent by 2012. This pattern applied not only to wealthy markets in the West, but also to labor-rich markets like China, India, and Mexico.[10] Instead of a path upward, those in the global working class increasingly face economic insecurity and even a descent into a new kind of serfdom.

The Road to Serfdom

Serfdom emerged out of the wreckage of the Roman Empire, replacing slavery but reducing free peasants to another form of dependency and subjection. Slaves had been imported from the far ends of the empire as it expanded and were put to work in the huge estates that grew in the countryside. "Today these are large estates," wrote a fourth-century poet; "at one time they were little villages." In the later empire, smallholders began submitting themselves to a large landowner, providing labor in exchange for protection from tax collectors and barbarian invaders. Imperial law in 332 bound these *coloni* to their lord's estate and made labor services mandatory. Out of this system would grow the serfdom that powered the medieval agrarian economy.[11]

After the Roman Empire collapsed, slavery waned, but most of the remaining free peasantry, seeking safety in a chaotic world, devolved into a subject class not much better off than slaves. Speaking of a serf attached to his estate, a French abbot claimed: "He is mine from the soles of his feet to the crown of his head."[12] Serfs could not themselves be bought and sold, but they were legally "unfree" and regarded as inferior. They and their descendants came to have the right to remain on their lord's estate, but not to leave it. They were required to work the lord's untenanted land (or demesne), to pay their lord a portion of what they produced on the plot of land they worked for their own needs, and to give a tithe to the parish church. This would be the condition of at least three-quarters of the European population in the feudal era.[13]

Various factors began to undermine European serfdom, including peasant rebellions that became more frequent in the later Middle Ages. The catastrophic population loss caused by the Black Death (1347–1352) resulted in a labor shortage, giving more leverage to laborers. An increasing use of coinage enabled some serfs to buy their freedom, while urban growth provided new opportunities to make a livelihood. By the fifteenth century, agricultural labor was done more by paid workers than by serfs.[14]

Life remained hard even for free peasants, however. Despite some technological advances and increasing commerce, there was little sustained economic growth for centuries.[15] Fernand Braudel paints the grim reality of life for European peasants in the Middle Ages and into the Early Modern era, a life of "almost total deprivation." Peasants had practically no furniture, often not even a table, and they sold their better food products—like wheat, eggs, poultry and lambs—to their social superiors, contenting themselves with millet and maize supplemented by salt pork once a week.[16]

Similar feudal structures with highly concentrated property ownership, wide disparities in wealth, and economic stagnation lasted even longer in Asia than in the West.[17] By 1913, China's population was four times its size in 1500, but most people were still peasants living in a state of poverty, if not near-starvation. "The bondage of feudalism" remained well in place into the 1940s, Mao observed.[18]

The Triumph of the Working Class

Centuries after serfdom ended in western Europe, a new serflike working class developed in the early industrial era. Displaced peasants and small farmers who went to work in urban factories in the early nineteenth century powered Britain's robust economic growth, but endured conditions arguably worse than those of the poorest inhabitants of ancient cities. Even Rome's slaves had readily available water, but some British industrial workers had to walk a mile and wait in line for it. "Science was improving the mechanical contrivances of life," wrote Philip A. M. Taylor, "but the arts of life were in decline."[19] In the mid-nineteenth century, upwards of 30 percent of the British population owned practically nothing. From these poor laborers would come demands for a greater share of the vast wealth produced by their own labor.[20]

The French bourgeoisie and some peasants, along with their intellectual allies, overthrew the monarchy and ended the privileges of the aristocracy and clergy. But decades later, Alexis de Tocqueville saw widening disparities in property distribution in the emerging capitalist economy. "The great field of battle will be property," he predicted. The next political struggles would begin "between those who possess and those who have nothing."[21] It would be a struggle that the upper classes might lose. Tocqueville was writing in 1847, the year before *The Communist Manifesto* appeared.

But there would not be another revolutionary upheaval in France, or a Marxist-style revolution anywhere in western Europe. The working classes would not need to overthrow the system to improve their prospects.[22] Instead, governments gradually, with considerable nudging, began to address their grievances and accommodate their needs, thus escaping Marxist revolution and autocratic socialism. In the 1850s, living and working conditions were already beginning to improve for laborers in British factories: shorter working days, higher wages, lower taxes on food. The Reform Bills of 1832 and 1867 expanded the franchise, giving a greater political voice to rural smallholders and urban workers. Across Europe, life continued to improve for the working classes, despite some painful periods, especially the Great Depression.[23] Marx never anticipated this development, which undermined the belief in his infallibility held by some acolytes.[24]

In the United States, Alexander Hamilton's vision was congruent with a European-style class system, vesting power in propertied worthies.[25] But populists, notably during the presidency of Andrew Jackson, pushed an agenda that offered the promise of expanded opportunities for both rural freeholders and urban workers.[26] Despite its nasty racial history, brutal policies toward Native Americans, and tolerance of slavery, Jacksonian democracy represented something of a revolution not only in politics but in expectations for average Americans.

After the Civil War, the old merchant and planter elites were displaced by a new industrial aristocracy with enormous and sometimes very conspicuous wealth, but the country as a whole continued to prosper. In 1861 there were three millionaires in the United States, and by the end of the century the number had risen to 3,800. "The swiftness of their accumulations rivaled all previous achievements in the history of lucre," wrote Charles and Mary Beard.[27]

These great fortunes elicited the resentment of many in the middle class and the old upper class, and anger among the industrial workers whose labor helped build that wealth but who had little way to protect themselves from exploitation by the powerful corporations. Social reforms during the Progressive Era and under the New Deal brought substantial gains for laborers, such as the right to organize. The swelling ranks of unionized workers achieved major victories, in particular the so-called Treaty of Detroit in 1950 between the major auto companies and auto workers.[28]

A growing economy as well as union contracts brought improving conditions for communities that had previously been left behind or suffered discrimination, especially African Americans. Large numbers migrated away from the fields of the South to take factory jobs that paid better and offered protection from discrimination. Black women found employment in service jobs and other occupations instead of working as domestic servants. In the three decades after the end of the Depression, the income gap between black and white men shrank by about one-third, and black women made even bigger gains. Racial prejudice persisted, shamefully, but life expectancy, college enrollment, and homeownership rates for black Americans all rose dramatically.[29]

The entire working class was moving upward at the same time. Between 1940 and 1950, the incomes of the bottom 40 percent of American workers surged by roughly 40 percent, while the gains in the top quintile were a modest 8 percent and the top 5 percent saw their incomes drop slightly.[30] The "new industrial state" gave workers an escape from "the wretched freedom of the slums," as John Kenneth Galbraith put it.[31] By the 1960s, the American labor movement could boast of "developing a whole new middle class," said Walter Reuther, president of the United Auto Workers. Industrial laborers could afford to buy homes, send their kids to college, and live the kind of life only the affluent had previously enjoyed.[32]

Goodbye to Reuther's Universe

This promise of a better future for all has been evaporating, and one reason is the decline of private-sector unions. In the United States, membership in trade unions fell from 28 percent in 1954 to 11 percent in 2017. Similar declines have occurred in other countries, including those in northern and western Europe. Since 1985, the proportion of union-ized workers in the higher-income countries dropped from 30 percent to below 20 percent.[33]

Unionization of the workforce has declined in large part because industrial jobs have been disappearing. As early as the 1950s, automation was beginning to eliminate some industrial labor jobs, but such jobs have also been particularly vulnerable to globalization. U.S. trade with China alone, according to the labor-backed Economic Policy Institute, cost 3.4 million jobs between 1979 and 2017.[34] This trend in the United States has been accelerated by some other countries' more jealous protection of their workers. Great Britain too has seen a rapid decrease in the numbers of industrial jobs. Even promising sectors like medical equipment shrank from 150,000 to 30,000 jobs between 1995 and 2015.[35]

In various parts of the world, rustbelts have spring up: in the British Midlands, in the old industrial cities of eastern Germany and northeast-ern France, in Ontario, in Wuhan, in Osaka, in the American Midwest. John Russo and Sherry Linkon have described how the loss of jobs in communities like Youngstown, Ohio, an old steelmaking center, under-mines the sense of worth and optimism among residents, many of whom can recall better days:

> In places like Youngstown, many people still remember what life was like when employment was high, jobs paid well, workers were protected by strong unions, and industrial labor provided a source of pride— not only because it produced tangible goods but also because it was

recognized as challenging, dangerous, and important. The memory of what it felt like to transform raw ore into steel pipes and to be part of the connected, prosperous community that work generated still haunts the children and grandchildren of those workers. They long for the sense of purpose that industrial labor brought, even as they stock shelves at Walmart, wait tables at Applebee's, and try to persuade strangers to make donations from a cubicle at the local call center.[36]

As the numbers of industrial jobs have declined, so have working-class incomes—a sharp reversal from the trend after World War II. For the past four decades in the United States, those below the top 20 percent, including much of what is regarded as the middle class, have enjoyed no consistent gains.[37] The median lifetime incomes (over an assumed thirty-year working life) of American men in all occupations who entered the labor market in 1983 were up to one-fifth lower than those of the cohorts who began work in 1967. This does not mean that all American incomes dropped across the board, but the overall trend was downward.[38]

Upward mobility—the essence of capitalist promise—has declined markedly in virtually all high-income countries.[39] In Ontario, the economic center of historically egalitarian Canada, middle-class jobs are disappearing and being replaced by a mix of highly technical jobs and low-end work.[40] The "job polarization" resulting from shrinkage of the middle-wage sector can be seen in Europe as well, notably Germany, France, and Sweden—countries long associated with social democracy.[41] In the United Kingdom, between 2010 and 2014, urban wages dropped 5 percent even as a million jobs were created.[42] In France, a majority of citizens could not save more than 50 euros ($56) a month.[43]

Future technological advances could further intensify the pressure on the working class globally. In 2017, a British report predicted that about 30 percent of jobs in the UK would be automated within fifteen years, with a higher risk of automation for jobs typically held by men (35 percent) than for those normally done by women (26 percent). It's easier to automate trucking than nursing.[44] Artificial intelligence could accelerate the loss of many kinds of jobs that once provided a means of upward mobility: postal workers, switchboard operators, machinists, computer operators, bank tellers, travel agents. For the 90 million Americans who work in such jobs—and their counterparts elsewhere—the future could be bleak.[45]

CHAPTER 14

The Future of
the Working Class

I n the past, fears of job losses from automation were often over-stated. Technological progress eliminated some jobs but created others, and often better-paying ones. In the early days of the high-tech revolution, many of the pioneering firms—such as Hewlett-Packard, Intel, and IBM—were widely praised for treating their lower-level workers as part of the company and deserving of opportunities for advancement, as well as benefits including health insurance and a pension.[1]

The labor policies of the newer generation of tech giants tend to be vastly different. Firms like Tesla have been sued for failing to pay contract workers the legally mandated overtime rates, and for depriving them of meal and rest breaks. The Tesla plant has wages below the industry average, according to workers, and risk of injury higher than the industry average, notes a pro-labor nonprofit.[2] Given that the high housing prices keep them living far from the workplace, some workers sleep in the factory hallways or in their cars. "Everything feels like the future but us," complained one worker.[3]

The largest tech employer today is Amazon, with 798,000 employees worldwide in 2019.[4] Amazon tends to pay its workers less than rivals do. Many employees rely on government assistance, such as food stamps, to make ends meet. When the company announced it was adopting a minimum wage of $15 an hour, it also cut stock options and other benefits, largely wiping out the raises, at least for long-term employees.[5]

The average Amazon worker in 2018 made less than $30,000 annually, about the same as the CEO made every ten seconds.[6]

Working conditions at Amazon are often less than optimal. Warehouse workers in Britain were reportedly urinating in bottles to avoid being accused of "time-wasting" for taking breaks. Amazon has also patented wristbands that track employee movements, described as a "labor-saving measure." Those who can't keep up the pace are written up and then fired, said one British worker. "They make it like the Hunger Games. That's what we actually call it."[7]

Apple manufactures virtually all its products abroad, mostly in China, although both medical concerns and political factors might change that. In addition to its own employees there, the company relies on the labor of more than 700,000 workers—roughly ten times its U.S. employment—to build Apple products at contractors like Foxconn. These workers suffer conditions that have led to illegal strikes and suicides; workers often claim they are treated no better than robots.[8]

From Proletariat to Precariat

In the old working-class world, unions often set hours and benefits, but many low-status workers today are sinking into what has been described as the "precariat," with limited control over their working hours and often living on barely subsistence wages.[9] One reason for this descent is a general shift away from relatively stable jobs in skill-dependent industries or in services like retail to such occupations as hotel housekeepers and home care aides.[10] People in jobs of this kind have seen only meager wage gains, and they suffer from "income volatility" due to changing conditions of employment and a lack of long-term contracts.[11]

This kind of volatility has become more common even in countries with fairly strong labor laws. In Canada, the number of people in temp jobs has been growing at more than triple the pace of permanent employment, since many workers who lose industrial jobs fail to find another full-time permanent position.[12] The same patterns can be seen in traditionally labor-friendly European countries. From 20 to 30 percent of the working-age population in the EU15 and the United States, or up to 162 million individuals, are doing contract work.[13] A similar trend shows up in developing countries such as Kenya, Nigeria, South Africa, Vietnam, Malaysia, and the Philippines.[14]

Even in Japan, long known as a country of secure long-term employment, the trend is toward part-time, conditional work. Today, some 40 percent of the Japanese workforce are "irregular," also known as "freetors," and this group is growing fast while the number of full-time jobs is decreasing. The instability in employment is widely seen as one reason for the country's ultra-low birth rate.[15]

Many of today's "precariat" work in the contingent "gig" economy, associated with firms such as Uber and Lyft. These companies and their progressive allies, including David Plouffe (who managed Barack Obama's presidential campaign in 2008), like to speak of a "sharing" economy that is "democratizing capitalism" by returning control of the working day to the individual. They point to opportunities that the gig economy provides for people to make extra money using their own cars or homes. The corporate image of companies like Uber and Lyft features moonlighting drivers saving up cash for a family vacation or a fancy date while providing a convenient service for customers—the ultimate win-win.[16]

Yet for most gig workers there's not very much that is democratic or satisfying in it. Most are not like the middle-class driver in Uber ads, picking up some extra cash for luxuries. Instead, they depend on their "gigs" for a livelihood, often barely making ends meet. Almost two-thirds of American gig workers in their late thirties and forties—the age range most associated with family formation—were struggling to pay their bills. Nearly half of gig workers in California live under the poverty line. One survey of gig workers in seventy-five countries including the United States found that most earned less than minimum wage, leading one observer to label them "the last of Marx's oppressed proletarians."[17]

The reasons for their precarious situation are not hard to locate. Gig workers lack many basic protections that full-time workers might have, such as enforcement of civil rights laws. Workers without representation, or even set hours, do not have the tools needed to protect their own position; they are essentially fungible, like day laborers anywhere. Robert Reich, former U.S. secretary of labor, has gone so far as to label the "sharing" economy a "share-the-scraps" economy.[18] Rather than providing an "add on" to a middle-class life, gig work for many has turned out to be something closer to serfdom.

Cultural Erosion in the Working Class

The downward economic trajectory of the working class has been amplified by cultural decline. The traditional bulwarks of communities—religious institutions, extended family, neighborhood and social groups, trade unions—have weakened generally, but the consequences are most damaging for those with limited economic resources.[19]

Social decay among the working class echoes what occurred in the first decades of the industrial revolution, when family and community structures and bonds of religion buckled and often broke. Rampant alcoholism spread "a pestilence of liquor across all of Europe," wrote the Marxist historian E. J. Hobsbawm. In the mid-nineteenth century, forty thousand prostitutes plied their trade in London. The physical condition of British workers was horrible: most were malnourished and suffered various job-related maladies. As late as 1917, only one-third of the young males were considered to be in good health.[20]

In America and elsewhere today, the working classes lag behind the affluent in family formation, academic test scores, and graduation rates. Marriages may be getting more stable in the upper classes, as the sociologist Stephanie Coontz has shown, but as many as one in three births in the nation occurs outside matrimony. In some working-class neighborhoods, particularly those with a large proportion of ethnic minorities, four-fifths of all children are born to unmarried mothers. The rate of single parenting is the most significant predictor of social immobility across the United States and in Europe as well.[21]

These social patterns parallel changes in economic trends. A detailed study in the United States published in 2017 shows that when towns and counties lose manufacturing jobs, fertility and marriage rates decrease, while out-of-wedlock births and the share of children living in single-parent homes increase.[22] In addition, a variety of health problems—obesity, diabetes, disease of the heart, kidney, or liver—occur at much higher rates when family income is under $35,000 than when it is over $100,000. Between 2000 and 2015, the death rate increased for middle-aged white Americans with a low educational level. Anne Case and Angus Deaton say this trend owes primarily to "deaths of despair": suicides as well as deaths related to alcohol and drugs, including opioids.[23] In Europe likewise, a health crisis including drug addiction and drug-related deaths has emerged in old industrial areas, especially in Scotland.[24]

In East Asia, traditionally known for strong family structures, the working class is showing signs of social erosion. Half of all South Korean households have experienced some form of family crisis, mostly involving debt, job loss, or issues relating to child or elder care, notes one recent study.[25] Japan has a rising "misery index" of divorces, single motherhood, spousal and child abuse—all of which accelerate the country's disastrous demographic decline and deepen class division.[26]

An even greater social challenge may emerge in China, where some authorities are concerned about the effects of deteriorating family relations, particularly in care for aging parents. The government has started a campaign to promote the ideal of "filial piety," a surprising revival of Confucian ideals by a state that previously attempted to eradicate them.[27] The problem of family breakdown is especially severe in the countryside. The flow of migrants into the cities in search of work has resulted in an estimated 60 million "left behind children" and nearly as many "left behind elderly." The migrants themselves suffer from serious health problems, including venereal disease at rates far higher than the national norm, but the children left behind in rural villages face especially difficult challenges. Scott Rozelle, a professor at Stanford University, found that most of these children are sick or malnourished, and as many as two in three suffer from anemia, worms, or myopia. Rozelle predicts that more than half the left-behind toddlers are so cognitively delayed that their IQs will never exceed 90.[28] This portends a future as something like the Gammas and Epsilons of *Brave New World*.

The Gentrification of the Left

In developed nations, as the middle classes are being proletarianized and the working classes fall further behind, the longstanding alliance between the intellectual left and the working class is dissolving. Already in the 1960s, New Left radicals such as C. Wright Mills and Ferdinand Lundberg disparaged the mental capacity of average Americans. Most of the population, according to Lundberg, were "quite misinformed, and readily susceptible to be worked upon, distracted."[29] The general acceptance of capitalism by the working class, as well as questions of race and culture, led many on the left to seek a new coalition to carry the progressive banner. For its part, the working class has moved away from its traditional leftist affiliation not only in the United States but also across Europe and the United Kingdom.[30]

"The more than 150-year-old alliance between the industrial working class and what one might call the intellectual-cultural Left is over," notes Bo Rothstein, a Swedish political scientist. He suggests that a "political alliance between the intellectual left and the new entrepreneurial economy" could replace the old "class struggle" model and provide a way to "organize public services in a new and more democratic way."[31] Across Europe, traditional parties of the left now find their backing primarily among the wealthy, the highly educated, and government employees.[32] Germany's Social Democrats, France's Socialists, and the British and Australian Labor parties have been largely "gentrified," as has America's Democratic Party, despite the resurgence of "democratic socialism" as part of its ideology. They have shifted their emphasis away from their historic working-class base, toward people with college and graduate degrees.[33]

Even more than disagreements over immigration and cultural values, differences in economic interests have driven a wedge between the established left and the working class. The agenda promoted by the leftist clerisy and the corporate elite—on immigration, globalization, greenhouse gas emissions—does not threaten their own particular interests. But it often directly threatens the interests of working-class people, especially in resource-based industries, manufacturing, agriculture, and construction. Environmental policy in places like California and western Europe has tended to ignore the concerns of working-class families.[34]

The continuing heavy use of coal, oil, and other fossil fuels—still increasing in countries like India and China—may present a danger to humanity's future, but it has contributed greatly to wealth creation and the comfort of the working class since the eighteenth century.[35] Plans for a drastic reduction in the use of carbon-based energy by 2050 would force middle-class Americans to be more like North Koreans in their energy consumption. In Europe, green energy mandates have caused a spike in energy costs. As many as one in four Germans and over half of Greeks have had to spend 10 percent or more of their income on energy, and three-fourths of Greeks have cut other spending to pay their electricity bills, which is the economic definition of "energy poverty."[36] These mandates have far less impact on the wealthy.

In their zeal to combat climate change, the clerisy have taken aim at things like suburban homes, cars, and affordable airfare. The lifestyles of the middle and working classes are often criticized by the very rich, who will likely maintain their own luxuries even under a regime of "sustainability." A former UK environment minister said that cheap airfare represents the "irresponsible face of capitalism." Apparently the more expensive travel done by the wealthy, including trips by private jet to conferences on climate change, is not so irresponsible.[37] New regulations and taxes on fuel imposed by France's aggressively green government sparked the *gilets jaunes* uprising, as well as the previous *bonnets rouges* protests in Brittany.[38]

Those in today's intellectual left are concerned about the planet and about international migrants, but not so much about their compatriots in the working class. The French philosopher Didier Eribon, a gay man who grew up in a struggling working-class family in provincial Reims, describes a deep-seated "class racism" in elite intellectual circles toward people like his family. Working-class voters in France were joyful at the Socialist victory in the 1981 election, but then found themselves supporting a government whose priorities turned out to be "neoliberalism," multiculturalism, and modernization. One result is widespread cynicism toward the political establishment. Eribon recalls his socialistically inclined mother saying, "Right or left, there's no difference. They are all the same, and the same people always end up footing the bill."[39]

Realignment

As the major left-leaning parties in high-income countries have become gentrified, the political orientation of working-class voters is realigning. Populist and nationalist parties in Sweden, Hungary, Spain, Poland, and Slovakia have done particularly well among younger votes. In fact, many of the right-wing nationalist parties are led by millennials.[40] American millennials too are surprisingly attracted to right-wing populism. In

November 2016, more white American millennials voted for Donald Trump than for Hillary Clinton. Their much-ballyhooed shift toward the Democratic Party has reversed, and now less than a majority identify as Democrats.[41]

More broadly, a sense of betrayal among those being left behind by progress is leading to defections from mainstream parties of both right and left. Among the working classes and the young, there is a steady growth of far-left opposition to the established liberal order, as well as strong support for the far right. This increasing movement away from the center and toward the fringes is not an ideal formula for a stable democratic society.

As Tocqueville put it, we may be "sleeping on a volcano."[42]

CHAPTER 15

Peasant Rebellions

Will the world's working classes accept their continuing decline? We are already seeing what might be described as "peasant rebellions" against the globalist order that is being constructed by the oligarchs and their allies in the clerisy.[1] In recent years, an insurrectionary spirit has surfaced in the Brexit vote, the rise of neonationalist parties in Europe and authoritarian populists in Brazil and the Philippines, and of course the election of Donald Trump.[2]

At the core of these rebellions against the political mainstream lies the suspicion among the lower classes that the people who control their lives—whether corporate bosses or government officials—do not have their interests at heart. The slow-growth economy that emerged from the Great Recession benefited the financial elite and property speculators, but did little for the vast majority of people. Firms like Apple have profited from soaring stock prices and low-wage Chinese production while less capital-rich businesses have struggled.[3]

These lopsided economic results have prompted attrition from the traditional mainstream political parties in many countries. In multiparty democracies, a reaction against economic globalization and mass immigration, among other policies, has resulted in pronounced movement to the political fringes. One Harvard study found that anti-establishment populist parties across Europe expanded their share of the electorate from 10 percent in 1990 to 25 percent in 2016.[4] At the same time, center-left parties are losing ground to far-left parties or candidates. Is this only a prelude to a more serious kind of rebellion—one that could undermine democratic capitalism itself?

A Brief History of Peasant Rebellions

Admirers of medieval feudalism highlight the concept of mutual obliga-tion between the classes. The upper clergy and the military aristocracy practiced a kind of noblesse oblige that provided a floor (albeit often insufficient) for the lower classes. But the obligations of the lower to the higher classes may have been no more voluntary than those binding the Cosa Nostra.[5]

The medieval poor did not always accept their miserable situation quietly. Uprisings broke out as early as Charlemagne's reign in the ninth century, and became more common in the later Middle Ages. Violent peasant armies actually bested aristocratic knights in the Low Countries in 1227, in northern Germany in 1230, and in the Swiss Alps in 1315.[6] The brutal fourteenth century brought a rash of peasant rebellions and urban insurrections. French peasants burned down manors of the wealthy in the Jacquerie of 1358, aiming to "destroy all the nobles and gentry in the world and there would be none any more." After being routed by armies of nobility and gentry, the insurgents were subjected to a campaign of reprisal that cost an estimated twenty thousand lives.[7]

In England, a labor shortage following the great plague resulted in higher pay and more mobility for laborers, but Parliament and big landowners took measures to hold down wages and keep peasants on their estates. Then, a new poll tax sparked a large-scale uprising led by Watt Tyler in 1381. A radical priest named John Ball traveled up and down England stirring up peasants, and in a speech outside London he famously asked: "When Adam delved and Eve span, who was then the gentleman?" The rebels' demands included abolition of serfdom and feudal service, an end to market monopolies and other restrictions on buying and selling, and confiscation of clerical property.[8]

Violent uprisings of peasants or urban poor also broke out in many other places, including Flanders, Florence, Lübeck, Paris, Transylvania, Croatia, Estonia, Galicia, and Sweden. But the biggest social upheaval before the French Revolution was the great Peasants' Rebellion of 1525 in Germany. Among the demands presented in the "Twelve Articles of the Peasantry" were the abolition of serfdom, restrictions on feudal dues, the right to fish and hunt, and the right of peasants to choose their own priest. The rebels took inspiration from Martin Luther's doctrine of a "priesthood of all believers," but Luther himself became horrified by their violence. The rebellion was put down so savagely that it dissuaded further uprisings in Germany.

Only rarely did such rebellions prove successful, like the one by the Swiss peasants. The ruling powers sometimes used treachery to quell uprisings by offering pardons that were eventually revoked.[9] In seventeenth-century England, Cromwell's "respectable revolution" quashed the efforts of the Levellers to extend Parliament's war against the monarchy into a radical egalitarian reordering of society.[10] Southern and western France endured frequent rural protests through much of the seventeenth century.

Peasant rebellions also occurred in other parts of the world, often with greater ferocity. Japan had numerous *ikki* or peasant uprisings, particularly in the fifteenth century; the consolidation of power under the shogun in 1600 finally put an end to the disturbances.[11] There were numerous uprisings and revolutions in Mexico, but it was only in the early twentieth century that the *peones* finally overturned the quasi-feudal regime left over from the Spanish legacy. They achieved significant land reform, but at the cost of well over a million lives.[12]

In Russia, with its overwhelmingly rural society, peasant rebellions were commonplace by the seventeenth century. A revolt among Ural Cossacks under Emelian Pugachev threatened the czarist regime in 1773, during the reign of Catherine the Great. The rebellion failed, as did some 550 others, but in 1917 the peasants rose up to support Lenin's seizure of power. When the Soviet regime began to confiscate land for collectivization, the property-loving *muzhiks* rebelled, only to be put down ruthlessly.[13]

Arguably the most powerful peasant rebellion occurred in China, in 1843. After failing civil service exams several times, Hung Hsiu-ch'uan read some Christian tracts and connected their message with hallucinations he had experienced. He designed his own religion, in which he was part of the Holy Trinity, but with doctrines based mainly on the Ten Commandments, and he preached it to destitute laborers.[14] His Taiping

Rebellion called for the overthrow of the Manchu Ch'ing dynasty, land reform, improving the status of women, tax reduction, eliminating bribery, and abolishing the opium trade. The rebellion was finally put down more than a decade later, with massive loss of life. Some of the Taiping program would later be adopted by Sun Yat-sen, who would overthrow the imperial regime, and then by Mao Tse-tung and the Communists.[15]

The Revolt against Mass Migration

The contemporary versions of peasant rebellions, particularly in Europe and the United States, are in large part a reaction against globalization and the mass influx of migrants from poor countries with very different cultures. The numbers of international migrants worldwide swelled from 173 million in 2000 to 258 million in 2017; of these, 78 million were living in Europe and 50 million in the United States.[16]

Mass migration from poorer to wealthier countries seems all but unstoppable, given the great disparities between them. According to a Gates Foundation study, 22 percent of the people in sub-Saharan Africa live in extreme poverty, defined as subsisting on less that $1.90 a day. By 2050, the region will be home to 86 percent of the world's poorest people, and about half that number will live in just two countries, Nigeria and the Democratic Republic of the Congo.[17] For the extremely poor in such countries, who see little to no chance of improving their condition at home, a dangerous trek to Europe or some other wealthy place would seem worth the risk.

Many people in Europe have welcomed migrants from poorer countries, including former colonies. Political and cultural elites in particular have elevated cosmopolitanism and "diversity" above national identity and tradition. Tony Blair's "Cool Britannia" was an effort to highlight cultural diversity as a central part of modern Britain's identity.[18] Herman Lebovics, in *Bringing the Empire Back Home: France in the Global Age* (2004), pondered how to redefine what it means to be French in a multicultural age.

When Germany's chancellor, Angela Merkel, flung the doors wide open to a huge wave of refugees and migrants from the war-ravaged Middle East in 2015, many ordinary Germans were eager to show *Gastfreundschaft*, or hospitality, as were many people elsewhere in Europe.

By the end of that year, nearly a million refugees had entered Germany alone, and the public welcome turned cold. Chancellor Merkel's decision came to be widely unpopular with Germans and the vast majority of Europeans.[19] A year after the rapid influx of refugees began, Pew Research found that 59 percent of Europeans thought immigrants were imposing a burden on their country, while only a third said that immigrants made their country a better place to live. Among Greeks, 63 percent said that immigrants made things worse, as did 53 percent of Italians.[20] In 2018, Pew found 70 percent of Italians, almost 60 percent of Germans, half of Swedes, and 40 percent of French and British citizens wanting either fewer or no new immigrants; barely 10 percent wanted more.[21]

In the years following Merkel's decision to set out the welcome wagon, virtually all European countries—including such progressive ones as the Netherlands, France, Denmark, Norway, and Germany itself—have tightened their immigration controls. This has been done chiefly to counter the populist (and at times quasi-fascist) nativist movements growing in many countries: Hungary, Poland, Austria, France, the Netherlands, Sweden, Finland, Slovakia, and most importantly in Germany. Much of the support for populist parties comes from the working class and lower-middle class, who are more exposed to the disruptions and dangers that the migrants have often brought, and are generally more burdened by the public expense of accommodating them.[22] Even in Sweden, where the citizens have long prided themselves on tolerance, there is widespread anger about rising crime and an unprecedented level of social friction in a formerly homogeneous country.[23]

Some of the anti-immigrant movements that have sprung up espouse racist views, but others are far less odious, being simply opposed to the globalizing policies of elites and their indifference to the concerns of average citizens.[24] Some have found inspiration in the Middle Ages, such as the example of the Frankish king Charles Martel, who defeated Muslim invaders in the eighth century. Fans of Donald Trump presented images of him as a Crusader clad in chain mail with a cross embroidered on the front.[25]

The conflict over immigration divides largely along class lines. There is a huge divergence between elite opinion, which generally favors mass immigration, and that of majorities in the working and middle classes. France's president, Emmanuel Macron, acknowledged this divergence in

2015 when he said, "The arrival of refugees is an economic opportunity. And too bad if [it] isn't popular."[26]

If political elites in Europe regard open borders as good for the economy, corporate elites in the United States are eager to import skilled technicians and other workers, who typically accept lower wages. The tech oligarchs in particular like to hire from abroad: in Silicon Valley, roughly 40 percent of the tech workforce is made up of noncitizens. Steve Case, the former CEO of America Online, has suggested that immigrant entrepreneurs and workers could offset middle-class job losses from automation.[27] Some conservative intellectuals have even thought that hardworking newcomers should replace the "lazy" elements of the working class.[28] Some of the earliest opposition to the Trump administration focused on his agenda of curtailing immigration.[29]

Somewheres vs. Anywheres

Ironically, the people who most strongly favor open borders are welcoming large numbers of immigrants who do not share their own secular, progressive values. That is particularly true in Europe, where migrants and refugees from Muslim countries often hold very conservative or reactionary views on things such as homosexuality and women's rights; many even support female genital mutilation. Some European politicians and other leaders, including the archbishop of Canterbury, have proposed that elements of Muslim *sharia* law, such as a prohibition of blasphemy, could be applied on top of existing national standards.[30]

Giles Kepel, one of France's leading Arabists, observes that Muslims coming to Europe tend to possess "a keen sense" of cultural identity rooted in religion, while the media and academia tend to promote the "erasing of identities," at least for the native population. Rather than defend their own values, Europeans and others in the West have been told by their leaders that "they must give up their principles and soul—it's the politics of *fait accompli*."[31] This "erasing of identities" is not widely popular among the working and middle classes.

The British writer David Goodhart describes a cultural conflict between the cosmopolitan, postnational "anywheres" and the generally less educated but more rooted "somewheres." If the media and most high-level government and business leaders in Europe have an "anywhere" perspective, people in less cosmopolitan precincts outside the capital cities tend to remain more strongly tied to national identities, local communities, religion and tradition. These divisions were particularly evident in the vote on Brexit and the Conservative sweep in 2019.[32]

The "somewhere" sentiment has repeatedly been expressed in votes concerning the European Union. In addition to the Brexit referendum of 2016, French, Danish, and Dutch voters have opted against deeper or broader EU ties, preferring a stronger national "somewhere." Less than 10 percent of EU residents identify themselves as Europeans first, and 51 percent favor a more powerful nation-state, while only 35 percent want power in Brussels to be increased.[33]

As long as the political and economic elites ignore these preferences, populist rebellions against establishment parties will likely continue and could become more disruptive. Elite disdain for traditions of country, religion, and family tends to exacerbate class conflict around cultural identity.[34] "Liberalism is stupid about culture," observed Stuart Hall, a Jamaican-born Marxist sociologist.[35]

In the United States, discontent with the globalist and open-borders agenda of the oligarchs and the upper clerisy resulted in strong working-class support for Donald Trump in 2016. He won two out of every five union voters and an absolute majority among white males.[36] Like his European counterparts, Trump ran strongest in predominantly white, working-class and lower-middle-class areas—precisely the areas hardest hit by globalization. He appealed most to people who work with their hands, own small shops, or are employed in factories, the logistics industry and energy sector; those who repair and operate machines, drive trucks, and maintain our power grid. Among white voters at least, he did poorest with well-educated professionals.[37]

To many voters, Trump was "a champion for forgotten millions."[38] When surveyed, these voters put a high priority on bringing back manufacturing jobs, protecting Social Security and Medicare, and getting conservatives on the Supreme Court—ahead of building a wall to keep out undocumented immigrants, who are widely seen as cutting into labor wages for American citizens. Even though he came from the business elite, Trump met almost universal opposition from the dominant classes. Instead, he won over voters who see big corporations as indifferent to the well-being of working people. Like some of the populist movements in Europe, the American populist right has adopted many of the class-based talking points, although usually not the policies, associated with the pregentrified left.[39]

In the higher echelons of the clerisy, the response to the populist revolt has mostly been revulsion. "It's Time for the Elites to Rise Up Against the Ignorant Masses" was the title of an article by James Traub in *Foreign Policy* in the summer of 2016. A former *New York Times* writer, Traub asserted that the Brexit vote and the nomination of Donald Trump, among other developments, indicate that the "political schism of our time" is not between left and right, but "the sane vs. the mindless angry."[40]

Larry Summers, a former Obama administration official, took a more astute view of the matter: "The willingness of people to be intimidated by experts into supporting cosmopolitan outcomes appears for the moment to have been exhausted."[41]

Is There a Mass Insurrection in the Making?

In the late 1920s and early 1930s, the proletarianization of the middle class resulted in widespread support for Communism, Fascism, and National Socialism.[42] Today, as in Europe before World War II, people on both right and left often blame financial institutions for their precarious situation.[43] Anger at the financial services sector gave rise to the Occupy Wall Street movement in New York City and the many spinoff Occupy protests in 2011–12. Marching under the slogan "We are the 99 percent," protesters around the world decried the heavy concentration of wealth in a few hands.

Alienation from the political mainstream today is resulting in strong support for far-left parties and candidates among youth in various high-income countries.[44] In France's presidential election of 2017, the former Trotskyite Jean-Luc Mélenchon won the under-24 vote, beating the more youthful Emmanuel Macron by almost two to one among that age group.[45] In the United Kingdom, the Labour Party under the neo-Marxist Jeremy Corbyn in 2018 won more than 60 percent of the under-40 vote, while the Conservatives got just 23 percent.[46] He won the youth vote similarly in 2020, even amidst a crushing electoral defeat. In Germany, the Green Party enjoys wide support among the young.[47]

A movement toward hard-left politics, particularly among the young, is also apparent in the United States, which historically has not been fertile ground for Marxism.[48] In the 2016 primaries, the openly socialist Bernie Sanders easily outpolled Hillary Clinton and Donald Trump *combined* among under-30 voters.[49] He also did very well among young people and Latinos in the early 2020 primaries, even as other elements of the Democratic Party rejected him decisively.[50] Support for socialism, long anathema in America, has gained currency in the new generation. A poll conducted by the Communism Memorial Foundation in 2016 found that 44 percent of American millennials favored socialism while 14 percent chose fascism or communism.[51] By 2024, millennials will be the country's biggest voting bloc by far.[52]

The core doctrines of Marxism are providing inspiration for labor unrest in China today, particularly among the younger generation of migrants to the cities. Activists often find themselves prosecuted for threatening "the social order."[53] Communist officials have been put in the awkward position of cracking down on Marxist study groups at universities, whose working-class advocacy conflicts with the policies of the nominally socialist government.[54]

Democratic capitalist societies need to offer the prospect of a brighter future for the majority. Without this belief, more demands for a populist strongman or a radical redistribution of wealth seem inevitable. A form of "oligarchic socialism," with subsidies or stipends for working people, might stave off destitution while allowing the wealthiest to maintain their dominance.[55] But the issue boils down to whether *people*—not just those with elite credentials and skills—actually matter in a technological age. Wendell Berry, the Kentucky-based poet and novelist, observed that the "great question" hovering over society is "what are people *for?*" By putting an "absolute premium on labor-saving measures," we may be creating more dependence on the state while undermining the dignity of those who want to do useful work.[56]

The future of the working class should concern us all. If too many lack any hope of improving their condition, we could face dangerous upheaval in the near future.

PART VI

The New Geography of Feudalism

A metropolitan economy, if it is working well, is constantly transforming many poor people into middle-class people, many illiterates into skilled (or even educated) people, many greenhorns into competent citizens.... Cities don't lure the middle class. They create it.

—Jane Jacobs, *The Death and Life of Great American Cities*

CHAPTER 16

The New Gated City

F ew sights are more thrillingly suggestive of artful modernity than the Chicago skyline. The city center along Lake Michigan is one of the most vibrant business districts in the nation, boasting numerous corporate headquarters and drawing affluent, highly skilled people from across America's vast Midwest.[1] In 2017, Chicago ranked second only to the tech hub Seattle among major American cities for the number of active construction cranes.[2]

Yet just a short drive away from the cranes and gleaming towers is a landscape of utter devastation. Minutes from the affluent neighborhood that was home to the nation's first African American president are old commercial districts now mostly deserted, with small shops, barbecue restaurants, and even longstanding churches lying derelict. Gangs proliferate in the decayed and rat-infested environment, and murder rates are among the highest for a large city in the high-income world.[3] Chicago's crime is heavily concentrated in the poorer districts, as is typical of big cities: according to one study, 5 percent of the nation's streets account for half of the urban crime.[4]

In the late nineteenth century, the muckraking journalist Frank Norris described Chicago as "the heart of the nation."[5] Today it is becoming essentially two different cities: one-third is what the local analyst Pete Saunders calls "global Chicago," which is something of a Midwestern San Francisco, while the other two-thirds is more like Saunders's hometown of Detroit as it is today, much of it a depopulated ruin or a dangerous netherworld of crime.[6]

Globalization and rapid deindustrialization together have led to the attrition of relatively well-paying jobs tied to the steel industry, meat processing, and manufacturing of agricultural equipment. Over a period of fifteen years, the number of manufacturing jobs in Chicago was cut in half, and it now stands at the lowest level in modern history.[7] Meanwhile, the middle class has been decimated. In 1970, half of Chicago's residents were middle-class; by 2019 the proportion was down to 16 percent, according to a University of Illinois study.[8]

The once large black urban middle class has been particularly ravaged. Many have left for the suburbs or moved to other states. Many of those remaining are worse off than their predecessors half a century ago. Today, around 40 percent of black 20-to-24-year-olds in Chicago are out of work and out of school, compared with 7 percent of their white counterparts.[9] William Lee, a *Chicago Tribune* reporter who grew up in the South Shore neighborhood, says that the large-scale exodus has left those remaining on the South Side "feeling like life after the rapture, with relatives, good friends and classmates vanishing and their communities shattering."[10]

The forces of globalization and deindustrialization have likewise transformed many big cities around the world from centers of opportunity to places that are starkly divided between rich and poor.[11] Today the world's great cities—Paris, London, Tokyo, New York, San Francisco—are attractive to those who already have wealth or the most impressive academic credentials, but less promising to the middle and working classes. The engines of upward mobility have stalled.

Urban Hierarchy

Since ancient times, cities have offered a chance for multitudes to gain prosperity. Rome nurtured the ambitious middle orders who found in the city a perfect environment for improving their condition. But the large numbers of slaves brought in as the empire grew displaced many self-sufficient farmers and artisans, who then became dependent on the public provision of bread for sustenance. The best advice for Romans, said Juvenal, was to emigrate from the Eternal City.[12]

Urban culture deteriorated after the empire collapsed, and especially after the Muslim conquests and incursions cut off lucrative trade routes.[13] Cities turned into fortresses where barbarian chieftains and ecclesiastical authorities could live sheltered behind protective walls. But for centuries these fortress-towns were peripheral to the lives of most people: barely 5 percent of the medieval European population lived in cities. As commerce quickened again in the later Middle Ages and a substantial merchant class emerged, city walls were extended to include growing populations.[14] During the Early Modern era, cities became generators of prosperity again.

In China, the major cities were mostly intended for Mandarins and aristocrats, served by a permanent lower class. The imperial bureaucrats were generally hostile or indifferent to the trading classes, seeing commerce as morally inferior to either scholarship or agriculture. As in Europe, the population overwhelmingly lived outside the city gates.[15]

With industrialization, huge fortunes came to be concentrated in big cities. Of course, the wealthy will always tend to congregate in particular places. In the nineteenth century, the Rockefellers famously moved from Cleveland, their original base, to New York. Many other moguls likewise brought their wealth to the city that the Beards called "the most powerful center of accumulation," and lived gloriously insulated from the poverty around them.[16] Globally, today's billionaires now cluster in a handful of cities led by New York but also including San Francisco, Moscow, Tokyo, Shanghai, Mumbai, Beijing, Singapore, London, and Paris. Fifteen cities together hold roughly 11 percent of the planet's total wealth.[17]

These "superstar cities" are becoming more bifurcated, with oligarchs and the upper clerisy living in the gentrified urban core, surrounded by propertyless and often impoverished masses on the periphery.[18] The elite urban cores constitute only a small percentage of the metropolitan area both in the United States and in Europe. In France, over 60 percent of the population live in the increasingly neglected periphery—the suburbs, provincial cities and small towns, and rural areas.[19]

The new urban paradigm is what Michael Bloomberg, the former mayor of New York, famously labeled a "luxury city," built around the preferences of his ultra-rich compadres.[20] But within the dominant cities are clear divisions by class, education, and sometimes race. The wealthy live in safe, gentrified areas, while the poor and minority populations are mostly consigned to neglected peripheral neighborhoods. In a distinctly neo-feudal vision of the urban future, the city core naturally attracts the best and brightest, while those living in the suburban periphery or the smaller cities and towns are doomed to struggle.[21]

Urban Bifurcation

Rather than a base for upward mobility, the great cities have largely become magnets for those who are already well-to-do. Few working-class or middle-class families can now afford to move to places like Paris, London, Tokyo, New York, San Francisco. Many former residents, like Chicago's black middle class, have left to make their future elsewhere. Many who still work in those cities are forced into intolerably long commutes.[22] As the middle class dwindles, it leaves behind a marginal urban population who depend on the city for a livelihood but often can barely get by. Reporters and politicians might swoon over the city's newest upscale restaurant or hip art gallery, but in the urban centers there are still many poor neighborhoods, and poverty rates are more than 65 percent higher than in the suburbs.[23]

America's major cities in general are not producing inclusive economic growth.[24] As a result, they now have higher levels of inequality than Mexico, according to a recent study.[25] The largest gaps between the top bottom and income quintiles among the fifty-three major metropolitan areas of the United States are in some of the most celebrated cities, including San Francisco, New York, San Jose, Los Angeles, and Boston.[26] If New York City were a country, it would have the fifteenth highest inequality level out of 134 countries, landing between Chile and Honduras, according to the Fiscal Policy Institute. Roughly 25 percent of the city's children live in poverty, more than twice the rate for the surrounding population.[27]

Nowhere is the urban class division more obvious than in the San Francisco Bay Area, the favored locale of the tech oligarchy. Two decades into the tech boom, nearly 40 percent of families in the city of San Francisco are "struggling" to make ends meet. Wages and job opportunities soared in the affluent, predominantly white precincts but dropped in the minority-dominated areas.[28] Hugely inflated housing prices have chased many working-class and even middle-class people away to locations hours distant. Increasing numbers of residents sleep on friends' couches, in their cars, or to a shameful extent in homeless encampments. San Francisco also suffers the highest rate of property crime per capita of any city in the United States.[29] These patterns extend to other parts of the Bay Area, particularly in Silicon Valley. More than half of the Bay Area's lower-income communities are in danger of mass displacement, according to a UC Berkeley study.[30]

Gated Cities: A Global Perspective

Similar patterns can be seen in big cities around the world. Even historically egalitarian Toronto has become bifurcated. In 1970, two-thirds of the neighborhoods were middle-income, but by 2001 it was down to one-third, while poor districts had more than doubled, to 40 percent of the city. University of Toronto researchers in 2007 projected that middle-class neighborhoods would fall to less than 10 percent of the city by 2020, with the balance being partly affluent neighborhoods but a far larger portion characterized by "very low" incomes.[31]

The pattern is even more striking in Britain, where wealth has become heavily concentrated in London. "It has felt as if the whole country had been turned upside down and shaken, until most of the wealth and talent has pooled in the capital," observes Peter Mandler. Home of the Cockney and postwar socialism, London is no longer a city of aspiration for the working and middle classes; it now exists mainly for investors, their student offspring, and highly educated professionals who are taking over the traditional blue-collar areas like Hackney.[32] Today only three of the city's thirty-two boroughs are affordable for people of median income. While many of the world's richest people live in London, four of its boroughs rank among the twenty poorest in England, and 27 percent of the city's population live in poverty.[33]

London's polarized economic landscape is typical of "superstar" cities. Other leading cities of Europe—Oslo, Amsterdam, Athens, Budapest, Madrid, Oslo, Prague, Riga, Stockholm, Tallinn, Vienna, Vilnius—also suffer widening gaps between the top and the bottom of the social hierarchy.[34]

Heavy immigration from developing countries, or from less wealthy parts of Europe, has exacerbated urban polarization. As the indigenous working and middle classes move out to the urban periphery, immigrants and their offspring crowd into the urban centers. They often fill positions at the lower end of the economy, particularly in services. In France, the proportion of young foreign-born people in the populations of larger cities reaches as high as 35 percent, notes Michele Tribalat, a demographer.[35] Immigrants, mostly from outside Europe, account for 37 percent of London's population, and more than 40 percent in Brussels, Zurich, and Geneva.[36]

Unlike earlier newcomers, today's immigrants find it difficult, in rapidly deindustrializing economies with slow growth, to secure the kind of work that might provide a ladder to the middle class.[37] Mass migration has not created the vibrant multicultural future expected by some, but instead has recreated much of the poverty and social disorder that characterized large European cities in the nineteenth century. Even close to their historic centers, the great cities have become graffiti-scarred, with large numbers of aimless young men loitering on street corners.[38]

Crime has become a major problem in the immigrant-heavy parts of the major European cities. Even in cities once known as remarkably safe and orderly, such as Stockholm, crime has risen dramatically over the past decade, and according to numerous official sources this trend has coincided with the large increase in new immigrants.[39] Europe's multicultural capital, London, by some measures now has a higher crime rate than New York, although fewer homicides.[40]

Densification and Gentrification

The social fabric of big cities is being further frayed by efforts to redesign the urban landscape on an upscale model. In many cities, a push for "densification" often replaces affordable older apartments and single-family houses with expensive apartment complexes geared toward affluent singles and childless couples. Los Angeles, for example, once had an abundance of middle-class housing, but some parts of the city, such as around Central Los Angeles, have seen a major drop in homeownership rates. Middle-class and working-class families—many of them minorities—have been displaced by hipsters and often pushed to the far periphery.[41]

Jane Jacobs spoke passionately about the solidity and "staying power" of New York's neighborhoods.[42] But the middle-class families that provide the social ballast for such neighborhoods are disappearing in places like Manhattan, West Los Angeles, San Francisco, Central London, and Paris. This is not simply a result of market forces, but of planning by urban political and economic leaders. Seeking to lure elite businesses, the global rich, and the highly educated, they often adopt policies that push the poor and middle classes outside the city.[43]

A former longtime Chicago resident and urban analyst, Aaron Renn, notes that the city has been losing much of its black population, as well as middle-class and low-income residents more broadly, and seeing a "collapse" of immigration from Mexico. He observes:

> None of these forces appear to make the upscale classes of Chicago sad. You certainly don't hear anyone sounding the alarm about black population loss and saying that the city needs to do something about it. In fact, the city's ineffective policing would appear to be a contributor to driving blacks out, meaning black population decline is de facto public policy.[44]

This is part of a process that has come to be called gentrification, a term whose origins lie in mid-1960s London.[45] At first it was unplanned, but over time it became a matter of design to rebuild urban centers around arts districts, cultural institutions, and sports facilities—using funds that could have gone toward improving infrastructure and education, or creating long-term middle-class jobs.[46] One consequence is that much of what made cities culturally distinct and interesting has been lost. The new urban landscape is remarkably similar—often with the same repetitive streetscape, shops, and even similar people—in major cities throughout the high-income world.[47]

For many people, this gentrification means a worsening quality of life. In fact, the urban world now being fashioned in London does not resemble "the social democracy imagined after the Second World War" so much as the bifurcated city of Victorian times, notes James Heartfield, a socialist writer.[48] Some who have chosen to stay in the hyper-expensive capital city have resorted to living in converted bathrooms, garden sheds, and old double-decker buses. Across the UK, there were an estimated

320,000 people living without permanent shelter in 2018, and the number continues to grow. Some urban "visionaries" even suggest that in the future people will need to live in shipping crates or water tubes.[49]

Even in nominally socialist China, old urban neighborhoods are being physically destroyed and residents uprooted to build "global cities." Maggie Shen King's novel *An Excess Male*, set a few years in the future, has a longtime Beijing resident remembering the brutal razing of the old blocks of *hutong*, or courtyard houses, once common in the capital, and the displacement of residents:

> Stately eight- and ten-lane boulevards crisscross the city, and we rarely walk down one without... pointing out that countless properties were seized and lives disrupted and, in the most egregious cases, cut short to make possible their construction. Relegated to tiny stacked boxes, ordinary citizens pour into parks and scenic streets, thirsting for open air and elbowroom, so that our leaders could have their show of grandeur.[50]

From "Creative Class" to a "New Urban Crisis"

The principal concern of many city leaders around the world has been to attract the young, educated professionals identified by the urban theorist Richard Florida as "the creative class."[51] To be sure, these people bring wealth and economic advantage to cities, but they are mostly single or childless, and not likely to recreate the stable, family-oriented neighborhoods of the historic city, with a thriving middle class and working class.

The most favored cities naturally draw the very rich, but they also attract many young people in the "creative class" who cannot afford to stay very long, particularly if they want to buy property or have children.[52] The average millennial with college debt would need twenty-seven years to save up for a down payment in the San Francisco metro area, according to one study.[53] Most of the young people who move to elite cities are likely to be short-timers indulging the "urban phase" of their life before heading elsewhere. According to the U.S. Census Bureau, urban core residents on average live barely two and a half years in the same place, whereas the average for suburbanites is about seven years.[54]

Given the mass exodus of middle-income residents—especially those with children—from elite cities like New York, they no longer resemble the welcoming urban havens so lovingly portrayed by Jane Jacobs.[55] Her hope that middle-class urbanites could recover their place in the city core seems unrealistic.

Decades ago, the National Urban Coalition noted that urban revitalization programs generally produced some overall economic benefit for cities, but at the cost of "the deprivation, frustration and anger of those who are becoming the new urban serfs."[56] Today, big cities continue to draw the wealthy and the well-educated, with impoverished residents pushed to the margins, and little in between.[57] The result is "rising inequality, deepening economic segregation, and increasingly unaffordable housing," which Richard Florida describes as a "new urban crisis."[58]

Some of those living in the cities outside the "glamour zone" feel trapped—victims of an urban system that doesn't provide opportunity for them. A backlash against gentrification has appeared in many cities, such as Ontario, Berlin, San Francisco, Los Angeles, Atlanta, and New Orleans.[59] Tactics for repelling gentrifiers have included vandalism and even arson.[60]

Jawanza Malone, executive director of Chicago's Kenwood-Oakland Community Organization, says that city leaders purposely neglect some neighborhoods while giving priority to the high-end economy and real estate speculation. "This isn't natural; this was created," said Malone. The lack of investment in certain areas by the city government or the private sector reflects their "perceived lack of importance to the city. It's a signal that residents here aren't as important."[61]

CHAPTER 17

The Soul of the Neo-feudal City

A n "inventory of the possible" is how René Descartes described the city of Amsterdam in the seventeenth century.[1] The growth of cities from the later Middle Ages into the modern era provided the ground for the development of a prosperous middle class. When the industrial revolution generated stark new inequities, pressure from labor unions and from middle-class reformers led to urban improvements, in sanitation and transportation systems, for example, and the creation of public parks.[2]

Today's urban world with its shrinking middle class is a departure from the ideal of the city as an engine of upward mobility, so emblematic of the industrial capitalist era.[3] Some of the very people who keep a city running—teachers, firemen, police officers—often cannot afford to live there. It is much the same for many skilled blue-collar workers—technicians, construction workers, mechanics—whose ranks are thinning in the high-priced cities.[4] Many people in such occupations find the cost of living in the city far greater than whatever premium it might bring in higher wages or convenience.[5]

At the same time, economic opportunity has been declining in smaller cities and towns throughout the high-income world.[6] In Japan, for example, mostly childless professionals cluster in the hyper-expensive and congested urban core, often in extremely cramped housing. Meanwhile, many smaller cities and suburbs are fading, notes Tomohiko Makino, a real estate expert focused on vacant houses. "Tokyo could end up being surrounded by Detroits."[7]

Arguably the starkest example of class division based on urban status is China's "two-tier" classification system. Under *hukou*, those who do not have the hereditary right of urban residency will always have an inferior, unprotected status even if they seek opportunity in the city.[8] Among the most common themes in contemporary Chinese science fiction is rigid class divisions in the urban world. Hao Jingfang's "Folding Beijing," for example, portrays a megacity divided into sharply delineated communities for the elite, the middle ranks, and a vast poor population living mainly by recycling the waste generated by the city.[9] This vision represents a shocking divergence from the Maoist ideal.

The Polarized Global City

Despite their population growth and economic dynamism, the sprawling megacities of the developing world have not nurtured a substantial middle class.[10] Power and money tend to be highly concentrated in a handful of elite urban districts, while opportunities for the middle and working classes are limited. A century after the Mexican Revolution, Mexico City is still composed of a few rich neighborhoods and numerous slumlike communities such as Ciudad Nezauhualcoyotl, where upwards of two million people live in ramshackle dwellings.[11]

In many countries, such as India, the oligarchy and well-connected professionals concentrate in and around the urban core, while migration from the countryside only adds to the slum population. In 1971, one in six residents of Mumbai lived in the slums, but now a majority do. The promise of city living is not working as the migrants may have anticipated. Life expectancy in Mumbai is now fifty-seven years, which is nearly seven years below the national average.[12]

Urban leaders in some of the fastest-growing large cities try to create special spaces to accommodate wealthy and well-educated residents. Places like Santa Fe in Mexico City, Bandra Kurla in Mumbai, Ortigas in Manila, or Luis Berrini in Sao Paulo resemble the residential and commercial developments typical of cites in the high-income world.[13] These are what Rajiv Desai has called "the VIP zones of cities," where luxury stores, hotels, and office towers mimic those in the West, but surrounding them are extensive slums.[14] As the urban scholar Saskia Sassen observes, "The elites in Sao Paolo and the elites in Manila both share an emergent geography of centrality that connects them—rather comfortably—with elites in New York, or in Paris." Much of the world is now divided between "urban glamour zones and urban slums."[15]

Beyond the glamour zones are the extensive, improvised favelas that have grown helter-skelter on the outskirts. City residents outside the "VIP zones," like the denizens of Chicago's South Side, are not benefiting from the global economy. The "shining India" that people talk about, for example, does not include the vast majority of the population, notes the sociologist R. M. Sharma. "We must ask, the 'Shining India' is for whom?"[16]

The Childless Urban Future

Another characteristic of the neo-feudal city is a dearth of children and families. The great metropoles like Hong Kong, London, New York, Los Angeles, Berlin, and Tokyo have exceptionally low percentages of families among their residents.[17] In the United States, birth rates are now at historic lows nationally, but especially in the biggest cities.[18] Between 2011 and 2019, the number of babies born annually in Manhattan dropped by nearly 15 percent, while the decrease across the city was 9 percent. The nation's premier urban center could see its infant population shrink by half in the next thirty years.[19] The share of nonfamily households grew three times as fast in gentrifying neighborhoods as in the city overall.[20] In the future, writes Steve LeVine, shifting local priorities "could write kids out of urban life for good."[21]

In Hong Kong, the most crowded high-income city, two-thirds of women want either one child only or no children at all, mainly due to the price of housing and a harried lifestyle.[22] Major Chinese cities such as Beijing and Shanghai have fertility rates among the lowest in the world, and only about one-third the replacement level.[23]

The neo-feudal urban order appears to incubate not only an aversion to having children, but also difficulty in relations with the opposite sex. In Japan, roughly a third of men enter their thirties as virgins, and a quarter of men are not married at age fifty.[24] This sex recession even affects places like Hong Kong's famous Wan Chai "red light" district, which is now being remade into an upscale hipster area as the sex trade plummets.[25] China's young men are so disconnected socially that the Communist Party and some private firms are teaching them how to approach women. This is being tried elsewhere too. "The problem is not getting people married or having kids," said one researcher in Singapore. "They don't even date."[26]

This is clearly a product of modern urbanism, but in China the problem has been exacerbated by the former one-child policy, which in combination with a strong cultural preference for male offspring has resulted in a demographic challenge. There is now a great surplus of young men, who often face difficult odds for getting married. If they lack a car or an apartment, they are likely to become "leftover men," also called *guang gun* or "bare branches," the "biological dead ends of their family tree." Shuzhuo Li, a leading demographer at Xian Jiaotong University in Shaanxi province, warns that in the future "there will be millions of men who can't marry, and that could pose a very big risk to society."[27]

The Middle Class and Suburbia

As cities became overcrowded in the industrial era, the middle classes found an alternative by settling in satellite neighborhoods on the expanding periphery. H. G. Wells foresaw the old city center becoming "essentially a bazaar, a great gallery of shops and places of concourse and rendezvous, a pedestrian place, its pathways reinforced by lifts and moving platforms, and shielded from the weather, and altogether a very spacious, brilliant, and entertaining agglomeration." Outside the center, he suggested, would be "suburban nuclei," functioning as "restorations of the old villages and country towns," with the services that most people needed nearby, and opportunity for people to use their skills profitably.[28] In these suburban neighborhoods, the middle class could grow and thrive.

Many other reformers of the Victorian and Edwardian era, including radicals like Engels and Wells, favored the outward expansion of cities. Similarly, more conservative figures such as Thomas Carlyle and Ebenezer Howard wished to provide an alternative to the overcrowded inner city for the middle and working classes.[29] In the United States, the architect Frank Lloyd Wright envisioned what he called the "Broadacre city," where average people could own a home and a plot of land. Wright broke with many of the old nostrums of urbanism, maintaining that there was no need to force high-density development in the modern era.[30]

In Britain, dispersion and suburbanization began in the 1850s but accelerated rapidly as soldiers came home from World War II. The result was a new level of comfort for people who were not aristocrats.[31] In places like Milton Keynes, a low-density edge city outside London, the expanding middle class could find safety, privacy, and a spot of lawn. Urban planners and green activists may find much to dislike in such car-oriented places, but they succeed for prosaic reasons, notes Mark Clapson, an urban historian. The landscape embodies the preferred "Englishness" of tidy homes and greenery. Milton Keynes now counts over 200,000 residents, who have gardens, easy access to shopping, and convenient trains to London. Communities like this are home to a great diversity of people, with a mix of professionals, skilled workers, and manual laborers. Recalling his childhood in a South London suburb, the filmmaker John Boorman asked, "Was there ever such a stealthy social revolution as the rise of this semi-detached suburbia?"[32]

The War on the Dream

In most high-income countries—including Canada, Australia, and the United States—suburban living still predominates.[33] Among Americans under 35 who buy homes, four-fifths choose single-family detached houses. A recent report from the National Association of Realtors found that over 66 percent of American adults, including those living in cities, prefer a house in the suburbs.[34] Since 2010, a net 1.8 million people have moved away from the urban core counties of major metropolitan areas, mainly to lower-density counties where single-family houses are the norm.[35]

Despite the continuing appeal of suburbia, planners, academics, and pundits sneer at this lifestyle. "The suburbs are about boredom, and obviously some people like being bored and plain and predictable," said Elizabeth Farrelly, an Australian urbanist and architecture critic. She continued: "I'm happy for them...even if their suburbs are destroying the world."[36] Farrelly is among those who argue for densification to create a green "global city," even though majorities of Australians, like Americans, appear less than enthusiastic about what critics describe as "cramming."[37]

Some pro-density activists operate from a sense of moral purpose to oppose what is a clearly demonstrated popular preference. While environmental arguments are most common, some activists claim that single-family neighborhoods are inherently racist because they used to be overwhelmingly white. This notion has been central to the push against single-family zoning in cities such as Seattle and Minneapolis.[38]

Others dislike the very idea of property ownership and family privacy. Victoria Fierce of the YIMBY pro-density lobby in California favors increasing urban density in part because it "promotes collectivism."[39] Of course, this is reminiscent of the orthodoxy seen in the late, great Soviet Union. In 1957, several architects from the University of Moscow set out to create "a concrete spatial agenda for Marxism," emphasizing small apartments densely built near public transit, with close proximity to the workplace. The plan of Alexei Gutnov and his team was later published in Italian and then English, as *The Ideal Communist City*. Gutnov acknowledged the appeal of suburbia, but rejected it as unsuitable for a society that prioritizes equality and social control.[40]

Those who dictate the urban form today come from the clerisy, along with elements of the financial aristocracy who seek to capitalize on high rents. As the architectural historian Robert Bruegmann observes, urban planners have a long history of ignoring or even disdaining middle-class aspirations for a suburban lifestyle. He adds that the motive is often "class based," an effort to revive the patterns of the premodern past, with defined hierarchies and limited opportunities for upward mobility or for improving the condition of those outside the upper classes.[41]

The attack on suburbia is, in effect, a way of socially deconstructing the middle class. Even as middle-income families are squeezed out of the urban core, planners wish to close off an alternative that majorities in fact prefer.

CHAPTER 18

The Totalitarian Urban Future

he new urban paradigm elevates efficiency and central control above privacy, local autonomy, class diversity, and broad-based property ownership. The same oligarchs who dominate our commercial culture, seek to profit from manipulating our moods, and influence the behavior of our children want to structure our living environment as well.[1]

Major tech firms—Y Combinator, Lyft, Cisco, Google, Facebook— are aiming to build what they call the "smart city." Promoted as a way to improve efficiency in urban services, these plans will also provide more opportunity for oligarchs to monitor our lives, as well as sell more advertising. The "smart city" would replace organic urban growth with a regime running on algorithms designed to rationalize our activities and control our way of life.[2]

This urban vision appeals to tech oligarchs' belief that their mission is to "change the world," not simply make money by meeting customers' needs and desires. In the urban landscape, changing the world means replacing the old physical and social structure with what the futurist William Mitchell in 1999 called "a city of bits." Our former understanding of the city gives way to an "electronically augmented environment" where everything is determined by digital code. Mitchell prophetically foresaw that the high-tech metropolis would intensify the concentration of wealth in a few places.[3]

The digital city is perfectly suited to the neo-feudal order. A new class of urban serfs are forced into small apartments and work sporadically, often remaining dependent on subsidies or "income maintenance" provided by the state.[4] Except for those who own or operate the technology or write the algorithms, people will become like bystanders in the computerized city much like the plebeians in imperial Rome whose jobs were taken over by slave labor. Human beings will exist largely for the machines, rather than be served by them. "Bees exist on Earth to pollinate flowers, and maybe humans are here to build the machines," said Andrew Hudson-Smith, from the Centre for Advanced Spatial Analysis at University College London. "Urban robots are just starting to appear, and in 200 years time, machines may run the urban form. The city will be one big joined-up urban machine, and humans' role on Earth will be done."[5]

The Oligarchic "Moral Imperative"

The emerging urban form perfectly fits the belief, shared by most top internet founders, that growing inequality is inevitable, a natural cost of technological progress. Silicon Valley first grew out of the suburbs, but many tech leaders now believe that "urbanization is a moral imperative," writes Greg Ferenstein.[6] If startups in suburban garages represented the individualism of cranky inventors and entrepreneurs, the future Silicon Valley will feature densely packed apartment complexes for workers who will become ever more corporate and controlled.[7]

The focus on apartment living for employees makes some sense for tech companies—like Facebook, Lyft, Salesforce, Square, Twitter, Yelp, and Google—that rely on a youthful, childless workforce.[8] This kind of urban experience does not spur individuals toward independent adulthood and family formation, but recreates "life as close to the college experience as possible," as Ferenstein notes, or a kind of prolonged adolescence.[9]

With traditional family-friendly housing near their workplaces out of reach for all but the wealthiest people, most tech employees will live in something like dormitories, perhaps well into their thirties. Their salaries may be relatively high, but often not enough to cover the cost of a conventional apartment, much less a house.[10] Adjusting for inflation, the average programmer earns about as much today as in 1998.[11] But housing costs have soared too high for most to have a chance to break out of renting. Urbanists have argued that ever higher densities will reduce housing costs, though higher-density housing in reality tends to be far more costly per square foot, and also carries the additional costs of the regulatory burdens associated with many large cities. More housing might be built in urban centers, but it will almost always come at a high price and usually be too small for families.[12]

Meanwhile, most tech oligarchs themselves live in the Bay Area's pricey bucolic suburbs, or have rural properties at their disposal.[13] Such options may never exist for most of their own employees, particularly the younger ones. The *Guardian* characterized Google's move to build high-density units near its offices as "well-wishing feudalism."[14]

Company Town or Dystopia?

What will the cities created by our tech overlords be like? They certainly will not be like those of postwar America or Britain, with their spreading suburbs, but more akin to the old company towns, such as Lowell, Massachusetts, built around textile mills, or the Pullman company town in Illinois.[15] Such developments have been sold as public-spirited accommodations, but they also offered a convenient way to increase control over employees and boost productivity.

Perhaps more concerning is what today's tech oligarchs expect for their employees. Unlike the executives of the typical large firm of the late twentieth century, they are not expecting their employees to aspire to buy a house and raise children. Instead, they prefer workaholic employees who embrace a modern version of "monasticism."[16]

Firms like Google are planning to build cities suited to such workers, using their technology to create a version of Mitchell's "city of bits." In an undeveloped twelve-acre portion of Toronto called Quayside, Google is spearheading a drive to build a city "from the internet up ... merging the physical and digital realms."[17] This vision of "smart" urbanism revolves around surveillance and relentless gathering of data. Ubiquitous monitoring sensors inside and outside buildings and on streets would be constantly on duty. Google would collect data about everything from water use to air quality to the movements of Quayside's residents, and use that data to run energy, transport, and all other systems.[18]

Constant monitoring will no doubt produce some efficiency in things such as trash collection, but at an enormous cost to privacy. The data gathered from monitoring people's daily lives will also be fed into the advertising and marketing machine that generates the oligarchs' fortunes. Meanwhile, the big tech firms will gain insights about urban life—including energy use, transit efficiency, climate mitigation strategies, and social service delivery—and sell the information to cities around the world.[19] "The whole point of a smart city is that everything that can be collected will be collected," says Al Gidari, the director of privacy at Stanford University's Center for Internet and Society.[20]

Global Cities of the Damned

Canadians, Americans, and most Europeans still have the option of objecting to heavy surveillance and control, but citizens of many other countries—Russia, China, and African nations—may have less ability to say no.[21] Data collection is totally unfettered in China's "techno-utilitarian" system, with no privacy protections for the individual.[22]

In its drive to dominate the next generation of artificial intelligence, the Chinese Communist Party works closely with tech oligarchs, both foreign and domestic, giving little consideration to public concerns. For example, if tech companies identify a district they want to turn into an "innovative ecosystem" like Silicon Valley, they wouldn't need to wait for organic urban development to take place, writes Kai-Fu Lee, former president of Google China. Instead, they can work with the government to speed things up by clearing out the inhabitants and "brute-forcing the geographic proximity" of the desired elements. The politically connected tech developer need not worry overmuch about the kind of opposition to development that often arises in Western cities.[23]

The Chinese Communist Party is clearly aware that artificial intelligence brings huge potential for controlling a city and its residents. China's large population of well-educated people and its enormous underclass both could pose challenges to the regime. The government uses technology in a complex "social credit" system to track citizens' activities and maintain control over all segments of the population. There's even an app that rewards people for reporting signs of dissent to authorities, such as illegal publications.[24] Christina Larson, an MIT researcher, likens China's surveillance system to the "electronic democracy" that Isaac Asimov described. As she puts it, "Who needs democracy when you have data?"[25]

In Maggie Shen King's novel *An Excess Male*, the surveillance system has been totally integrated into all dimensions of personal life, including access to good jobs, an apartment, or the right to marry. Since the one-child policy along with a preference for males has led to a demographic crisis, the government pursues and punishes anyone whose behavior, such as homosexuality, might impede the production of desperately needed children, something already much on the mind of Chinese planners and government officials.[26]

The Chinese regime has been implementing facial recognition systems around the country to track the movement of citizens, beginning in the Xinjiang region of western China, where Muslim Uighur dissidents are seen as a serious threat to the regime. This is a place where simply wearing a beard, or giving your child a Muslim name, can catch the attention of police. The facial recognition system alerts authorities when someone on a watchlist strays more than 300 meters from home or workplace, and that person could be arrested. Once an individual is caught up in the criminal law system, the chances of acquittal are estimated at less than one in a hundred. The regime is also aiming to collect DNA from every resident of Xinjiang, and implementing a satellite tracking system for every vehicle in the region. "They are combining all of these things to create, essentially, a total police state," said William Nee, a China campaigner at Amnesty International.[27]

But it isn't only Xinjiang province where the police state is growing. The government planned to deploy over 400 *million* surveillance cameras in cities across the country by 2020. Along with the facial recognition system, this surveillance is designed to regulate behavior, making it much more dangerous to express dissent, or even to commit a minor violation of traffic laws.[28] The regime is also tracking smartphones and harvesting biometric data. Brain-reading technology is destined to become more commonplace in Chinese factories, ostensibly to improve productivity, but also with a clear potential to monitor and manipulate the thoughts of workers.[29]

This kind of digital surveillance is likely spread to major urban areas in developing countries, many of which regard China as the ultimate role model. Given that many of these cities do not generate enough prosperity to improve the lives of their residents, it's not at all surprising that governments might find appeal in a technological approach to social control.[30]

Can We Resist the "Surveillance Society"?

What is now brewing in Silicon Valley, and proposed in Toronto, and being implemented in China could be the model for our future urban civilization. The British academic David Lyon sees the all-immersive data-driven city as part of a "surveillance society," where all individual activities are under the gaze of the ruling classes.[31]

These "smart cities" will prove to be essentially the opposite of the real thing, substituting machine-driven interfaces for the free and spontaneous human interactions that are the glory of the traditional city.[32] Averting the arrival of this contrived and controlled urban form, or at least slowing its development, will require new measures to limit the power of the oligarchic tech companies, and of the clerisy who promote their agenda.[33] Europeans may be in the lead here, seeking to curb information monopolies and to limit intrusions into personal lives; EU citizens are being given the tools to "erase" personal data collected by tech services.[34]

Some people will no doubt see pushback against the "smart city" as a case of rejecting technology or impeding efficiency, or shackling free enterprise and seizing intellectual property. But for democracy to work, the citizens need to control their own environment rather than hand it over to a few powerful corporations or a small tech elite who profit by stealing our privacy and manipulating our behavior. Cities must be suited to human aspiration, and not serve to nudge their inhabitants into a new kind of serfdom.

PART VII

A Manifesto for the Third Estate

Technology is perhaps the body rather than the soul of a civilization.
—Fernand Braudel, *The Perspective of the World*

CHAPTER 19

The Technological Challenge

W e are moving toward a future that most of us may not desire, with highly concentrated property ownership, a concerted drive for ever greater urban density, fewer families, and a declining middle class. The power of today's dominant classes is based on an accumulation of wealth and assets not seen since the emergence of the great industrial trusts in the late nineteenth and early twentieth centuries. In fact, the tech oligarchs often control 80 to 90 percent of their markets, surpassing the market share enjoyed by J. P. Morgan's U.S. Steel, which controlled two-thirds of America's steel manufacturing.[1]

As in the Gilded Age, this market dominance comes with grotesque levels of inequality.[2] In Europe and North America, and increasingly in East Asia, we are seeing what Robert Putnam calls "an incipient class apartheid."[3] The main beneficiaries of our current economy lord it over the commoners in a way reminiscent of the medieval nobility. "The new feudalism is like the older model, with class, privilege and wealth still highly influential," writes Satyajit Das in the *Independent*.[4]

"Experts" and "Problems"

The oligarchs and a privileged clerisy might be seen as fulfilling the role of a ruling "expert" class as proposed during the Enlightenment and in the Progressive Era. The ideal of rule by experts presupposes a society in which all problems—including those of morality, faith, and justice—are thought to have scientifically derived solutions. It is simply a matter of finding the "right" policy, irrespective of whether it enjoys broad public assent or reflects popular aspirations.[5]

If the exercise of power in the Middle Ages was justified by force of arms or divine ordination, today's dominant classes claim their right to control our lives on the basis of supposedly superior knowledge and morality. Unchecked and unchallenged, they may brew up a dystopian future out of monopoly capital, intrusive technology, and coercive ideology.

China, having been at the leading edge through much of history, may again prove to be the preeminent role model, representing an alternative to liberal capitalism with an advanced economy run from above, and offering little in the way of individual rights or freedom of expression. The Chinese regime does not much respect personal privacy, and it unabashedly practices a strict censorship. This model is appealing to rulers of many other countries, particularly in the developing world and among autocrats everywhere.[6]

In democratic countries, the greatest threat to the independence of ordinary citizens comes not directly from the state but from those oligarchs who are heralding what Amazon's Jeff Bezos describes, apparently without irony, as the "beginning of a Golden Age."[7] Yet the futurist Valhalla imagined by the oligarchy and the clerisy could be antithetical to democratic values and to the aspirations of the Western middle and working classes.[8]

As Irving Kristol wrote almost two decades ago, the fundamental problem is that technological and scientific elites "have the inclination to think that the world is full of 'problems' to which they should seek 'solutions.' But the world isn't full of problems; the world is full of other people." Of course, he adds, "there is no 'solution' to the existence of other people. All you can do is figure out a civilized accommodation with them."[9]

Eroding the Real

Technology adds to or enhances some human capacities, but it has limited ability to address some of humanity's biggest problems.

Experts in fields such as artificial intelligence have been very successful at solving problems in circumscribed domains, such as a chess match or cataloging records. But when confronted with more complex problems involving emotions or nuance, technological systems become "brittle and mistake prone," notes one leading computer scientist.[10] Many dimensions of human life are not reducible to digital code. "You cannot code intuition; you cannot code aesthetic beauty; you cannot code love or hate," says Miguel Nicolelis, a neurologist at Duke University.[11]

On our current technocratic path, we can see a developing society much like that portrayed in Stanley Bing's chilling novel *Immortal Life*. Set in the near future, it depicts a society where artificial intelligence has become dominant and life extension has emerged as the obsession of the ruling oligarchy. The world's richest man develops a technique for transferring his consciousness into the body of a "lesser" young person. The masses have essentially been neutralized by the availability of cheap commodities peddled by a handful of global corporations, and are largely removed from "any so-called real experience." While the oligarchs aspire to digital immortality, their technology renders the average human "prone to inertia, indolence and virtual existence."[12]

Technology itself may, however, be less of a problem than our dependency on machine interfaces, as opposed to genuine human interactions. According to Amazon, half of the conversations that users hold with the company's smart-home device Alexa are of a nonutilitarian nature—jokes, existential questions, groans about life. A study conducted by the Institute for Creative Technologies in Los Angeles in 2014 found that people display their sadness more intensely and are less scared about self-disclosure when they believe they're interacting with a virtual person instead of a real one. "By 2022, it's possible that your personal device will know more about your emotional state than your own family," said Annette Zimmermann, research vice president at the consulting company Gartner.[13]

This emotional reliance on technology provides more opportunity for the oligarchy and the clerisy to gain access to our inner feelings and profit from them.[14] No matter how strongly a public relations staffer at Facebook or Google contends otherwise, the algorithms that govern social media are not neutral or objective, but reflect the assumptions of those who create the programs. "Algorithms are opinions embedded in code," writes Cathy O'Neil, a data scientist.[15]

The most concerning effects of the new intrusive technology can be seen in younger people. Research published in 2017 by Jean Twenge, a psychologist at San Diego State University, indicates that more screen time and social media activity correlate with a higher rate of depression and elevated suicide risk among American adolescents. Not incidentally, depressed youths are more susceptible to buying products pitched to them, as one Facebook executive famously told the company's advertisers.[16] The influence of social media on the mood of users, whether by design or otherwise, has been called "brain hacking."[17] "I am convinced the devil lives in our phones and is wreaking havoc on our children," said Athena Chavarria, a former executive assistant at Facebook and an employee of Mark Zuckerberg's philanthropy, the Chan Zuckerberg Initiative.[18]

The effects of digital saturation appear to be profound. Young people today have been found to be less assertive and more risk-averse than earlier generations. Many lack basic soft skills, such as knowing how to interact with other people. In Australia, researchers have found that excessive time glued to screens has resulted in a younger generation "incapable of small talk, critical thinking and problem-solving." A survey of American millennials found that 65 percent did not feel comfortable engaging with another person in a face-to-face conversation, and 80 percent preferred conversing digitally.[19]

We may be witnessing a deterioration of the real-world human interaction that has always been fundamental to our species. For example, today's tech-savvy children clearly have problems relating to the opposite sex, a phenomenon traced in part to their immersion in social media and easy access to internet porn. In America, Finland, Sweden, Denmark, Japan, and the United Kingdom, younger people have been disproportionately contributing to what researchers have characterized as a "sex recession."[20] Artificial beings even appear poised to replace actual people in the most intimate of human activities. One entrepreneur invested in a sex robot shop to fill a perceived need for "a safe space for men to practice healthy sexual interactions without the complexity of a normal human relationship."[21]

As the French novelist Michel Houellebecq notes acidly, the price of improved technology appears to be a weakening of our capacity for real human interaction:

> The world is becoming ever more uniform before our eyes. Telecommunications are improving; apartment interiors fill with new gadgets. Human relations become progressively impossible, which greatly reduces the quantity of anecdote that goes to make up a life.... The third millennium augurs well.[22]

Wiring for Feudalism

It was once widely hoped that emerging technologies would create a world of "new opportunities for personal growth, adventure and delight," as the visionary Alvin Toffler wrote in *Future Shock* almost three decades ago. The prospect of a technologically advanced economy dangled like a bright gem for generations of utopian socialists, and for political thinkers on the right as well. Even today, some Marxists long for "a fully automated luxury communism" where technology has ended scarcity and created a "post-work society."[23]

Sadly, such utopian visions can lead to frighteningly dystopian results. Technology may connect people in unprecedented ways, but it appears to be constraining intellectual debate under the control of a few powerful companies. The widespread censorship and "de-platforming" of unapproved views already being practiced, notes law professor and author Glenn Reynolds, could presage a new form of technologically enhanced thought control.[24]

The rewiring of society could be accelerated by an even more remarkable, and somewhat terrifying, biological transformation. For a half century, scientists have been dreaming of engineering humans to limit reproduction, or to transmit information directly into the brain. To many modern scientists, Huxley's *Brave New World* may seem less a dystopia than a blueprint for technological paradise. Eugenics, once discredited by its association with fascism, is now "the ghost at the table" as scientists aim to edit genes to produce a "superior" human being.[25]

Rather than simply serve humanity, biotechnology could enable ruling classes to engineer people to fit their own preferences. The philosopher Yuval Noah Harari believes that technology will usher in a society controlled by a small, godlike caste of what he calls *Homo deus*, who will completely dominate run-of-the-mill *Homo sapiens*. Below them will be an underclass who don't work and depend utterly on alms from their betters. The relationship between them and the reengineered elite beings could be compared to our present relationship with animals. "You want to know how super-intelligent cyborgs might treat ordinary flesh-and-blood humans?" Harari asks. "Better start by investigating how humans treat their less intelligent animal cousins."[26]

Armed with the power of algorithms to control our social interactions and with unlimited cash, our overlords will be able to run society for their own benefit without worrying about the popular will or the aspirations of their fellow citizens. The technocratic future now being envisioned will have little need for the labor of the lower classes or the messiness of democracy. "A hundred years hence," writes Harari, "our belief in democracy and human rights might look...incomprehensible to our descendants."[27]

CHAPTER 20

The Shaping of Neo-feudal Society

ll human systems, from the primitive village to medieval feudalism to liberal democracy, are shaped not only by ideas but also by control of the physical environment and resources.[1] Democratic systems rest to some degree on the recognition and nurturing of individual property rights. Most democratic or republican societies in history—in Athens, Rome, the Netherlands, Britain, France, North America, Oceania—were created and sustained by a broad property-owning middle class.

In the twentieth century, middle-class asset growth was accomplished in large part by the expansion of an urban footprint beyond the city core that allowed many more citizens to buy property in spacious, safe environments offering a measure of privacy.[2] The ideal of broadly dispersed property ownership has long been promoted by politicians both right and left in most high-income countries. "A nation of homeowners, of people who own a real share in their land, is unconquerable," said President Franklin D. Roosevelt. He saw homeownership as critical not only to the economy but to democracy and the very idea of self-government.[3]

Today, the democratization of landownership is being reversed. In the United States and across the world, more and more people are being pushed into living in rented apartments or houses, with little chance of gaining financial independence. This trend is not simply a product of market forces. Rented housing—whether apartments or single-family houses—has been heavily promoted by much of the oligarchy and more so by the planning gurus of the clerisy, even though homeownership is favored by the great majority in the United States, Europe, Australia, and Canada.[4] Given the high cost of dense development, future generations may well become ever more dependent on subsidies or affordable unit set-asides.[5] An economy where most people rely upon wealth transfers from the lucky few cannot easily coexist with a tradition of individual initiative and self-governance.[6]

Undermining Familialism

Perhaps no institution is more threatened by the neo-feudal order than the traditional family structure. Since 1960, the percentage of people in the United States living alone has grown from about 12 percent to 28 percent. In the Scandinavian countries, around 40 percent of the population live alone.[7]

Even East Asia is seeing early signs of a breakdown of family structures.[8] Kyung-Sook Shin's highly praised bestseller *Please Look After Mom*, which sold two million copies, focused on the "filial guilt" of children over failing to look after aging parents.[9] Rapidly urbanizing China, traditionally a bastion of familialism, now has 200 million unmarried adults, including 58 million single people between 20 and 40 years of age. The proportion of people living alone in China, once a virtually unimaginable situation, has risen to 15 percent.[10]

This phenomenon is particularly marked in the urban centers that dominate the world's economy and culture. Today many large cities—such as Beijing, Tokyo, New York, Los Angeles, Boston, and San Francisco—are becoming childless demographic graveyards.[11] Workers in San Francisco's tech economy, forced to live in small apartments or shared living arrangements, are unlikely candidates for parenting, and perhaps will never achieve what prior generations considered to be full adulthood. Perhaps it is not surprising that identity politics based on such things as race, gender, or sexual orientation have taken a strong hold in places with few children and weakening family ties.[12]

The prevalence of singlehood and the culture of childlessness are often portrayed as matters of choice.[13] But as generational researchers Morley Winograd and Mike Hais have pointed out, American millennial attitudes about family are not significantly different from prior generations, albeit with a greater emphasis on gender equality.[14] Among American childless women under age 44, barely 6 percent are "voluntarily childless."[15] The vast majority of millennials want to get married and have children.[16]

A major reduction in childbearing may well be a blessing in some impoverished parts of the globe, but lower birth rates in higher-income countries will likely inhibit economic growth, due to rapid shrinkage of the labor force. Already in the United States, workforce growth has slowed to about one-third the level in 1970 and seems destined to fall even more.[17]

The demographic transition is even more marked in Japan, South Korea, Taiwan, and much of Europe, where finding younger workers is becoming a major problem for employers and could result in higher costs or increased movement of jobs to more fecund countries. As the employment base shrinks, some countries have raised taxes on the existing labor force to pay for the swelling ranks of retirees.[18] In certain places, the prospect of an inexorable depopulation looms: in Russia between 1991 and 2011, around 13 million more people died than were born.[19]

China's working-age population (those between 15 and 64 years old) peaked in 2011 and is projected to drop 23 percent by 2050.[20] This decline will be exacerbated by the effects of the now discarded one-child policy, which led to the aborting of an estimated 37 million Chinese girls since it came into force in 1980.[21] These grim statistics have created an imbalance between the sexes that could pose an existential threat to President Xi's "China dream," and perhaps to the stability of the Communist state.[22]

Getting Beyond Dogma

Given the likely effects of greenhouse gas emissions on the world's future climate, it will probably be necessary to change how we live, produce energy, and get around—even if such changes have significant economic costs. But this issue needs to be addressed rationally, and with attention to other concerns such as economic opportunity and the maintenance of the middle class.

As in the feudal era, genuine concerns about human sins and excesses can become excessively dogmatic and lead to socially destructive results.

Climate scientists have long recognized that the earth's climate is "a non-linear chaotic system," and that we lack the analytical tools to predict future climate conditions with much accuracy. Real and serious concerns, such as sea-level increases due to rising temperatures, need to be studied in the context of complex weather cycles whose fluctuations may not be as extreme as sensationalized reports have suggested.[23]

The oft-repeated notion that "the science is settled" is profoundly unscientific. Steve Koonin, former scientific adviser to President Obama's Department of Energy, believes there is "well-justified prudence in accelerating the development of low-emissions technologies and in cost-effective energy-efficiency measures" as well as various other means of mitigating the problem. At the same time, Koonin argues that well-informed public discussions on policy "should not be sidelined."[24] Like any serious challenge, climate change should be tackled with pragmatic measures that take the needs of human society into account.

But some policies being implemented today—such as wide-scale wind power and battery-powered cars—may be less beneficial than promised, with unexpected costs and other disadvantages.[25] The Paris Agreement on climate change appears to be having little effect, according to some observers.[26] Draconian climate policies in California and Germany have managed to hurt the middle class and the poor while producing little meaningful reduction in greenhouse gas emissions.[27] Extravagant policy proposals such as the recent "Green New Deal" floated in the U.S. Congress would cost trillions of dollars for uncertain benefits and divert resources from other priorities, such as reducing poverty or cleaning the oceans. In developing countries, an agenda like the Green New Deal could have the unintended effect of entrenching mass poverty, thus creating more dependency, and could bring new risks to health and sanitation as well.[28]

Most people naturally support environmental protection and efforts to address climate change, but are generally not willing to give up a large portion of their income for those purposes, especially when the benefits are dubious. In the 2019 elections in Australia, a country widely dependent on fossil fuel exports, the sometimes over-the-top antics of the environmentalist group called GetUp were widely credited with moving voters away from the progressive Labor Party and toward the conservatives.[29] In Canada, opposition to the Trans Mountain Pipeline project has led to a feud between British Columbia and Alberta, pitting environmental concerns against economic interests.[30] Even in Europe, policies that reduce living standards for middle- and working-class citizens are not widely popular, as evidenced for example by the *gilets jaunes* uprising in France.[31] Climate activists risk a widespread class-based backlash as long as they fail to consider the economic dislocation caused by the policies they prescribe.

How We View Humanity Matters

Approaches to environmental concerns are often conditioned by our view of humanity. Austin Williams describes a conflict around the question whether humanity represents "the biggest problem on the planet" or the "creators of a better future."[32] The negative view is somewhat similar to the early Christian idea that humanity's sins were to blame for everything from inclement weather to plagues to defeat in war. Having a family, like engaging in commerce, was viewed as secondary to the state of the individual soul.[33] But there's one big difference: in most religious faiths, especially monotheistic ones, humanity is seen as the pinnacle of creation, for whose benefit all else was created, while today's environmentalists are inclined to regard humans as no more worthy of respect than any other creature, and perhaps less so.

Climate change could well be a contributor to crop failures, hurricanes, floods, unusual weather patterns, or even war. But attempting to solve the problem by discouraging family formation or reducing living standards, as is often proposed, could have serious social ramifications, besides being politically unfeasible. One problem is that a Malthusian approach to demographics and economics tends to favor those who are already rich, to empower the clerisy, and generally to reinforce social hierarchy.[34]

Moreover, the measures taken by Western nations are unlikely to affect climate change much when virtually all the growth in emissions comes from developing countries, led by China.[35] Poorer developing countries also must accommodate the needs of large populations living in poverty and lacking basic amenities such as adequate electricity or clean water. Globally over one billion people lack reliable electricity. Leaders in countries such as India tend to be more concerned about the availability of energy than about reducing greenhouse gas emissions.[36]

Investing in Resilience

In order to find effective solutions to climate change and other problems, the environmental movement needs to give up "utopian fantasies," writes Ted Nordhaus, a longtime California environmentalist, and "make its peace with modernity and technology."[37] Given existing technologies, the much-anticipated shift to solar and wind energy seems largely impractical as a way of cutting emissions without dramatically raising energy costs, reducing reliability, and increasing poverty. A mix of diverse options, from nuclear power and hydroelectric generation to replacing coal with abundant, cleaner natural gas, seems more likely to reduce emissions in the short run without catastrophic economic and social consequences, particularly in the developing world.[38]

The best approach overall may be to emphasize resilience in preparation for future climate changes of any kind, including those that may be induced by human activities.[39] This idea is gradually taking root in policy discussions. Some proposals include more investment in coastal walls, a more decentralized power system, desalination plants, and better storage of water as well as conservation to alleviate possible harms from climate change. And after years of opposition, some environmentalists now acknowledge that poorly managed forests in states like California must be trimmed to forestall massive firestorms.[40]

We can find inspiration in the example of the Netherlands, where catastrophic flooding in the sixteenth century prompted an extensive and successful expansion of coastal berms to prevent future floods.[41] By contrast, failure to make on-the-ground improvements to mitigate risks contributed to the decline of ancient civilizations in Mesoamerica, the Indus Valley, and Cambodia.[42] A more recent example is New Orleans, where the dangers of storm-related flooding were widely recognized but the city's system of protective levees was not adequately maintained, and it failed during Hurricane Katrina. "Floods are 'acts of God,' but flood losses are largely acts of man," observed the geographer Gilbert F. White in 1942.[43]

Confronting the "Iron Law of Oligarchy"

The current approach to reducing climate-altering emissions has succeeded in enhancing the power of the oligarchy and the clerisy, illustrating the "iron law of oligarchy." Articulated by the sociologist Robert Michels in the early twentieth century, the law says: the more complex the issue, the greater the need for elite-driven solutions that bypass popular input.[44] In recent years, voices in the mainstream media have advocated the creation of a global "technocracy" that would preempt popular control and allow experts to implement policies of their own design.[45]

"Democracy is the planet's biggest enemy," asserted an article in the establishmentarian *Foreign Policy* magazine in 2019.[46] In this view, solving the climate problem requires an effort comparable to "mobilizing for war," with draconian measures unlikely to gain secure approval from legislative bodies or the general populace. Undemocratic means would be used to impose limits on such mundane popular pleasures as cheap air travel, cars, freeways, and suburbs with single-family houses.[47]

This approach to the issue perfectly matches the Chinese authoritarian system of governance. China's top-down way of solving problems has been praised by some environmental activists, such as Jerry Brown, former governor of California, who favors applying "the coercive power of the state" to achieve environmental goals. A strong supporter of the Beijing regime's current climate policies, Brown even recommends the "brainwashing" of the uncomprehending masses, a concept very much congruent with the logic behind Chinese thought control.[48]

CHAPTER 21

Can We Challenge Neo-feudalism?

he hope that we might see a global convergence toward democracy, as was once predicted by Francis Fukuyama and Thomas Friedman among others, seems increasingly remote. As China has grown both richer and more powerful, it has not become more like us, but instead has developed an authoritarian form of state capitalism.[1] Globally, democratic governance appears to have peaked in 2006, and many countries—including Turkey, Russia, and China—have become far more authoritarian. Even democratic India and many European countries have seen their own constitutional order frayed by internal dissension and racial and religious divisions.[2]

China's "civilization state," deeply rooted in thousands of years of history, represents the most profound philosophical challenge to liberal values since the end of the Cold War.[3] Jorgen Randers, a professor emeritus of climate strategy at the BI Norwegian Business School, predicts a Chinese-dominated global future, despite the country's many environmental and other challenges. "Western nations are not going to collapse, but the smooth operation and friendly nature of Western society will disappear, because inequity is going to explode," Randers argues. "Democratic, liberal society will fail, while stronger governments like China will be the winners."[4]

Even without the Chinese challenge, Western countries are already seeing more economic centralization, albeit in private hands. Over the past few decades, a small group of oligarchs, like Warren Buffett, have made vast fortunes by buying up businesses with little competition as a way to ensure monopoly profits.[5] More important still, the technological elite, highly adept at manipulating the tax code for their own benefit, continue to consolidate power in critical market sectors, making themselves into overlords more influential and powerful than most governments.[6]

The Importance of the Third Estate

How can those who believe in liberal democracy respond to the challenge of a rising oligarchy and clerisy? The nascent "peasant rebellions" in North America and Europe generally lack a coherent program to challenge the power of the dominant estates. All too often, they resort to a primitive nativism and cultural nostalgia that have little place in a twenty-first-century democracy.[7]

The key to resisting neo-feudalism today lies in the same kind of people who brought the first version to an end: what the leftist sociologist Barrington Moore described as "a numerous and politically vigorous class of town dwellers."[8] In other words, people who tend to own some property, and often their own business, and who build communities around the needs of their families. In the late eighteenth century, such people joined with independent peasants to challenge the hereditary aristocracy and the ecclesiastical hierarchy. Later on, the working classes successfully restrained the predatory power and disproportionate wealth accumulation of monopoly capitalists in the Gilded Age.

What is needed today is a new kind of politics that focuses primarily on fulfilling the aspirations of the Third Estate—on expanding opportunities for the middle and working classes. The current emphasis on social justice through redistribution and subsidies does not increase opportunities for upward mobility, but instead fosters dependency while consolidating power in a few hands.[9]

Off with Their Heads?

Today's oligarchs are the people who have benefited most from free markets, protection of property rights, and the meritocratic ideal. But their arrogance and greed could provoke a backlash against their privilege.

Consider the popular outrage over the recent college admissions scandal in the United States, with Hollywood and business elites cheating, bribing officials, and falsifying records to get their unqualified children into top colleges.[10]

Yet the oligarchy could be undermining the basis of their own good fortune. Much of the oligarchic class is allied with militant progressives whose basic agenda is hostile to classical liberalism and capitalist enterprise.[11] This is similar to what happened in the run-up to the French Revolution, when many French aristocrats not only lived dissolute lives but supported writers whose polemics ended up threatening "their own rights and even their existence," as Tocqueville noted.[12]

Up to now, policies advocated by the progressive left have come mostly at the expense of the lower and middle classes.[13] But the new breed of progressives are growing bolder and coming to resemble the Jacobins of the French Revolution, or the Red Guards unleashed during the Cultural Revolution in China in the late 1960s.[14] In the future, young activists may not tolerate the oligarchy's excesses as did earlier generations of environmental campaigners. After all, if the world is on the verge of a global apocalypse, and also suffering elevated levels of inequality, how can the luxurious lifestyles of so many of the world's most public green advocates—from Prince Charles and Richard Branson to Leonardo DiCaprio and Al Gore—be acceptable? The environmental left may well turn against the billionaires who lament climate change but fly their private jets to discuss the "crisis" in places like Davos.[15]

The activists who are melding environmentalist green with socialist red do not distinguish between good billionaires and bad ones. Some, like Bernie Sanders, believe that billionaires should not exist at all. The red-green contingent generally agree with the view of Barry Commoner, a founding father of modern environmentalism, that "Capitalism is the earth's number one enemy."[16]

Over time, our fashionably left-leaning oligarchs may discover that their apparent political allies and even their own employees are rebelling against them. While oligarchs give heavy financial backing to Democrats, some surveys indicate that more party members now support socialism than capitalism.[17] There's even a growing socialist movement among tech employees in Silicon Valley who have little chance of replicating the wealth accumulation enjoyed by prior generations in the Bay Area.[18]

Unsurprisingly, some tech titans and Wall Street oligarchs are already making emergency escape plans in case of civil unrest.[19]

The Rebellion We Need

To date, opposition to the neo-feudal order has all too often morphed into hatred of minorities, such as immigrants, Jews, and Muslims, and a belief that the society is threatened by migrants from different cultures.[20] Given the demographic trends not only in Europe but also in North America and Oceania, such a xenophobic agenda is likely to be counterproductive, and is incompatible with a liberal society that can successfully integrate newcomers into the national culture.

Great societies are by nature expansive, not closed in. Rome became great, Gibbon suggested, in part because it permitted religious heterodoxy and provided outsiders, including former slaves, a chance to rise above their station. In contrast to Athens, where citizenship was restricted, Rome extended citizenship to the farthest boundaries of its empire, and by 212 all free people were eligible to be citizens. "The grandsons of Gauls, who besieged Julius Caesar at Alesia, commanded legions, governed provinces and were admitted into the Senate of Rome," wrote Gibbon.[21]

Just as diverse peoples found much to emulate in Roman civilization, the liberal institutions that developed in the West appeal to people from radically different backgrounds. These institutions and their underpinning ideals are not tied to any set of racial characteristics. Chinese, Muslims, and Latin Americans migrate mostly to countries that have embraced the liberal values of citizenship, tolerance, and the rule of law.[22] China under the autocratic Xi Jinping may offer "the Chinese dream," but the number of immigrants from China living in the United States more than doubled between 2000 and 2018, reaching nearly 2.5 million. Similar patterns have been seen in both Canada and Australia. There is little such movement to China or most other Asian countries.[23]

Those with the good fortune to live in pluralistic Western-style democracies, rooted in classical culture, should recognize how rare such open societies have been through history, and how much the vitality of these societies is threatened today. Historically, democracy has been like a flame that shines bright for a while—as in Greece and Rome—and then succumbs to autocracy or ossifies into hierarchy.[24]

The Values Proposition

"Civilizations are fragile, impermanent things," wrote the historian Joseph Tainter.[25] Amidst our civilization's long period of success and stability, we may not recognize that things are shifting dangerously until it's far too late.[26] We are no more prepared for a regression to a less enlightened, less mobile society than the citizens of ancient Rome were prepared for the collapse of their empire.

A civilization can survive only if its members, especially those with the greatest influence, believe in its basic values. Today our key institutions—the academy, the media, the corporate hierarchy, and even some churches—reject many of the fundamental ideals that have long defined Western culture.[27] Activists on both left and right, instead of emphasizing what binds a democratic society together, have focused on narrow identity politics that cannot sustain a pluralistic democracy.[28]

A loss of faith in the basic values of our society is particularly marked among the young; nearly 40 percent of young Americans think the country lacks "a history to be proud of." Far fewer place a great emphasis on family, religion, or patriotism than in previous generations. Europe is, if anything, moving faster toward cultural deconstruction by anathematizing its own heritage.[29] The "Paris Statement" put forward in 2017 by a group of scholars from several European countries, titled "A Europe We Can Believe In," says that the EU bureaucracy is invested in an "ersatz religious enterprise" based on postnationalism and the rejection of a distinct, historical culture in favor of multiculturalism.[30]

Given the high-level commitment to cultural deconstruction in Western societies, it isn't surprising that we are seeing decreased cultural literacy and a greatly reduced interest in history among the young.[31] Maybe we won't quite see a reprise of the early Middle Ages, when "the very mind of man was going through degeneration," as Henri Pirenne put it, but we could be creating what Roderick Seidenberg called "posthistoric man," cut off from the traditions and values of our civilizational past.[32] If one doesn't know the foundational principles of our democracy, including individual freedom and open discussion, one is not likely to recognize when they are lost. Regaining a sense of pride in Western culture and its achievements—while remaining open to newcomers and influences from elsewhere—is essential to recovering the ambition and self-confidence that drove the West's ascent, from the Age of Exploration to the Space Age.[33]

Some scholars believe that Japan now provides a model for high-income countries that can dispense with growth and instead focus on spiritual or quality-of-life issues. Japan will not conquer the world, one observer suggests, but it could settle into being something like an Asian Switzerland with a rapidly aging but comfortable population.[34]

Similarly, the neo-feudal order would replace a focus on upward mobility and family with a desire for a comfortable, subsidized life, indulging in the digital mind-sinks that keep the masses in their metaphorical basements.[35] Already, roughly half of all Americans support the idea of a guaranteed basic income of about $2,000 a month if robots put them out of work.[36] A universal basic income enjoys even stronger support in most European countries, particularly among younger people.[37]

To slow or reverse neo-feudalism, with its constraints on upward mobility and creation of more dependency, requires awakening the political will of the Third Estate to resist it. "Happy the nation whose people have not forgotten how to rebel," wrote the British historian R. H. Tawney.[38] Whether we can muster the resolve to assert our place as engaged citizens will determine the kind of world our children inherit.

ACKNOWLEDGMENTS

Like my other books, this one benefited greatly from input by many people who put hours into reviewing and critiquing early drafts. These reviewers were invaluable in pointing out inconsistencies or adding nuance to the analysis.

Among these reviewers are Aaron Renn, Michael Lind, and Fred Siegel. The sections on housing and environmental policy were greatly enhanced by input from Wendell Cox, a demographer, and David Friedman, an attorney. My brother Mark, former director of survey research at *Consumer Reports*, lent his keen analytical skills and historical perspective, to great effect.

This effort would not have been possible without the support of Chapman University in Orange, California. I am particularly grateful to Daniele Struppa, Chapman's president, and Lisa Sparks, dean of the School of Communications, which houses the Center for Demographics and Policy. The California Feudalism project was shaped in large part in a collaboration with Marshall Toplansky, who teaches in the Argyros School of Business. I owe a great deal also to our research team including Karla del Rio Lopez, Alex Thomas, Andre Cabrera, Luke Edwards, Chad Lonski, Doug Havard, and Mike Christensen. This work was supported by Tom Piechota, head of research at Chapman, and two great assistants, Morgan Sohrabian and Mahnaz Asghari.

Parts of this book, particularly the sixth chapter, drew upon work done for the Urban Reform Institute, formerly the Center for Opportunity Urbanism, based in Houston. Our work on alternatives to gentrification were shaped in large part by Wendell Cox, Pete Saunders, Karla del Rio Lopez, and Cullum Clark, now at the Bush Center in Dallas. I also want to express appreciation to Tom Lile, chairman, and Leo Linbeck, vice chairman, and the entire board of the institute.

Particular mention should be made of Alicia Kurimska, who helped on all these projects and worked extensively on the book. A native of Slovakia and former Chapman student, Alicia is now living in Stockholm. Her contributions in terms of research and copy-editing were critical to the completion of the book.

Some parts of this book grew out of articles for various news outlets. I want to thank editors including Sal Rodriguez at the Southern California News Group, Brian Anderson and Paul Beston of *City Journal* (Manhattan Institute), Harry Siegel at the *Daily Beast*, *Quillette*'s Jamie Palmer in London and Claire Lehmann in Sydney, and Julius Krein at *American Affairs*. Many articles also appeared in New Geography, a website run efficiently by Rhonda Howard and Mark Schill from Praxis Strategy in Grand Folks, North Dakota.

I also want to express my gratitude for the staff at my publisher, Encounter Books. The president, Roger Kimball, comes from a different political tradition but saw the value of the book. Without his support this book may never have been published. I benefited from terrific editing by Encounter's Carol Staswick, whose background in medieval studies was particularly helpful. I also want to thank members of Encounter's marketing staff, including Sam Schneider, Lauren Miklos and Amanda DeMatto.

Finally my deepest gratitude belongs to my wife, Mandy Shamis. Besides putting up with my long disappearances into my office, she also helped edit the earlier drafts of the book. Her emotional support was critical and her intellectual acuity contributed mightily to the effort.

Joel Kotkin
Orange, California

NOTES

CHAPTER 1—THE FEUDAL REVIVAL

1   Nicholas Riasanovsky, *A History of Russia* (New York: Oxford University Press, 1963), 127–31, 204–7; Daniel Pipes, *Russia Under the Old Regime* (New York: Scribner, 1974), 48–49, 144.

2   Emmanuel Saez and Gabriel Zucman, "Wealth Inequality in the United States since 1913: Evidence from Capitalized Income Tax Data," *Quarterly Journal of Economics*, vol. 131:2 (May 2016), 519.

3   Michael Savage, "Richest 1% on target to own two-thirds of all wealth by 2030," *Guardian*, April 7, 2018, https://www.theguardian.com/business/2018/apr/07 /global-inequality-tipping-point-2030.

4   Christophe Guilluy, *Twilight of the Elites: Prosperity, the Periphery, and the Future of France*, trans. Malcolm Debevoise (New Haven: Yale University Press, 2019), 100.

5   Daniel Henninger, "Socialism? Yes, Be Afraid," *Wall Street Journal*, March 13, 2019, https://www.wsj.com/articles/socialism-yes-be-afraid-11552518646.

6   Michael Grant, *The Fall of the Roman Empire* (New York: Collier, 1990), 58.

7   Robert S. Lopez, *The Birth of Europe* (New York: M. Evans & Co., 1967), 170.

8   Max Roser, "Economic Growth," Our World in Data, https://ourworldindata. org/economic-growth.

9   George W. Bush, "Remarks by President George W. Bush at the 20th Anniversary of the National Endowment for Democracy," November 6, 2003, U.S. Chamber of Commerce, Washington, D.C., https://www.ned.org/remarks -by-president-george-w-bush-at-the-20th-anniversary/; David A. Graham, "The Wrong Side of 'the Right Side of History,'" *Atlantic*, December 21, 2015, https://www.theatlantic.com/politics/archive/2015/12/obama-right-side-of -history/420462/.

10   OECD, "Governments must act to help struggling middle class," October 4, 2019, https://www.oecd.org/newsroom/governments-must-act-to-help -struggling-middle-class.htm.

11   Estelle Sommeiller and Mark Price, "The new gilded age: Income inequality in the U.S. by state, metropolitan area, and county," Economic Policy Institute, Table 10, July 19, 2018, https://www.epi.org/publication/the-new-gilded-age -income-inequality-in-the-u-s-by-state-metropolitan-area-and-county/#epi -toc-14.

12   David DeGraw, "We're living in a system of new feudalism. Here's how to

change it," *New Statesman*, October 31, 2013, http://www.newstatesman.com/2013/10/were-living-system-new-feudalism-heres-how-change-it.

13 Shannon Tiezzi, "Report: China's 1 Percent Owns 1/3 of Wealth," *Diplomat*, January 15, 2016, https://thediplomat.com/2016/01/report-chinas-1-percent-owns-13-of-wealth/; Jonathan Kaiman, "China gets richer but more unequal," *Guardian*, July 28, 2014, https://www.theguardian.com/world/2014/jul/28/china-more-unequal-richer; David S.G. Goodman, *Class in Contemporary China* (Cambridge: Polity Press, 2014), 2–3, 45.

14 Satyajit Das, "Despite appearances, the idea of social progress is a myth," *Independent*, July 30, 2017, http://www.independent.co.uk/voices/despite-appearances-the-idea-of-social-progress-is-a-myth-a7867371.html.

15 Christopher Ingraham, "American land barons: 100 wealthy families now own nearly as much land as that of New England," *Washington Post*, December 21, 2017, https://www.washingtonpost.com/news/wonk/wp/2017/12/21/american-land-barons-100-wealthy-families-now-own-nearly-as-much-land-as-that-of-new-england/?utm_term=.89f1e78c55d0; *2018 Land Report 100: America's 100 Largest Landowners*, Magazine of the American Landowner, Special Report, Winter 2018, https://www.landleader.com/land-report-100.

16 Julie Turkewitz, "Who Gets to Own the West?" *New York Times*, June 22, 2019, https://www.nytimes.com/2019/06/22/us/wilks-brothers-fracking-business.html.

17 Elena L. Pasquini, "Land Concentration in Europe: What we know," Degrees of Latitude, November 28, 2017, http://www.degreesoflatitude.com/stories/land-concentration-in-europe-what-we-know/; Levente Polyak, "Exploring Property: Perspectives of Ownership," Cooperative City, October 22, 2017, https://cooperativecity.org/2017/10/22/ownership/; Palko Karasz, "Half of England Is Owned by Less Than 1% of Its Population, Researcher Says," *New York Times*, April 19, 2019, https://www.nytimes.com/2019/04/19/world/europe/england-land-inequality.html.

18 Michael D. Carr and Emily E. Wiemers, "The decline in lifetime earnings mobility in the U.S.: Evidence from survey-linked administrative data," Washington Center for Equitable Growth, September 7, 2016, https://equitablegrowth.org/working-papers/the-decline-in-lifetime-earnings-mobility-in-the-u-s-evidence-from-survey-linked-administrative-data/.

19 OECD, *Under Pressure: The Squeezed Middle Class* (Paris: OECD Publishing, 2019), 13, https://doi.org/10.1787/ 689afed1-en.

20 John W. Schoen, "Millennials will be renting for a lot longer," CNBC, September 9, 2016, https://www.cnbc.com/2016/09/09/millennials-will-be-renting-for-a-lot-longer.html; Leith van Onselen, "The sad death of Australian home ownership," Macrobusiness, August 7, 2018, https://www.macrobusiness.com.au/2018/08/sad-death-australian-home-ownership/; Richard Partington, "Home ownership among young adults has 'collapsed', study finds," *Guardian*, February 16, 2018, https://www.theguardian.com/money/2018/feb/16/homeownership-among-young-adults-collapsed-institute-fiscal-studies; Joel Kotkin, "The High Cost of a Home Is Turning American Millennials Into the New Serfs," *Daily Beast*, April 11, 2017, https://www.thedailybeast.com/the-high-cost-of-a-home-is-turning-american-millennials-into-the-new-serfs.

21 Robert E. Scott and Zane Mokhiber, "The China toll deepens," Economic Policy Institute, October 23, 2018, https://www.epi.org/publication/the-china-toll -deepens-growth-in-the-bilateral-trade-deficit-between-2001-and-2017-cost -3-4-million-u-s-jobs-with-losses-in-every-state-and-congressional-district/; Phillip Inman, "UK manufacturing has lost 600,000 jobs in a decade, says union," *Guardian*, June 4, 2018, https://www.theguardian.com/business/2018 /jun/04/uk-manufacturing-has-lost-600000-jobs-in-a-decade-says-union.

22 Guilluy, *Twilight of the Elites*, 2.

23 Joel Kotkin, "Progressives Have Let Inner Cities Fail For Decades. President Trump Could Change That," *Daily Beast*, April 13, 2017, https://www .thedailybeast.com/progressives-have-let-inner-cities-fail-for-decades -president-trump-could-change-that.

24 Michael Lind, "The New Class War," *American Affairs*, Summer 2017; Brody Mullins and Jack Nicas, "Paying Professors: Inside Google's Academic Influence Campaign," *Wall Street Journal*, July 14, 2017, https://www.wsj.com/articles /paying-professors-inside-googles-academic-influence-campaign-1499785286; Justin Danhof, "I Confronted Google about Its Liberal Groupthink at a Shareholder Meeting—Here's What Happened Next," *Investors*, August 9, 2017, https://www.investors.com/politics/commentary/i-confronted-google-about -its-liberal-groupthink-at-a-shareholder-meeting-heres-what-happened-next/.

25 Daniel Bell, *The Coming of Post-Industrial Society* (New York: Basic Books, 1973), 391.

26 Bruce Stokes, "Expectations for the Future," Pew Research Center, September 18, 2018, https://www.pewresearch.org/global/2018/09/18/expectations-for-the -future/.

27 Bruce Stokes and Kat Devlin, "Despite Rising Economic Confidence, Japanese See Best Days Behind Them and Say Children Face a Bleak Future," Pew Research Center, November 12, 2018, https://www.pewglobal.org/2018/11/12 /despite-rising-economic-confidence-japanese-see-best-days-behind-them -and-say-children-face-a-bleak-future/; Ameber Pariona, "The World's Most Pessimistic Countries," *World Atlas*, August 15, 2017, https://www.worldatlas .com/articles/the-world-s-10-most-pessimistic-countries.html.

28 "Employment and Wages," *China Labour Bulletin*, July 2019, https://clb.org.hk /content/employment-and-wages.

29 Lyman Stone, "More Thoughts on Falling Fertility," *Medium*, December 4, 2017, https://medium.com/migration-issues/more-thoughts-on-falling- fertility-366fd1a84d8; Rich Miller, "Powell's Puzzling U.S. Labor Market Looks Somewhat Like Japan's," Bloomberg, June 19, 2018, https://www.bloomberg. com/news/articles/2018-06-19/powell-s-puzzling-u-s-labor-market-looks -somewhat-like-japan-s; Peter Dockrill, "US Fertility Rates Have Plummeted Into Uncharted Territory, And Nobody Knows Why," *Science Alert*, May 21, 2018, https://www.sciencealert.com/us-birth-rate-hits-record-low-fertility -plummets-uncharted-territory-cdc-decline; Andrew Van Dam, "Toys R Us's baby problem is everybody's baby problem," *Washington Post*, March 15, 2018, https://www.washingtonpost.com/news/wonk/wp/2018/03/15/toys-r-uss-baby -problem-is-everybodys-baby-problem/?noredirect=on&utm_term= .fb1caf2d80c5; Justin Fox, "The Consequences of the U.S. Baby Bust,"

Bloomberg Opinion, September 20, 2017, https://www.bloomberg.com/view
/articles/2017-09-20/the-consequences-of-the-u-s-baby-bust; Wolfgang
Streeck, *How Will Capitalism End? Essays on a Failing System* (New York:
Verso, 2016), 219.

30 Phil Longman, *The Empty Cradle: How Falling Birthrates Threaten World
Prosperity* (New York: New America Books, 2004); Joel Kotkin, "Death Spiral
Demographics: The Countries Shrinking the Fastest," *Forbes*, February 1, 2017,
https://www.forbes.com/sites/joelkotkin/2017/02/01/death-spiral
-demographics-the-countries-shrinking-the-fastest/#4ae48b38b83c.

31 Alex Gray, "The troubling charts that show young people losing faith in
democracy," World Economic Forum, December 1, 2016, https://www.weforum
.org/agenda/2016/12/charts-that-show-young-people-losing-faith-in
-democracy/.

32 Amanda Taub, "How Stable Are Democracies? 'Warning Signs Are
Flashing Red,'" *New York Times*, November 29, 2016, https://www.nytimes.
com/2016/11/29/world/americas/western-liberal-democracy.html?_r=0.

33 Francis Fukuyama, *The End of History and the Last Man* (New York: Free Press,
1992), 12.

34 Emily Atkin, "Al Gore's Carbon Footprint Doesn't Matter," *New Republic*,
August 7, 2017, https://newrepublic.com/article/144199/al-gores-carbon
-footprint-doesnt-matter; "How Electricity Became a Luxury Good," *Spiegel*,
September 4, 2013, http://www.spiegel.de/international/germany/high-costs
-and-errors-of-german-transition-to-renewable-energy-a-920288-2.html;
Dagmara Stoerring, "Energy Poverty," European Parliament, November 9,
2016, http://www.europarl.europa.eu/RegData/etudes/STUD/2017/607350
/IPOL_STU(2017)607350_EN.pdf.

35 Salena Zito and Brad Todd, *The Great Revolt: Inside the Populist Coalition
Reshaping American Politics* (New York: Crown Forum, 2018), 3, 246.

36 Guilluy, *Twilight of the Elites*, 15; Pascal-Emmanuel Gobry, "The Failure of the
French Elite," *Wall Street Journal*, February 22, 2019, https://www.wsj.com
/articles/the-failure-of-the-french-elite-11550851097?mod=?mod=itp_wsj&ru
=yahoo&mod=djemITP_h.

37 Adam Nossiter, "France's Mayors, Feeling the Pinch, Lead a Quiet Rebellion
and Quit," *New York Times*, November 11, 2018, https://www.nytimes.
com/2018/11/11/world/europe/france-mayors-quit-macron.html; Adam
Nossiter, "As France's Towns Wither, Fear of a Decline in 'Frenchness,'" *New
York Times*, February 28, 2017, https://www.nytimes.com/2017/02/28/world
/europe/france-albi-french-towns-fading.html; Wendell Cox, "The Evolving
Urban Form: Paris," *New Geography*, March 19, 2018, http://www.
newgeography.com/content/005912-the-evolving-urban-form-paris.

38 Alan S. Blinder, "Democrats, Stop Pretending to Be Socialists," *Wall Street
Journal*, March 14, 2019, https://www.wsj.com/articles/democrats-stop
-pretending-to-be-socialists-11552603666.

39 Ibid.

40 Vasily Grossman, *Life and Fate*, trans. Robert Chandler (New York: New York
Review of Books, 1985), 537.

CHAPTER 2—THE ENDURING ALLURE OF FEUDALISM

1 Marc Bloch, *Feudal Society*, trans. L. A. Manyon (London: Routledge, 1961), xii–xiii.

2 Peter Heather, *Empires and Barbarians: The Fall of Rome and the Birth of Europe* (Oxford: Oxford University Press, 2010), 291–93; Frances and Joseph Gies, *Daily Life in Medieval Times* (New York: Barnes & Noble, 1969), 12–13; Jeffrey Barraclough, *The Crucible of Europe* (Berkeley: University of California Press, 1976), 33; J. Huizinga, *The Waning of the Middle Ages* (Garden City, N.Y.: Doubleday, 1954), 59–61.

3 Norman F. Cantor, *Medieval History: The Life and Death of a Civilization* (New York: Macmillan, 1963), 294.

4 Robert S. Lopez, *The Birth of Europe* (New York: M. Evans & Co., 1967), 163–66; Bloch, *Feudal Society*, 145–46, 161.

5 Bloch, *Feudal Society*, 232.

6 Pierre Riché, *Daily Life in the World of Charlemagne*, trans. Jo Ann McNamara (Philadelphia: University of Pennsylvania Press, 1978), 133.

7 Lopez, *The Birth of Europe*, 339; James Westfall Thompson and Edgar Nathaniel Johnson, *An Introduction to Medieval Europe* (New York: Norton, 1937), 229.

8 Riché, *Daily Life in the World of Charlemagne*, 51; Barbara Tuchman, *A Distant Mirror: The Calamitous 14th Century* (New York: Knopf, 1978), 27: Cantor, *Medieval History*, 97, 109; Lopez, *The Birth of Europe*, 149–50, 198; Bloch, *Feudal Society*, 98; Pitirim Sorokin, *The Crisis of Our Age* (Oxford: Oneworld Publications, 1992), 17–19.

9 Edward Gibbon, *The History of the Decline and Fall of the Roman Empire* (New York: Modern Library, 1931), vol. 2: 6, 93, 845, Cantor, *Medieval History*, 7.

10 Riché, *Daily Life*, 211–12; Gies, *Daily Life in Medieval Times*, 128.

11 Thompson and Johnson, *An Introduction to Medieval Europe*, 290–91; Riché, *Daily Life*, 67–68.

12 Arno Mayer, *The Persistence of the Old Regime: Europe to the Great War* (New York: Pantheon, 1981), 292–94; Raymond Williams, *Culture and Society* (New York: Harper & Row, 1958), 110–17, 258; Martin Wiener, *English Culture and the Decline of the Industrial Spirit* (Cambridge: Cambridge University Press, 1981), 31.

13 Karl Marx, *Capital*, trans. Ben Fowkes (New York: Vintage, 1957), 452–53.

14 Friedrich Engels, *The Condition of the Working Class in England*, trans. W. O. Henderson and W. H. Chalmers (Palo Alto: Stanford University Press, 1958), 207–8.

15 Karl Marx and Friedrich Engels, "The Manifesto of the Communist Party," in *The Essential Left* (New York: Barnes & Noble, 1961), 36–37.

16 Arnold Toynbee, *The Industrial Revolution* (Boston: Beacon, 1956), 121–22; Charles H. Kegel, "Lord John Manners and the Young England Movement: Romanticism in Politics," *Western Political Quarterly*, vol. 14:3 (1961), 691–97.

17 J. Hobsbawm, *The Age of Revolution* (New York: New American Library, 1962), 290–91.

18 Orlando Figes, *A People's Tragedy: The Russian Revolution, 1891–1924* (New York: Penguin, 1996), 87.

19   Mayer, *The Persistence of the Old Regime*, 293–94; Ernst Nolte, *Three Faces of Fascism*, trans. Leila Vennewitz (New York: New American Library, 1969), 28.

20   Frederick Hayek, *The Road to Serfdom* (Chicago: University of Chicago Press, 1972*)*, 17; Nolte, *Three Faces of Fascism*, 57, 75, 166; F. L. Carsten, *The Rise of Fascism* (Berkeley: University of California Press, 1967), 11–12.

21   Wiener, *English Culture and the Decline of the Industrial Spirit*, 107.

22   "The far right's new fascination with the Middle Ages," *Economist*, January 2, 2017, https://www.economist.com/blogs/democracyinamerica/2017/01/medieval-memes.

23   "Vladimir Putin embraces the Russian church," *Economist*, February 3, 2018, https://www.economist.com/europe/2018/02/03/vladimir-putin-embraces-the-russian-church; Andrey Pertsev, "President and Patriarch: What Putin Wants from the Orthodox Church," Carnegie Moscow Center, December 19, 2017, https://carnegie.ru/commentary/75058; Yaroslav Trofimov, "Russia's Turn to Its Asian Past," *Wall Street Journal*, July 7–8, 2018, https://www.wsj.com/articles/russias-turn-to-its-asian-past-1530889247.

24   Ya Hua, "In China, Feudal Answers to Modern Problems," *New York Times*, April 10, 2013, https://www.nytimes.com/2013/04/11/opinion/yu-in-china-feudal-answers-for-modern-problems.html; Jeremy Page, "Why China Is Turning Back to Confucius," *Wall Street Journal*, September 20, 2015, https://www.wsj.com/articles/why-china-is-turning-back-to-confucius-1442754000; Richard McGregor, *The Party: The Secret World of China's Communist Rulers* (New York: Harper, 2010), 26.

25   Lee Kwan Yew, *From Third World to First* (New York, Harper, 2000), 491–94; McGregor, *The Party: The Secret World of China's Communist Rulers*, 32–33.

26   Wiener, *English Culture and the Decline of the Industrial Spirit*, 93.

27   Robert Verkaik, "Just 96 months to save the world, says Prince Charles," *Independent*, June 9, 2009, https://www.independent.co.uk/environment/green-living/just-96-months-to-save-world-says-prince-charles-1738049.html; "Prince Charles: Feudal Critic of Capitalism," Socialist Party of Great Britain, February 2003, https://www.worldsocialism.org/spgb/socialist-standard/2000s/2003/no-1182-february-2003/prince-charles-feudal-critic-capitalism; Oscar Rickett, "What We Can Learn From Prince Charles from his Letters to Politicians," *Vice*, May 15, 2015, https://www.vice.com/en_us/article/yvxgzx/prince-charles-letters-284.

28   Michael Kimmelman, "The Kind of Thinking Cities Need," *New York Times*, October 28, 2016, https://www.nytimes.com/2016/10/30/opinion/sunday/the-kind-of-thinking-cities-need.html.

29   Dominic Green, "A Philosopher on the Decline of the English Countryside, Brexit, and the European Project," *Weekly Standard*, November 17, 2017, https://www.weeklystandard.com/a-philosopher-on-the-decline-of-the-english-countryside-brexit-and-the-european-project/article/2010521.

30   Karl Sharro, "Density over Sprawl," in *The Future of Community*, ed. Dave Clements et al. (London: Pluto Press, 2008), 72.

CHAPTER 3—THE RISE AND DECLINED OF LIBERAL CAPITALISM

1 R. R. Palmer, *The World of the French Revolution* (New York: Harper & Row, 1971), 268–69; Georges Lefebvre, *The Coming of the French Revolution,* trans. R. R. Palmer (Princeton: Princeton University Press, 1947), 177–81.

2 Robert S. Lopez, *The Birth of Europe* (New York: M. Evans & Co., 1967), 21–23.

3 Reuven Brenner, *Rivalry: In Business, Science, Among Nations* (Cambridge: Cambridge University Press, 1987), 37–41.

4 Edward Barbier, *Scarcities and Frontiers: How Economies Have Developed Through Natural Resource Exploitation* (Cambridge, Cambridge University Press, 2011), 84–91, 158, 176; Jeffrey A. Winters, *Oligarchy* (Cambridge: Cambridge University Press, 2011), 28–29; Bernard Lewis, *The Muslim Discovery of Europe* (New York: Norton, 1982), 27.

5 Peter Heather, *Empires and Barbarians: The Fall of Rome and the Birth of Europe* (Oxford: Oxford University Press, 2010), 465; Nathan Rosenberg and L. E. Birdzell, Jr., *How the West Grew Rich: The Economic Transformation of the Industrial World* (New York: Basic Books, 1986), 37; Fernand Braudel, *The Perspective of the World,* vol. 3 of *Civilization and Capitalism, 15th–18th Century,* trans. Sian Reynolds (New York: Harper & Row, 1982), 503, 511.

6 Barbier, *Scarcities and Frontiers,* 273; Immanuel Wallerstein, *The Modern World System: Capitalist Agriculture and the Origins of the European World Economy in the 16th Century* (New York: Academic Press, 1974), 14–17; Tony Smith, *The Patterns of Imperialism: The United States, Great Britain and the Late-Industrializing World since 1815* (Cambridge: Cambridge University Press, 1981), 27, 35.

7 Data from the World Bank.

8 Javier C. Hernandez, "Mao 101: Inside a Chinese Classroom Training the Communists of Tomorrow," *New York Times,* June 28, 2018, https://www.nytimes.com/2018/06/28/world/asia/chinese-classrooms-education-communists.html; Aaron L. Friedberg, "The Authoritarian Challenge: China, Russia and the Threat to the Liberal International Order," Sasakawa Peace Foundation, August 2017, https://www.spf.org/jpus-j/img/investigation/The_Authoritarian_Challenge.pdf; Anne-Marie Brady, "Magic Weapons: China's political influence under Xi Jinping," Kissinger Institute on China and the United States, September 18, 2017, https://www.wilsoncenter.org/article/magic-weapons-chinas-political-influence-activities-under-xi-jinping; Chun Han Wong, "China Celebrates Xi Jinping With Fervor Not Seen Since Mao," *Wall Street Journal,* December 10, 2017, https://www.wsj.com/articles/china-celebrates-xi-jinping-with-fervor-not-seen-since-mao-1512907201.

9 Salvatore Babones, "China's Middle Class Is Pulling Up the Ladder Behind Itself," *Foreign Policy,* February 1, 2018, https://foreignpolicy.com/2018/02/01/chinas-middle-class-is-pulling-up-the-ladder-behind-itself/; Richard McGregor, *The Party: The Secret World of China's Communist Rulers* (New York: Harper, 2010), 30; David S. G. Goodman, "The New Rich in China: Why There Is No New Middle Class," *Arts: The Journal of the Sydney University Arts Association,* vol. 32 (2010), https://openjournals.library.sydney.edu.au/index.php/ART/article/view/5715.

10 Maya Wang, "China's Chilling 'Social Credit' Blacklist," *Wall Street Journal*, December 11, 2017, https://www.wsj.com/articles/chinas-chilling-social -credit-blacklist-1513036054.

11 Hal Brands, "China's Master Plan: Exporting an Ideology," Bloomberg, June 11, 2018, https://www.bloomberg.com/opinion/articles/2018-06-11/china-s-master -plan-exporting-an-ideology.

12 Paul Kennedy, *Preparing for the Twenty-first Century* (New York: Random House, 1993), 25; Austin Williams, *The Enemies of Progress: The Dangers of Sustainability* (Exeter: Societas, 2008), 125–26; McGregor, *The Party: The Secret World of China's Communist Rulers*, 272; Howard W. French, *China's Second Continent: How a Million Migrants Are Building a New Empire in Africa* (New York: Vintage, 2015), 33–25, 261; Jason Horowitz and Jack Ewing, "Italy May Split With Allies and Open Its Ports to China's Building Push," *New York Times*, March 6, 2019, https://www.nytimes.com/2019/03/06/world/europe/italy -ports-china.html.

13 Martin Jacques, *When China Rules the World: The End of the Western World and the Birth of a New Global Order* (New York: Penguin, 2009), 363–64; Tunku Varadarajan, "India Turns West but Away from Western Values," *Wall Street Journal*, May 23, 2019, https://www.wsj.com/articles/india-turns-west -but-away-from-western-values-11558651907.

14 Karel van Wolferen, *The Enigma of Japanese Power: People and Politics in a Stateless Nation* (New York: Vintage, 1990), 1.

15 Robert J. Gordon, *The Rise and Fall of American Growth* (Princeton: Princeton University Press, 2016), 574–76, 601–4.

16 Fred Pearce, *The Coming Population Crash and Our Planet's Surprising Future* (Boston: Beacon, 2011), 94–95.

17 Emma Chen and Wendell Cox, "Six Adults and One Child in China," *New Geography*, October 9, 2011, http://www.newgeography.com/content/002474 -six-adults-and-one-child-china; Paul Yip, "Does China actually need more children to replace its declining working-age population?" *South China Morning Post*, January 28, 2018, https://www.scmp.com/comment/insight -opinion/article/2130666/does-china-actually-need-more-children-replace-its -declining.

18 Greg Wilford, "Young Japanese people are not having sex," *Independent*, July 8, 2017, https://www.independent.co.uk/news/world/asia/japan-sex-problem -demographic-time-bomb-birth-rates-sex-robots-fertility-crisis-virgins -romance-porn-a7831041.html; Bill Emmott, *The Sun Also Sets* (New York: Times Books, 1989), 31, 36; Pearce, *The Coming Population Crash*, 39; Jonathan V. Last, *What to Expect When No One's Expecting: America's Coming Demographic Disaster* (New York: Encounter, 2013), 110–11.

19 Anuradha Shroff, Ali Modarres, and Wendell Cox, "The Rise of Post-Familialism: Humanity's Future?" Civil Service College Singapore, 2012, https://www.chapman.edu/wilkinson/_files/the-rise-of-post-familialism.pdf.

20 Chen and Cox, "Six Adults and One Child in China."

21 Phil Longman, *The Empty Cradle: How Falling Birthrates Threaten World Prosperity* (New York: New America Books, 2004), 26–27, 63; Fred Pearce, "The bomb in 2076: The population bomb has imploded," *New Scientist*, November

16, 2016, https://www.newscientist.com/article/mg23231001-400-the-world-in
-2076-the-population-bomb-did-go-off-but-were-ok/.

22 Pearce, *The Coming Population Crash*, 147; "Experts Predict Global Population
Will Plateau," *Spiegel*, November 3, 2011, http://www.spiegel.de/international
/world/the-great-contraction-experts-predict-global-population-will-plateau-a
-795479.html.

23 Longman, *The Empty Cradle*, 5.

24 Shroff et al., "The Rise of Post-Familialism: Humanity's Future?"; Aisha
Majid and Sarah Newey, "Defusing the 'demographic timebomb': the world's
population in 13 charts," *Telegraph*, September 18, 2018, https://www.telegraph.
co.uk/news/0/defusing-demographic-timebomb-worlds-population
-challenges-13/.

25 Michael Grant, *The Fall of the Roman Empire* (New York: Collier, 1990), 17;
Taichi Sakaiya, *The Knowledge Value Revolution,* trans. George Fields and
William Marsh (Tokyo: Kodansha International, 1985), 138–39; George
Friedman, *The Next Hundred Years: A Forecast for the 21st Century* (New York:
Doubleday, 2009), 53.

26 James K. Galbraith, "Extreme Inequality Creates Global Disorder," *Nation*,
June 22, 2018, https://www.thenation.com/article/extreme-inequality-creates
-global-disorder/.

27 Robert D. Atkinson, "Unfortunately, Technology Will Not Eliminate Many
Jobs," Innovation Files, August 7, 2017, https://itif.org/publications/2017/08/07
/unfortunately-technology-will-not-eliminate-many-jobs; Carl Benedikt
Frey and Michael A. Osborne, "The Future of Employment: How Susceptible
Are Jobs to Computerisation?" Oxford Martin School, University of Oxford,
September 17, 2013, https://www.oxfordmartin.ox.ac.uk/downloads
/academic/The_Future_of_Employment.pdf; Greg Ip, "Workers: Fear Not the
Robot Apocalypse," *Wall Street Journal*, September 5, 2017, https://www
.wsj.com/articles/workers-fear-not-the-robot-apocalypse-1504631505?shareTok
en=stabbe53f26f544566a3b04fc3361af876&reflink=article_email_share; Deirdre
McCloskey, "The Myth of Technological Employment," *Reason*, August–
September 2017, http://reason.com/archives/2017/07/11/the-myth-of
-technological-unem; Vanessa Fuhrmans, "How the Robot Revolution Could
Create 21 Million Jobs," *Wall Street Journal*, November 15, 2017, https://www.
wsj.com/articles/how-the-robot-revolution-could-create-21-million-jobs
-1510758001; Oren Cass, "Is Technology Destroying the Labor Market?" *City
Journal*, Spring 2018, https://www.city-journal.org/html/technology
-destroying-labor-market-15829.html.

28 Martin Wolf, "Seven charts that show how the developed world is losing its
edge," *Financial Times*, July 19, 2017, https://www.ft.com/content/1c7270d2
-6ae4-11e7-b9c7-15af748b60d0; Gordon, *The Rise and Fall of American Growth*,
601–4.

29 David P. Goldman, "The Triumph of Inequality," *PJ Media*, August 14, 2017,
https://pjmedia.com/spengler/2017/08/14/the-triumph-of-inequality/.

30 See Joel Kotkin, "The Growth Dilemma," *Quillette*, January 9, 2020, https://
quillette.com/2020/01/09/the-growth-dilemma/.

31 Johannes Niederhauser, "An Interview with John Gray: 'Human Progress Is a Lie,'" *Vice*, March 28, 2013, https://www.vice.com/en_us/article/qbwqem/john-gray-interview-atheism.

32 Austin Williams, *The Enemies of Progress: The Dangers of Sustainability* (Exeter: Societas, 2008), 8–9, 59.

CHAPTER 4—HIGH-TECH FEUDALISM

1 Fernand Braudel, *The Perspective of the World*, vol. 3 of *Civilization and Capitalism, 1500–1800*, trans. Sian Reynolds (New York: Harper & Row, 1984), 68, 617; Geoffrey Barraclough, *The Crucible of Europe* (Berkeley: University of California Press, 1976), 97; William H. McNeill, *The Pursuit of Power: Technology, Armed Force, and Society since A.D. 1000* (Chicago: University of Chicago Press, 1982), 82–83, 117–18.

2 Gustavo Grullon, Yelena Larkin, and Roni Michaely, "Are US Industries Becoming More Concentrated?" *Review of Finance*, vol. 23:4 (July 2019), 697–743, https://academic.oup.com/rof/article/23/4/697/5477414; Mike Konczal, "There Are Too Few Companies and Their Profits Are Too High," *Nation*, August 5, 2019, https://www.thenation.com/article/industry-concentration-score/.

3 Taichi Sakaiya, *The Knowledge Value Revolution,* trans. George Fields and William Marsh (Tokyo: Kodansha International, 1985), 152.

4 Danny Yadron, "Silicon Valley tech firms exacerbating income inequality, World Bank warns," *Guardian*, January 15, 2016, https://www.theguardian.com/technology/2016/jan/14/silicon-valley-tech-firms-income-inequality-world-bank; Gemma Tetlow, "Blame Technology not Globalization for Rising Inequality, Says IMF," *Financial Times*, April 11, 2017, https://www.ft.com/content/cfbd0af6-1e0b-11e7-b7d3-163f5a7f229c.

5 Michael Anton, "The Frivolous Valley and Its Dreadful Conformity," Law & Liberty, September 4, 2018, https://www.lawliberty.org/liberty-forum/the-frivolous-valley-and-its-dreadful-conformity/.

6 Kevin Starr, *California: A History* (New York: Modern Library, 2005), 261–67; Kevin Starr, *The Dream Endures: California Enters the 1940s* (New York: Oxford University Press, 1997) 42–43; Gary Brechin, *Imperial San Francisco: Urban Power, Earthly Ruin* (Berkeley: University of California Press, 1999), 98–99, 322–23; Leslie Berlin, "Tracing Silicon Valley's Roots," *SFGate*, September 30, 2007, https://www.sfgate.com/business/article/Tracing-Silicon-Valley-s-roots-2520298.php.

7 Ruchir Sharma, "When Will the Tech Bubble Burst?" *New York Times*, August 5, 2017, https://www.nytimes.com/2017/08/05/opinion/sunday/when-will-the-tech-bubble-burst.html.

8 Kevin Starr, *Coast of Dreams: California on the Edge, 1990–2003* (New York: Knopf, 2004), 271–75.

9 Scott Galloway, "Silicon Valley's Tax-Avoiding, Job-Killing, Soul-Sucking Machine," *Esquire*, February 8, 2018, http://www.esquire.com/news-politics/a15895746/bust-big-tech-silicon-valley/.

10 Shira Ovide, "Big Tech Has Dug a Moat That Rivals and Regulators Can't Cross," Yahoo, July 5, 2019, https://finance.yahoo.com/news/big-tech-dug-moat-rivals-120012308.html.

11 Thomas Piketty, *Capital in the Twenty-First Century*, trans. Arthur Goldhammer (Cambridge, Mass.: Belknap/Harvard, 2014), 174; "Richest people in the world," CBS News, https://www.cbsnews.com/pictures/richest-people-in-world-forbes/12/.

12 Carter Coudriet, "13 Under 40: Here Are The Youngest Billionaires On The Forbes 400 2019," *Forbes*, October 31, 2019, https://www.forbes.com/sites/cartercoudriet/2019/10/02/forbes-400-youngest-under-40-zuckerberg-spiegel/#7fd35f5a5a0e.

13 Sally French, "China has 9 of the world's 20 biggest companies," *Market Watch*, May 31, 2018, https://www.marketwatch.com/story/china-has-9-of-the-worlds-20-biggest-tech-companies-2018-05-31.

14 Farhad Manjoo, "Tech's 'Frightful 5' Will Dominate Digital Life for Foreseeable Future," *New York Times*, January 20, 2016, https://www.nytimes.com/2016/01/21/technology/techs-frightful-5-will-dominate-digital-life-for-foreseeable-future.html; Dana Mattioli, "Takeovers Roar to Life as Companies Hear Footsteps From Tech Giants," *Wall Street Journal*, November 20, 2017, https://www.wsj.com/articles/takeovers-roar-to-life-as-companies-hear-footsteps-from-tech-giants-1511200327.

15 "Why startups are leaving Silicon Valley," *Economist*, August 30, 2018, https://www.economist.com/leaders/2018/08/30/why-startups-are-leaving-silicon-valley; Rex Crum, "Let's make a deal: SV150 firms spent $41 billion on acquisitions in 2016," *Mercury News*, May 1, 2017, https://www.mercurynews.com/2017/05/01/lets-make-a-deal-acquisitions-were-all-over-the-sv150-in-2016/; "Too much of a good thing," *Economist*, March 26, 2016, https://www.economist.com/briefing/2016/03/26/too-much-of-a-good-thing.

16 Christopher Mims, "Why Free Is Too High a Price for Facebook and Google," *Wall Street Journal*, June 8, 2019, https://www.wsj.com/articles/why-free-is-too-high-a-price-for-facebook-and-google-11559966411; Andy Kessler, "Antitrust Can't Catch Big Tech," *Wall Street Journal*, September 14, 2019, https://www.wsj.com/articles/antitrust-cant-catch-big-tech-11568577387; David Dayen, "Trump's Antitrust Cops Fail to Police Big Business—Again," *American Prospect*, July 24, 2019, https://prospect.org/power/trump-s-antitrust-cops-fail-police-big-business-again/; Andrew Orlowski, "Google had Obama's ear during antitrust probe," *Register*, August 18, 2016, https://www.theregister.co.uk/2016/08/18/google_had_obamas_ear_on_antitrust_probe/.

17 Bryan Clark, "Facebook's new 'early bird' spy tool is just tip of the iceberg," *Next Web*, August 10, 2017, https://thenextweb.com/insider/2017/08/10/facebooks-new-early-bird-spy-tool-is-just-the-tip-of-the-iceberg/#; Betsy Morris and Deepa Seetharaman, "The New Copycats: How Facebook Squashes Competition from Startups," *Wall Street Journal*, August 9, 2017, https://www.wsj.com/articles/the-new-copycats-how-facebook-squashes-competition-from-startups-1502293444.

18 Crunchbase, Google Acquisitions, updated January 15, 2020, https://www.crunchbase.com/organization/google/acquisitions/acquisitions_list#section-acquisitions; Ben Popper, "Failure is a feature: how Google stays sharp gobbling up startups," The Verge, September 17, 2012, https://www.theverge.com/2012/9/17/3322854/google-startup-mergers-acquisitions-failure-is-a-feature; Tim Wu and Stuart A. Thompson, "The Roots of Big Tech Run

Disturbingly Deep," *New York Times*, June 7, 2019, https://www.nytimes.com
/interactive/2019/06/07/opinion/google-facebook-mergers-acquisitions
-antitrust.html.

19 Jeff Desjardins, "How Google retains more than 90% of market share," *Business
Insider*, April 24, 2018, https://www.businessinsider.com/how-google-retains
-more-than-90-of-market-share-2018-4; Gordon Donnelly, "75 Super-Useful
Facebook Statistics for 2018," WordStream, August 12, 2019, https://www
.wordstream.com/blog/ws/2017/11/07/facebook-statistics; "Amazon Ebook
Market Share 2019—is it big enough?" PublishDrive, December 2019, https://
publishdrive.com/amazon-ebook-market-share/; Tanwen Dawn-Hiscox,
"Synergy: AWS dominates the public cloud market across the world," Data
Center Dynamics, June 26, 2018, https://www.datacenterdynamics.com/news
/synergy-aws-dominates-the-public-cloud-market-across-the-world/; Stat-
counter, "Mobile Marketing Share," http://gs.statcounter.com/os-market-share
/mobile/worldwide; Shanhong Lui, "Operating systems market share of
desktop PCs 2013-2019, by month," Statista, November 19, 2019, https://www
.statista.com/statistics/218089/global-market-share-of-windows-7/.

20 Li Yuan, "China's Startups Are Only Pawns in the Game," *Wall Street Journal*,
December 9, 2017, https://www.wsj.com/articles/chinas-startups-are-only
-pawns-in-the-game-1512642603.

21 Josh Marshall, "A Serf on Google's Farm," *Talking Points Memo*, September 1,
2017, https://talkingpointsmemo.com/edblog/a-serf-on-googles-farm.

22 Jonathan Taplin, "Can the Tech Giants Be Stopped?" *Wall Street Journal*, July
14, 2017, https://www.wsj.com/articles/can-the-tech-giants-be-stopped
-1500057243; Erin Griffith, "Silicon Valley's single degree of separation,"
Fortune, March 20, 2014, http://fortune.com/2014/03/20/silicon-valleys-single
-degree-of-separation/.

23 Kalev Leetaru, "The Perils to Democracy Posed by Big Tech," *Real Clear Politics*,
November 16, 2018, https://www.realclearpolitics.com/articles/2018/11/16
/the_perils_to_democracy_posed_by_big_tech.html; Sean Gallagher, "The
Internet has serious health problems, Mozilla Foundation report finds," *Ars
Technica*, October 4, 2018, https://arstechnica.com/information-technology
/2018/04/mozilla-foundation-report-details-decline-in-health-of-internet/;
Ariel Ezrachi and Maurice Stucke, "The EScraper and EMonopsony," Faculty of
Law, University of Oxford, April 10, 2017, https://www.law.ox.ac.uk/business
-law-blog/blog/2017/04/e-scraper-and-e-monopsony.

24 John Detrixhe, "Tech firms like Amazon and Facebook are the biggest
competitive threats to the banking industry," *Quartz*, August 22, 2017, https://
qz.com/1058590/tech-firms-like-amazon-amzn-facebook-fb-and-google
-googl-are-the-biggest-competitive-threats-to-the-banking-industry/?mc
_cid=ea17b615f3&mc_eid=d569232f9d; Andy Pasztor and Doug Cameron, "Jeff
Bezos' Space Startup to Supply Engines for Boeing-Lockheed Rocket Venture,"
Wall Street Journal, September 27, 2018, https://www.wsj.com/articles/jeff
-bezoss-space-startup-to-supply-engines-for-boeing-lockheed-rocket-venture
-1538035079?mod=hp_lead_pos3; Erin Griffith, "Google Is On the Prowl
for Cloud and AI Deals in 2017," *Fortune*, January 30, 2017, http://fortune.
com/2017/01/30/google-acquisitions-2017/; Cathy O'Neil, "Silicon Valley's

unchecked influence in the classroom," *Metro West Daily News*, June 16, 2017, http://www.metrowestdailynews.com/opinion/20170616/oneil-silicon-valleys -unchecked-influence-in-classroom; Jon Fingas, "Jeff Bezos outlines Blue Origin's space colony ambitions," Engadget, May 27, 2018, https://www .engadget.com/2018/05/27/jeff-bezos-outlines-blue-origin-space-colony -ambitions/; Gregory Zuckerman and Bradley Hope, "The Quants Run Wall Street Now," *Wall Street Journal*, May 21, 2017, https://www.wsj.com/articles /the-quants-run-wall-street-now-1495389108.

25 Evgeny Morozov, "Tech titans are busy privatizing our data," *Guardian*, April 24, 2016, https://www.theguardian.com/commentisfree/2016/apr/24/the-new -feudalism-silicon-valley-overlords-advertising-necessary-evil.

26 Matthew B. Crawford, "Algorithmic Governance and Political Legitimacy," *American Affairs*, Summer 2019, https://americanaffairsjournal.org/2019/05 /algorithmic-governance-and-political-legitimacy/.

27 Cade Metz, "As China Marches Forward on A.I., the White House Is Silent," *New York Times*, February 12, 2018, https://www.nytimes.com/2018/02/12 /technology/china-trump-artificial-intelligence.html; Li Yuan, "For These Young Entrepreneurs, Silicon Valley, Is, Like, Lame," *Wall Street Journal*, January 18, 2018, https://www.wsj.com/articles/for-these-entrepreneurs-silicon -valley-is-like-lame-1516270601.

28 Ezekiel Emanuel, "How the U.S. Surrendered to China on Scientific Research," *Wall Street Journal*, April 19, 2019, https://www.wsj.com/articles/how-the-u-s -surrendered-to-china-on-scientific-research-11555666200.

29 "Forbes 2017 Billionaires List: Mainland Chinese make up greatest number of new entrants," CNA, March 21, 2017, https://www.channelnewsasia.com/news /business/forbes-2017-billionaires-list-mainland-chinese-make-up-greatest --8582612; Megan Trimble, "The 10 Countries With the Most Billionaires," *U.S. News*, May 23, 2018, https://www.usnews.com/news/best-countries/articles /2018-05-23/the-10-countries-with-the-most-billionaires.

30 Richard McGregor, *The Party: The Secret World of China's Communist Rulers* (New York: Harper, 2010), 206–8; David S. G. Goodman, *Class in Contemporary China* (Cambridge: Polity Press, 2014), 26.

31 Friedrich Engels, "Socialism: Utopian and Scientific," in *The Essential Left*, trans. Edward Aveling (New York: Barnes & Noble, 1968), 138–42.

32 Goodman, *Class in Contemporary China*, 83; Kenneth Scott LaTourette, *The Chinese: Their History and Culture* (New York: Macmillan, 1967), 579–80; Jane Perlez, Paul Mozer, and Jonathan Ansfield, "China's Technology Ambitions Could Upset the Global Trade Order," *New York Times*, November 7, 2017, https://www.nytimes.com/2017/11/07/business/made-in-china-technology- trade.html; Li Yuan, "Growing Pains: What the Next Five Years Will Bring to Chinese Technology," *Wall Street Journal*, November 9, 2017, https://www.wsj .com/articles/a-look-at-the-future-of-tech-in-xis-china-1509013963; Liza Lin and Josh Chin, "China's Tech Giants Have a Second Job: Helping Beijing Spy on Its People," *Wall Street Journal*, November 30, 2017, https://www.wsj.com /articles/chinas-tech-giants-have-a-second-job-helping-the-government-see -everything-1512056284.

33 Kai-Fu Lee, *AI Superpowers: China, Silicon Valley, and the New World Order*

(Boston: Houghton Mifflin, 2018), 115; Julian E. Barnes and Josh Chin, "The New Arms Race in AI," *Wall Street Journal*, March 2, 2018, https://www.wsj .com/articles/the-new-arms-race-in-ai-1520009261.

34 Andrew Browne, "China's Big Brother Is Watching You Do Business," *Wall Street Journal*, May 23, 2017, https://www.wsj.com/articles/big-brother-comes -for-foreign-firms-in-china-1495531800.

35 Mara Hvistendahl, "Inside China's Vast New Experiment in Social Ranking," *Wired*, December 14, 2017, https://www.wired.com/story/age-of-social-credit/; Ryan Gallagher, "How U.S. Tech Giants Are Helping to Build China's Surveillance State," *Intercept*, July 11, 2019, https://theintercept.com/2019/07 /11/china-surveillance-google-ibm-semptian/; Mike Elgan, "Uh Oh: Silicon Valley is building a Chinese-style social credit system," Fast Company, August 26, 2019, https://www.fastcompany.com/90394048/uh-oh-silicon-valley-is -building-a-chinese-style-social-credit-system; Dan Strumpf and Wenxin Fan, "Who Wants to Supply China's Surveillance State? The West," *Wall Street Journal*, November 1, 2017, https://www.wsj.com/articles/who-wants-to-supply -chinas-surveillance-state-the-west-1509540111.

36 Stewart Brand, "Spacewar," *Rolling Stone*, December 7, 1972, http://www.wheels .org/spacewar/stone/rolling_stone.html.

37 Jaron Lanier, *Who Owns the Future?* (New York: Simon & Schuster, 2013), xii.

38 Will Oremus, "Most Americans Still Don't Fear Big Tech's Power," *Slate*, March 16, 2018, https://slate.com/technology/2018/03/most-americans-still-dont-fear -big-techs-power-survey-finds.html; Aaron Smith, "Public Attitudes Toward Technology Companies," Pew Research Center, June 28, 2018, http://www .pewinternet.org/2018/06/28/public-attitudes-toward-technology-companies/.

39 Wolfgang Streeck, *How Will Capitalism End?* (New York: Verso, 2016), 117.

40 Philip Elmer-DeWitt, "The Tea Party, Occupy Wall Street and Steve Jobs," *Fortune*, November 6, 2011, http://fortune.com/2011/11/06/the-tea-party -occupy-wall-street-and-steve-jobs/.

41 Piketty, *Capital in the Twenty-First Century*, 444.

42 David Callahan, *Fortunes of Change: The Rise of the Liberal Rich and the Remaking of America* (New York: Wiley, 2010), 67, 269.

43 "America's Gilded Age: Robber Barons and Captains of Industry," Maryville University, https://online.maryville.edu/business-degrees/americas-gilded-age/.

CHAPTER 5—THE BELIEF SYSTEM OF THE NEW OLIGARCHY

1 Anne VanderMey, "Why Are Young Billionaires So Boring?" Bloomberg, July 9, 2018, https://www.bloomberg.com/news/articles/2018-07-09/why-are -young-billionaires-so-boring.

2 Reuven Brenner, *Rivalry: In Business, Science, Among Nations* (Cambridge: Cambridge University Press, 1987), 31–39; Thomas Mahon, *Charged Bodies: People, Power, and Paradox in Silicon Valley* (New York: New American Library, 1985), 30–31.

3 Joel Kotkin and Paul Grabowicz, *California, Inc.* (New York: Rawson Wade, 1982), 142.

4 David Callahan, *Fortunes of Change: The Rise of the Liberal Rich and the*

Remaking of America (New York: Wiley, 2010), 22–24; Paige Leskin and Nick Vega, "Here's where the world's most influential tech CEOs went to college—and what they studied," *Business Insider*, June 14, 2019, https://www .businessinsider.com/college-degrees-and-majors-of-famous-tech-ceos #larry-page-ceo-alphabet-14.

5 Charles Murray, *Coming Apart: The State of White America, 1960–2010* (New York: Crown Forum, 2012), 46–47.

6 Aldous Huxley, *Brave New World and Brave New World Revisited* (New York: Harper Classics, 2004), 237.

7 Julie Charpentrat, "Labor unions face hard road in Silicon Valley," Phys.org, April 27, 2018, https://phys.org/news/2018-04-labor-unions-hard-road-silicon .html; Gregory Ferenstein, "Why Labor Unions and Silicon Valley Aren't Friends, in 2 Charts," Tech Crunch, July 29, 2013, https://techcrunch.com/2013 /07/29/why-labor-unions-and-silicon-valley-arent-friends-in-2-charts/.

8 Craft, "S&P 500 – Market Value Per Employee Perspective," https://craft.co /reports/s-p-500-market-value-per-employee-perspective; Jeff Desjardins, "Which Companies Make the Most Revenue Per Employee?" Visual Capitalist, June 15, 2017, http://www.visualcapitalist.com/companies-revenue-per -employee/; Jon Hilsenath and Bob Davis, "America's Dazzling Tech Boom Has a Downside: Not Enough Jobs," *Wall Street Journal*, October 12, 2016, https:// www.wsj.com/articles/americas-dazzling-tech-boom-has-a-downside-not -enough-jobs-1476282355; I. Wagner, "Number of General Motors employees between FY 2010 and FY 2018," Statista, February 2019, https://www.statista .com/statistics/239843/employees-of-general-motors/; Lockheed Martin, "About Lockheed Martin," https://www.lockheedmartin.com/en-us/who-we -are.html; Jan Conway, "Number of Employees Kroger 2014–2018," Statista, April 2019, https://www.statista.com/statistics/717646/kroger-number -employees/; Home Depot, "About Home Depot," https://corporate.homedepot .com/about.

9 Nikhil Swaminathan, "Inside the Growing Guest Worker Program Trapping Indian Students in Virtual Servitude," *Mother Jones*, September/October 2017, http://www.motherjones.com/politics/2017/09/inside-the-growing-guest -worker-program-trapping-indian-students-in-virtual-servitude.

10 Annalee Newitz, "Mark Zuckerberg's manifesto is a political trainwreck," *Ars Technica*, February 18, 2017, https://arstechnica.com/staff/2017/02/op-ed-mark -zuckerbergs-manifesto-is-a-political-trainwreck/; Ezra Klein, "Mark Zuckerberg's theory of human history," *Vox*, February 18, 2017, http://www.vox .com/new-money/2017/2/18/14653542/mark-zuckerberg-facebook-manifesto -sapiens.

11 Gregory Ferenstein, "The Disrupters," *City Journal*, Winter 2017, https://www .city-journal.org/html/disrupters-14950.html.

12 Gregory Ferenstein, "A Lot of Billionaires Are Giving to Democrats. Here's a Look at Their Agenda," *Forbes*, February 26, 2016, https://www.forbes.com /sites/gregoryferenstein/2016/02/26/a-lot-of-billionaires-are-giving-to -democrats-heres-a-data-driven-look-at-their-agenda/#2002ef134869; Greg Ferenstein, "Why are Billionaires Ditching the Republican Party?" *Medium*,

February 26, 2016, https://medium.com/@ferenstein/a-lot-of-billionaires-are
-giving-to-democrats-here-s-a-look-at-their-agenda-b5038c2ecb34.

13 Todd Haselton, "Mark Zuckerberg joins Silicon Valley bigwigs in calling for
government to give everybody free money," Yahoo, May 25, 2017, https://
finance.yahoo.com/news/mark-zuckerberg-joins-silicon-valley-202800717
.html; Patrick Gillespie, "Mark Zuckerberg supports universal basic income.
What is it?" CNN, May 6, 2017, https://money.cnn.com/2017/05/26/news
/economy/mark-zuckerberg-universal-basic-income/index.html; Chris
Weller, "Elon Musk doubles down on universal basic income: 'It's going to be
necessary,'" *Business Insider*, February 13, 2017, https://www.businessinsider
.com/elon-musk-universal-basic-income-2017-2; Patrick Caughill, "Another
Silicon Valley Exec Joins the Ranks of Universal Basic Income Supporters,"
Futurism, September 8, 2017, https://futurism.com/another-silicon-valley
-exec-joins-the-ranks-of-universal-basic-income-supporters; Sam Altman,
"Moving Forward on Basic Income," Y Combinator, May 31, 2016, https://blog
.ycombinator.com/moving-forward-on-basic-income/; Diane Francis, "The
Beginning of the End of Work," *American Interest,* March 19, 2018, https://
www.the-american-interest.com/2018/03/19/beginning-end-work/.

14 "The YIMBY Guide to Bullying and Its Results: SB 827 Goes Down in
Committee," *City Watch LA*, April 19, 2018, https://www.citywatchla.com
/index.php/los-angeles/15298-the-yimby-guide-to-bullying-and-its-results
-sb-827-goes-down-in-committee; John Mirisch, "Tech Oligarchs and the
California Housing Crisis," *California Political Review,* April 15, 2018, http://
www.capoliticalreview.com/top-stories/tech-Oligarchs-and-the-california
-housing-crisis/; Joel Kotkin, "Giving Common Sense a Chance in California,"
City Journal, April 26, 2018, https://www.city-journal.org/html/giving
-common-sense-chance-california-15868.html.

15 Thomas Piketty, *Capital in the Twenty-First Century*, trans. Arthur
Goldhammer (Cambridge, Mass.: Belknap/Harvard, 2014), 85.

16 VanderMey, "Why Are Young Billionaires So Boring?"

17 Fernand Braudel, *The Structures of Everyday Life,* vol. 1 of *Civilization and
Capitalism, 15th–18th Century,* trans. Sian Reynolds, (Berkeley: University of
California Press, 1992), 334.

18 Laura Sydell, "In Google's Vision of the Future, Computing is Immersive,"
NPR, May 20, 2017, https://www.npr.org/sections/alltechconsidered/2017
/05/20/529146185/in-googles-vision-of-the-future-computing-is-immersive.

19 Jason Pontin, "Silicon Valley's Immortalists Will Help Us All Stay Healthy,"
Wired, December 15, 2017, https://www.wired.com/story/silicon-valleys
-immortalists-will-help-us-all-stay-healthy/; Dom Galeon and Christianna
Reedy, "A Google Exec Just Claimed the Singularity Will Happen by 2029,"
Science Alert, March 16, 2017, https://www.sciencealert.com/google-s-director
-of-engineering-claims-that-the-singularity-will-happen-by-2029.

20 Alvin Toffler, *The Third Wave* (New York: Bantam, 1980), 158–59; Kevin Carty,
"Tech giants are the robber barons of our time," *New York Post*, February 3,
2018, https://nypost.com/2018/02/03/big-techs-monopolistic-rule-is-hiding
-in-plain-sight/; Jia Tolentino, "The End of the Awl and the Vanishing of
Freedom and Fun from the Internet," *New Yorker*, January 18, 2018, https://

www.newyorker.com/culture/cultural-comment/the-end-of-the-awl-and-the
-vanishing-of-freedom-and-fun-from-the-internet; Andrew Orlowski,
"Google, propaganda, and the new New Man," *Register*, September 4, 2017,
https://www.theregister.co.uk/2017/09/04/google_propaganda_and_the_new
_new_man; Aaron Renn, "How Apple and Google Are Censoring the Mobile
Web," *Real Clear Politics*, August 24, 2017, https://www.realclearpolitics.
com/2017/08/24/how_apple_and_google_are_censoring_the_mobile_web
_419092.html; Kenneth P. Vogel, "Google Critic Ousted From Think Tank
Funded by the Tech Giant," *New York Times*, August 30, 2017, https://www
.nytimes.com/2017/08/30/us/politics/eric-schmidt-google-new-america.html
?referer=https://www.google.com/.

21 Joseph Lichterman, "Nearly half of U.S. adults get news on Facebook, Pew
Says," Nieman Lab, May 16, 2016, http://www.niemanlab.org/2016/05/pew
-report-44-percent-of-u-s-adults-get-news-on-facebook/; Amy Gesenhues,
"Pew Research Center says 45% of Americans get their news from Facebook,"
Marketing Land, November 8, 2017, https://marketingland.com/pew-research
-center-says-45-americans-get-news-facebook-228001; Elisa Shearer and Jeffrey
Gottfried, "News Use Across Social Media Platforms 2017," Pew Research
Center, September 7, 2017, http://www.journalism.org/2017/09/07/news-use
-across-social-media-platforms-2017/.

22 Monica Anderson and Jingjing Jiang, "Teens, Social Media and Technology
2018," Pew Research Center, May 31, 2018, vhttp://www.pewinternet.
org/2018/05/31/teens-social-media-technology-2018/; Daniel Reed, "How do
Millennials Receive News?" Study Breaks, May 7, 2018, https://studybreaks.
com/sponsored/millennials-receive-news/.

23 Joel Kotkin and Michael Shires, "The Cities Winning the Battle for Information
Jobs," *New Geography*, May 23, 2013, http://www.newgeography.com/
content/003736-the-cities-winning-the-battle-for-information-jobs; Marc
Tracy, "Google Made $4.7 Billion From the News Industry in 2018, Study Says,"
New York Times, June 9, 2019, https://www.nytimes.com/2019/06/09/business
/media/google-news-industry-antitrust.html; Lucy Handley, "Google and
Facebook take 20% of Total Global Ad Spend," CNBC, May 2, 2017, https://
www.cnbc.com/2017/05/02/google-and-facebook-take-20-percent-of-total
-global-ad-spend.html.

24 Keach Hagey, Lukas Alpert, and Yaryna Serkez, "In News Industry, a Stark
Divide Between Haves and Have-Nots," *Wall Street Journal*, May 4, 2019,
https://www.wsj.com/graphics/local-newspapers-stark-divide/.

25 David Gelles, "Billionaires Can Seem Like Saviors to Media Companies, but
They Come with Risks," *New York Times*, September 19, 2018, https://www
.nytimes.com/2018/09/19/business/media/newspapers-billionaire-owners
-magazines.html; Jeffrey A. Trachtenberg, "Time Magazine Sold to Salesforce
Founder Marc Benioff for $190 Million," *Wall Street Journal*, September 16,
2018.

26 Javier C. Hernandez, "A Hong Kong Newspaper on a Mission to Promote
China's Soft Power," *New York Times*, March 31, 2018, https://www.nytimes
.com/2018/03/31/world/asia/south-china-morning-post-hong-kong-alibaba
.html.

27 Jeffrey A. Winters, *Oligarchy* (Cambridge: Cambridge University Press, 2011), xii, 277–80.

28 "*The Atlantic* Expands Its News Team and Adds Other New Roles," *Atlantic*, July 23, 2015, https://www.theatlantic.com/press-releases/archive/2015/07/the-atlantic-expands-its-news-team-and-adds-other-new-roles/399407/.

29 "Robert R. McCormick," *Britannica*, https://www.britannica.com/biography/Robert-R-McCormick.

30 Jim Rutenberg, "Behind the Scenes, Billionaires' Growing Control of News," *New York Times*, May 28, 2016, https://www.nytimes.com/2016/05/28/business/media/behind-the-scenes-billionaires-growing-control-of-news.html; John Sexton, "Audit: Google Favors a Small Number of Left-Leaning News Outlets," *Hot Air*, May 10, 2019, https://hotair.com/archives/2019/05/10/audit-concludes-google-favors-small-number-left-leaning-news-outlets/.

31 Mike Shatzkin, "A changing book business: it all seems to be flowing downhill to Amazon," The Idea Logical Company, January 22, 2018, https://www.idealog.com/blog/changing-book-business-seems-flowing-downhill-amazon/; David Steitfeld, "What Happens After Amazon's Domination Is Complete? Its Bookstore Offers Clues," *New York Times*, June 23, 2019, https://www.nytimes.com/2019/06/23/technology/amazon-domination-bookstore-books.html.

32 Nick Srnicek, "We need to nationalize Google, Facebook, and Amazon. Here's why," *Guardian*, August 30, 2017, https://www.theguardian.com/commentisfree/2017/aug/30/nationalise-google-facebook-amazon-data-monopoly-platform-public-interest.

33 Brittany Hodak, "How Fragmentation Is Hurting the Music Industry's Developing Artists," *Forbes*, July 9, 2018, https://www.forbes.com/sites/brittanyhodak/2018/07/09/how-fragmentation-is-hurting-the-music-industrys-developing-artists/#243d19502402; Peter Kafka, "Here's why the music labels are furious at YouTube. Again," *Vox*, April 11, 2016, https://www.recode.net/2016/4/11/11586030/youtube-google-dmca-riaa-cary-sherman.

34 Alex Shephard, "Can Netflix Take Over Hollywood?" *New Republic*, April 2, 2018, https://newrepublic.com/article/148102/can-netflix-take-hollywood; David Griffin, "Netflix Will Outspend Every Hollywood Studio in 2018," IGN, July 6, 2018, https://www.ign.com/articles/2018/07/05/netflix-will-outspend-every-hollywood-studio-in-2018.

35 Jeremy Carl, "How to Break Silicon Valley's Anti-Free-Speech Monopoly," *National Review*, August 15, 2017, https://www.nationalreview.com/2017/08/silicon-valleys-anti-conservative-bias-solution-treat-major-tech-companies-utilities/; John Hinderaker, "Google Does It Again," *Power Line*, May 31, 2018, https://www.powerlineblog.com/archives/2018/05/google-does-it-again.php; Aaron M. Renn, "Like, Share, Beware," *City Journal*, Autumn 2016, https://www.city-journal.org/html/share-beware-14801.html; Aaron M. Renn, "How Apple and Google Are Censoring the Mobile Web," *Real Clear Politics*, August 24, 2017, https://www.realclearpolitics.com/2017/08/24/how_apple_and_google_are_censoring_the_mobile_web_419092.html; Jim Treacher, "It Seems Twitter's 'Trust and Safety Council' Is Working Overtime to Ban Conservatives," *PJ Media*, August 15, 2018, https://pjmedia.com/trending/it-seems-twitters-trust-and-safety-council-is-working-overtime-to-ban

-conservatives/; Eric Lieberman, "Google's New Fact-Check Feature Almost Exclusively Targets Conservative Sites," *Daily Caller*, January 9, 2018, http://dailycaller.com/2018/01/09/googles-new-fact-check-feature-almost -exclusively-targets-conservative-sites/; Glenn Harlan Reynolds, "When Digital Platforms Become Censors," *Wall Street Journal*, August 18, 2018, https://www .wsj.com/articles/when-digital-platforms-become-censors-1534514122; Karl Zinsmeister, "How the Tech Worldview Affects Free-Speech Battles," *Real Clear Politics*, October 3, 2018, https://www.realclearpolitics.com/articles/2018/10/03 /how_the_tech_worldview_affects_free-speech_battles_138234.html.

36 Daniel Friedman, "How Free Speech Dies Online," *Quillette*, June 23, 2019, https://quillette.com/2019/06/23/how-free-speech-dies-online/.

37 Paul Bedard, "Social media companies back liberals, 72% 'censor' views they don't like," *Washington Examiner*, June 28, 2018, https://www. washingtonexaminer.com/washington-secrets/pew-social-media-companies -back-liberals-72-censor-views-they-dont-like; Brad Parscale, "Big Tech is becoming Big Brother," *Washington Examiner*, August 16, 2018, https://www .washingtonexaminer.com/opinion/op-eds/brad-parscale-big-tech-is -becoming-big-brother.

38 Mark Epstein, "The Google-Facebook Duopoly Threatens Diversity of Thought," *Wall Street Journal*, December 18, 2017, https://www.wsj.com/articles /the-google-facebook-duopoly-threatens-diversity-of-thought-1513642519; Robert Tracinski, "'Don't Be Evil'? Google Is Becoming a Police State," *Federalist*, January 12, 2018, http://thefederalist.com/2018/01/12/dont-be-evil -google-is-trying-to-become-a-police-state/.

39 Richard L. Hasen, "Speech in America is fast, cheap and out of control," *Los Angeles Times*, August 18, 2017, http://www.latimes.com/opinion/op-ed/la-oe -hasen-cheap-speech-democracy-20170818-story.html.

40 Ruchir Sharma, "When Will the Tech Bubble Burst?" *New York Times*, August 5, 2017, https://www.nytimes.com/2017/08/05/opinion/sunday/when-will-the -tech-bubble-burst.html.

41 Maurice E. Stucke and Ariel Ezrachi, "Looking up in the Data-Driven Economy," Competition Policy International, May 2017, https://www .competitionpolicyinternational.com/wp-content/uploads/2017/05/CPI-Stucke -Ezrachi.pdf; Kai-Fu Lee, *AI Superpowers: China, Silicon Valley, and the New World Order* (Boston: Houghton Mifflin, 2018), 70.

42 Joe Miller, "How Facebook's tentacles reach further than you think," BBC, May 26, 2017, https://www.bbc.com/news/business-39947942.

43 Gaspard Koenig, "We Are All Digital Serfs But the Time Is Ripe for Revolution," *Irish Examiner*, July 24, 2018, https://www.irishexaminer.com /breakingnews/views/analysis/we-are-all-digital-serfs-but-the-time-is-ripe-for -revolution-857216.html.

44 Jaron Lanier, *Who Owns the Future?* (New York: Simon & Shuster, 2013), 309.

45 Zac Hall, "Facebook might not spy on you now, but it has a patent for the ability," 9 to 5 Mac, June 27, 2018, https://9to5mac.com/2018/06/27/facebook -spy-patent/.

46 Alfred Ng, "Amazon's Alexa had a flaw that let eavesdroppers in," CNET, April 25, 2018, https://www.cnet.com/news/amazon-alexa-voice-assistant-had-a

-flaw-that-let-eavesdroppers-listen-in/; Surya Mattu and Kashmir Hill, "The house that spied on me," Gizmodo, February 7, 2018, https://gizmodo.com /the-house-that-spied-on-me-1822429852.

47 Michelle Malkin, "The Student Data-Mining Scandal Under Our Noses," *National Review*, April 11, 2018, https://www.nationalreview.com/2018/04 /the-student-data-mining-scandal-under-our-noses/.

48 Richi Jennings, "Google CEO: if you want privacy, do you have something to hide?" *Computer World*, December 11, 2009, https://www.computerworld .com/article/2468308/internet/google-ceo--if-you-want-privacy--do-you-have -something-to-hide-.html.

49 Ellie Mae O'Hagan, "No one can pretend Facebook is just harmless fun any more," *Guardian*, March 18, 2018, https://www.theguardian.com/commentisfree /2018/mar/18/facebook-extremist-content-user-data.

CHAPTER 6—FEUDALISM IN CALIFORNIA

1 Peter Leyden, "California Is the Future of American Politics," *Medium*, October 4, 2017, https://medium.com/s/state-of-the-future.

2 Kevin Starr, *Americans and the California Dream, 1850–1915* (New York: Oxford University Press, 1973), xii.

3 Public Policy Institute of California, "Californians and Their Government," PPIC Statewide Survey, September 2019, https://www.ppic.org/wp-content /uploads/ppic-statewide-survey-californians-and-their-government -september-2019.pdf.

4 George Skelton, "Capitol Journal: California's Legislature is less popular than Trump with state's voters, poll finds," *Los Angeles Times*, June 6, 2019, https:// www.latimes.com/politics/la-pol-sac-skelton-california-legislature-disapproval -rating-20190606-story.html; Morning Consult, "The 10 Most Popular and Unpopular Governors," https://morningconsult.com/governor-rankings-q2-19/.

5 Jonathan Lansner, "Bubble Watch: Why is California consumer confidence down? Is it Trump or Newsom?" *Orange County Register*, June 27, 2019, https://www.ocregister.com/2019/06/27/bubble-watch-california-consumer -confidence-plummets-to-near-3-year-low/.

6 Thomas Fuller, Tim Arango, and Louis Keene, "As Homelessness Surges in California, So Does a Backlash," *New York Times*, October 21, 2019, https:// www.nytimes.com/2019/10/21/us/california-homeless-backlash.html?emc =rss&partner=rss.

7 James Galbraith, "Inequality and the 2016 Election Outcome: A Dirty Secret and a Dilemma," *New Geography*, July 5, 2017, http://www.newgeography.com /content/005678-inequality-and-2016-election-outcome-a-dirty-secret-and-a -dilemma.

8 Jonathan Lansner, "California has No. 1 wage gap between middle-income pay and what wealthy earn," *Orange County Register*, April 25, 2019, https://www .ocregister.com/2019/04/23/california-has-no-1-wage-gap-between-middle -income-pay-and-what-wealthy-earn/.

9 Spencer P. Morrison, "California's Income Inequality Now Worse Than Mexico's, Poverty Level Highest in America," *National Economics Editorial*,

January 17, 2018, https://nationaleconomicseditorial.com/2018/01/17
/californian-income-inequality-tops-mexico/.

10 Liana Fox, "The Supplemental Poverty Measure: 2017," U.S. Census Bureau,
September 12, 2018, https://www.census.gov/library/publications/2018/demo
/p60-265.html.

11 "Is California the Welfare Capital?" *San Diego Union-Tribune*, July 28, 2012,
http://www.sandiegouniontribune.com/news/politics/sdut-welfare-capital-of
-the-us-2012jul28-htmlstory.html.

12 United Way, "Struggling to Stay Afloat: The Real Cost Measure in California
2018," United Ways of California, https://www.unitedwaysca.org/realcost.

13 David Friedman and Jennifer Hernandez, "California, Greenhouse Gas
Regulation, and Climate Change," *New Geography*, June 25, 2018, http://www
.newgeography.com/content/006014-california-greenhouse-gas-regulation
-and-climate-change.

14 Sarah Bohn, Caroline Danielson, and Tess Thorman, "Child Poverty in
California," Public Policy Institute of California, July 2019, http://www.ppic
.org/publication/child-poverty-in-california/.

15 David Friedman and Jennifer Hernandez, *California Environmental Quality
Act, Greenhouse Gas Regulation, and Climate Change*, Center for Demographics
and Policy, Chapman University, 2015, https://www.chapman.edu/wilkinson
/_files/ghg-fn.pdf.

16 Mark Hugo Lopez and Manuel Krogstad, "Will California ever become a
majority-Latino state?" Pew Research Center, June 4, 2015, http://www
.pewresearch.org/fact-tank/2015/06/04/will-california-ever-become-a-majority
-latino-state-maybe-not/.

17 Betsy Baum Block et al., "Struggling to Get By: The Real Cost Measure in
California 2015," United Ways of California, https://www.unitedwaysca.org
/images/StrugglingToGetBy/Struggling_to_Get_By.pdf.

18 Emma G. Gallegos, "Los Angeles Is the Poorest Big City," *LAist*, September 9,
2014, http://laist.com/2014/09/19/los_angeles_is_the_poorest_of_the_m
.php; Alejandro Lazo, "Homelessness Grows in California Despite New
Government Spending," *Wall Street Journal*, June 7, 2019, https://www.wsj.com
/articles/homelessness-grows-in-california-despite-new-government-spending
-11559899801.

19 Alex Thomas, "A Tale of Two SoCals: Poverty in Southern California," *New
Geography*, January 16, 2018, http://www.newgeography.com/content/005854
-a-tale-two-socals-poverty-southern-california.

20 Kerry Jackson, "California Leads the Nation in Bringing Back Medieval
Illnesses," *Daily Caller*, March 21, 2019, https://dailycaller.com/2019/03/21
/jackson-california-illness/; Joseph Curl, "Bubonic Plague 'Likely' Already
Present in Los Angeles, Dr. Drew Says," *Daily Wire*, May 31, 2019, https://www
.dailywire.com/news/47888/bubonic-plague-likely-already-present-los-angeles
-joseph-curl; David K. Randall, "Climate change could bring bubonic plague
back to Los Angeles," *Los Angeles Times*, May 16, 2019, https://www.latimes
.com/opinion/op-ed/la-oe-randall-plague-climate-change-rats-20190516-story
.html.

21   "California Economy: Annual Forecast Charts," California Lutheran University,
     September 14, 2017, https://blogs.callutheran.edu/cerf/files/2017/09/Annual
     _Pop_PerCapitaGDP_Forecast1.pdf; Friedman and Hernandez, *California,
     Greenhouse Gas Regulation, and Climate Change*, 67–68. Susan Shelley, "In
     California, a poor imitation of economic growth," *Los Angeles Daily News*,
     January 27, 2017, https://www.dailynews.com/2017/01/27/in-california-a-poor
     -imitation-of-economic-growth-susan-shelley/.

22   Joel Kotkin, "California Preening," *City Journal*, December 20, 2019, https://
     www.city-journal.org/california-high-tech-feudalism.

23   Marisa Kendall, "Buying a Bay Area home now a struggle even for Apple,
     Google engineers," *Mercury News*, February 15, 2018, https://www
     .mercurynews.com/2018/02/14/buying-a-bay-area-home-now-a-struggle
     -even-for-apple-google-engineers/.

24   Amy Graff, "$303K is the annual income needed to buy a median priced home
     in San Francisco," *SFGate*, February 15, 2018, https://www.sfgate.com/realestate
     /article/income-needed-buy-home-San-Francisco-real-estate-12614111.php;
     Alan Berube, "All Cities Are Not Created Unequal," Brookings, February 20,
     2014, https://www.brookings.edu/research/all-cities-are-not-created-unequal
     /; Frederick Kuo, "San Francisco has become one huge metaphor for economic
     inequality in America," *Quartz*, June 21, 2016, https://qz.com/711854/the
     -inequality-happening-now-in-san-francisco-will-impact-america-for
     -generations-to-come/.

25   Luke Redenbach et al., "The Growth of Top Incomes Across California,"
     California Budget and Policy Center, February 2016, https://calbudgetcenter
     .org/wp-content/uploads/The-Growth-of-Top-Incomes-Across-California
     -02172016.pdf; Chris Roberts, "How California's Homeless Crisis Grew
     Obscenely Out of Control," *Observer*, May 30, 2019, https://observer.com
     /2019/05/california-homeless-crisis-san-francisco/.

26   Amy Graff, "San Francisco metro area has lost 31,000 home-owning families in
     10 years," *SFGate*, July 13, 2018, https://www.sfgate.com/mommyfiles/article
     /San-Francisco-low-percentage-families-homeowners-13069287.php; Megan
     Cassidy and Sarah Ravani, "San Francisco ranks No. 1 in US in property crime,"
     San Francisco Chronicle, October 2, 2018, https://www.sfchronicle.com/crime
     /article/The-Scanner-San-Francisco-ranks-No-1-in-13267113.php?psid=bwGGn;
     Aria Bendix, "San Francisco's homelessness crisis is so bad, people appear to be
     using poop to graffiti the sidewalks," *SFGate*, November 20, 2018, https://www
     .sfgate.com/technology/businessinsider/article/Meet-the-guy-in-charge-of
     -tackling-San-8331836.php.

27   Chris Brenner and Manuel Pastor, *Equity, Growth, and Community: What
     the Nation Can Learn from America's Metro Areas* (Oakland: University of
     California Press, 2015), 167.

28   Rachel Massaro, "Silicon Valley Index," Joint Venture, 2016, https://
     jointventure.org/images/stories/pdf; Dylan Wittenberg, "These Bay Area
     FinTech Companies Are Revolutionizing the Lending Space," Benzinga, July 25,
     2017, https://www.benzinga.com/fintech/17/07/9816489/these-bay-area-fintech
     -companies-are-revolutionizing-the-lending-space/index2016.pdf.

29   Issie Lapowsky, "Silicon Valley's Biggest Worry Should Be Inequality, Not a

Bubble," *Wired*, February 4, 2015, https://www.wired.com/2015/02/silicon
-valley-inequality-study/.

30 Gabriel Metcalf, "Four Future Scenarios for the San Francisco Bay Area," SPUR
Regional Strategy, August 2018, https://www.spur.org/sites/default/files
/publications_pdfs/SPUR_Future_Scenarios_for_the_SF_Bay_Area.pdf;
Alex Thomas, "The Demographics of Poverty in Santa Clara County," *New
Geography*, January 10, 2017, https://www.newgeography.com/content/005501
-the-demographics-poverty-santa-clara-county; Jeff Desjardins, "Which
Companies Make the Most Revenue Per Employee?" Visual Capitalist, June 15,
2017, http://www.visualcapitalist.com/companies-revenue-per-employee/.

31 Nikhil Swaminathan, "Inside the Growing Guest Worker Program Trapping
Indian Students in Virtual Servitude," *Mother Jones*, September/October 2017,
http://www.motherjones.com/politics/2017/09/inside-the-growing-guest
-worker-program-trapping-indian-students-in-virtual-servitude.

32 Sam Levin, "Black and Latino representation in Silicon Valley has declined,
study shows," *Guardian*, October 3, 2017, https://www.theguardian.com
/technology/2017/oct/03/silicon-valley-diversity-black-latino-women-decline
-study.

33 Seung Lee, "'These are poverty-level jobs in Facebook': Silicon Valley security
officers protest for better wages," *Mercury News*, June 18, 2018, https://www
.mercurynews.com/2018/06/15/these-are-poverty-level-jobs-in-facebook-
silicon-valley-security-officers-protest-for-better-wages/; Julia Carrie Wong,
"Silicon Valley subcontracting makes income inequality worse, report finds,"
Guardian, March 30, 2016, https://www.theguardian.com/us-news/2016
/mar/30/silicon-valley-subcontracting-income-inequality-worse-report.

34 Kathleen Elkins, "Several Google employees say they've lived in the company
parking lot—here's why they did it," *Business Insider*, October 30, 2015,
https://www.businessinsider.com/why-google-employees-live-in-the-parking
-lot-2015-10; Robert Johnson, "Welcome to 'The Jungle': The Largest Homeless
Camp in Mainland USA Is Right in the Heart of Silicon Valley," *Business
Insider*, September 7, 2013, https://www.businessinsider.com/the-jungle-largest
-homeless-camp-in-us-2013-8.

35 Brenner and Pastor, *Equity, Growth and Community*, 168.

36 Antonio García Martínez, "How Silicon Valley Fuels an Informal Caste System,"
Wired, July 9, 2018, https://www.wired.com/story/how-silicon-valley-fuels-an
-informal-caste-system/.

37 Ibid.

38 Jeff Daniels, "Nearly half of California's gig economy workers struggling with
poverty," CNBC, August 28, 2018, https://www.cnbc.com/2018/08/28/about
-half-of-californias-gig-economy-workers-struggling-with-poverty.html.

39 Nick Srnicek, "We need to nationalize Google, Facebook, and Amazon. Here's
why," *Guardian*, August 30, 2017, https://www.theguardian.com/commentisfree
/2017/aug/30/nationalise-google-facebook-amazon-data-monopoly-platform
-public-interest; Jonathan Taplin, "Is It Time to Break Up Google?" *New York
Times*, April 22, 2017, https://www.nytimes.com/2017/04/22/opinion
/sunday/is-it-time-to-break-up-google.html?ref=opinion&_r=0; Franklin
Foer, "Amazon Must Be Stopped," *New Republic*, October 10, 2014, https://

newrepublic.com/article/119769/amazons-monopoly-must-be-broken-radical-plan-tech-giant; Andrew Clement and David Lyon, "Facebook: A mass media micro-surveillance monopoly," *Globe and Mail*, April 23, 2018, https://www.theglobeandmail.com/opinion/article-facebook-a-mass-media-micro-surveillance-monopoly/; James Pethokoukis, "Conservatives turn on Silicon Valley—and the free market," *The Week*, August 17, 2017, http://theweek.com/articles/718558/conservatives-turn-silicon-valley--free-market.

40 David Dayen, "Big Tech: The New Predatory Capitalism," *American Prospect*, December 26, 2017, http://prospect.org/article/big-tech-new-predatory-capitalism; K. Sabeel Rahman, "Up Against Big Tech," *American Prospect*, February 5, 2018, http://prospect.org/article/against-big-tech; Elizabeth Kolbert, "Who Owns the Internet?" *New Yorker*, August 21, 2017, https://www.newyorker.com/magazine/2017/08/28/who-owns-the-internet.

41 Daniel Bell, *The Coming of Post-Industrial Society* (New York: Basic Books, 1973), 33.

42 Mike Elgan, "Why the Public's Love Affair With Silicon Valley Might Be Over," *Fast Company*, September 27, 2017, https://www.fastcompany.com/40472189/why-the-publics-love-affair-with-silicon-valley-might-be-over.

43 Stanley Bing, *Immortal Life: A Soon to Be True Future* (New York: Simon & Schuster, 2017).

CHAPTER 7—THE NEW LEGITIMIZERS

1 Alexandra Alter, "Uneasy About the Future, Readers Turn to Dystopian Classics," *New York Times*, January 27, 2017, https://www.nytimes.com/2017/01/27/business/media/dystopian-classics-1984-animal-farm-the-handmaids-tale.html.

2 Andrew S. Ross, "In Silicon Valley, age can be a curse," *SFGate*, August 20, 2013, https://www.sfgate.com/business/bottomline/article/In-Silicon-Valley-age-can-be-a-curse-4742365.php.

3 Aldous Huxley, *Brave New World and Brave New World Revisited* (New York: Harper Classics, 2004), 237, 259.

4 Eleanor Duckett, *Death and Life in the Tenth Century* (Ann Arbor: University of Michigan Press, 1967), 251; Norman F. Cantor, *Medieval History: The Life and Death of a Civilization* (New York: Macmillan, 1963), 50–51, 69–70, 97, 101.

5 Pitirim Sorokin, *The Crisis of Our Age* (London: Oneworld Publication, 1992), 20–21, 67–69, 81.

6 Adam K. Webb, "Class and Clerisy," Front Porch Republic, October 19, 2010, https://www.frontporchrepublic.com/2010/10/class-and-Clerisy.

7 Max Weber, *Economy and Society* (Berkeley: University of California Press, 1978), vol. 1: xcviii; Thomas Piketty, *Capital in the Twenty-First Century*, trans. Arthur Goldhammer (Cambridge, Mass.: Belknap/Harvard, 2014), 345.

8 Barbara Tuchman, *The March of Folly: From Troy to Vietnam* (New York: Ballantine, 1984), 6–7; John Hale, *The Civilization of Europe in the Renaissance* (New York: Touchstone, 1993), 413–19.

9 H. G. Wells, *Anticipations of the Reaction of Mechanical and Scientific Progress Upon Human Life and Thought* (1901; Mineola, N.Y.: Dover Books, 1999),

85–87, 99, 151; Fred Siegel, *The Revolt Against the Masses: How Liberalism Has Undermined the Middle Class* (New York: Encounter, 2015), 100.

10 Peter Bachrach, *The Theory of Democratic Elitism* (Boston: Little Brown & Co., 1967), 58–60; Arthur Herman, *The Idea of Decline in Western History* (New York: Free Press, 1997), 17; Talcott Parsons, "The Distribution of Power in American Society," in *The Power Elite*, ed. C. Wright Mills (Boston: Beacon, 1968), 79; J. Hobsbawm, *The Age of Revolution* (New York: New American Library, 1962), 327.

11 C. Wright Mills, *The Causes of World War Three* (1958; Armonk, N.Y.: M. E. Sharpe, 1985), 170.

12 Robert B. Reich and Ira C. Magaziner, *Minding America's Business* (New York: Harcourt Brace, 1982), 13, 378.

13 Thomas L. Friedman, "Our One-Party Democracy," *New York Times*, September 8, 2009, https://www.nytimes.com/2009/09/09/opinion/09friedman .html; John Hudson, "Peter Orszag Is So Over Democracy," *Atlantic*, September 26, 2011, https://www.theatlantic.com/politics/archive/2011/09/peter-orszag -so-over-democracy/337475/; Joseph C. Sternberg, "The European Union's Democracy Deficit," *Wall Street Journal*, February 15, 2018, https://www.wsj .com/articles/the-european-unions-democracy-deficit-1518739588.

14 Daniel Bell, *The Coming of Post-Industrial Society* (New York: Basic Books, 1973), 15, 51, 213, 387.

15 "An hereditary meritocracy," *Economist*, January 22, 2015, https://www .economist.com/briefing/2015/01/22/an-hereditary-meritocracy; Kevin Carey, "'I Do' Between Elites Widens Class Gap, Researchers Say," WRAL, March 31, 2018, https://www.wral.com/-i-do-between-elites-widens-class-gap -researchers-say/17456597/.

16 Bell, *The Coming of Post-Industrial Society*, 427.

17 Michael Lind, "The New Class War," *American Affairs*, Summer 2017, https:// americanaffairsjournal.org/2017/05/new-class-war; Michael Lind, *The New Class War: Saving Democracy from the Managerial Elite* (New York: Portfolio, 2020).

18 Charles Murray, *Coming Apart: The State of White America, 1960–2010* (New York: Crown Forum, 2012), 19–20.

19 Marge Anderson, "The Clergy and the Nobility: The French Revolution," Big Site of History, June 9, 2008, https://bigsiteofhistory.com/the-clergy-and-the -nobility-the-french-revolution/.

20 Christophe Guilluy, *Twilight of the Elites: Prosperity, the Periphery, and the Future of France* (New Haven: Yale University Press, 2016), 2, 9.

21 U.S. Bureau of Labor Statistics, "Employment by industry, 1910 and 2015," *Economics Daily*, March 3, 2016, U.S. Department of Labor, https://www.bls .gov/opub/ted/2016/employment-by-industry-1910-and-2015.htm.

22 Analysis of job data by Mark Schill based on EMSI calculations.

23 Julian Mischi et al., "The world of the blue-collar worker: changed, but not gone," trans. Olivier Waine, *Metropolitics*, February 19, 2014, https://www .metropolitiques.eu/The-world-of-the-blue-collar.html.

24 Jeremy Warner, "Small Business Owners Explain Why France Is a Nation in

Decline," *Business Insider*, October 19, 2014, https://www.businessinsider.com/small-business-owners-explain-why-france-is-a-nation-in-decline-2014-10.

25 Orlando Figes, *A People's Tragedy: The Russian Revolution, 1891–1924* (New York: Penguin, 1996), 737.

26 Ibid., 511, 551; Dmitri Volkogonov, *Autopsy for Empire: The Seven Leaders Who Built the Soviet Regime* (New York: Free Press, 1998), 63.

27 Eric D. Weitz, *Weimar Germany: Promise and Tragedy* (Princeton: Princeton University Press, 2007), 334.

28 Frederic Spotts, *Hitler and the Power of Aesthetics* (New York: Overlook Press, 2003), 30, 79–82, 98.

29 Klaus P. Fischer, *Nazi Germany: A New History* (New York: Continuum, 1996), 17.

30 Nate Silver, "There Really Was a Liberal Media Bubble," FiveThirtyEight, March 10, 2017, https://fivethirtyeight.com/features/there-really-was-a-liberal-media-bubble/; "Media Bias: Pretty Much All of Journalism Now Leans Left, Study Shows," *Investor's Business Daily*, November 16, 2018, https://www.investors.com/politics/editorials/media-bias-left-study/.

31 Christopher M. Finan, "A Shameful Season for American Journalism," *Wall Street Journal*, September 24, 2018, https://www.wsj.com/articles/a-shameful-season-for-american-journalism-1537830679; Justin Ward, "The death of the working class reporter," *Medium*, June 25, 2019, https://blog.usejournal.com/the-death-of-the-working-class-reporter-48b467300f4d; Amee LaTour, "Do 97 percent of journalist donations go to Democrats?" Ballotopedia, August 16, 2017, https://ballotpedia.org/Fact_check/Do_97_percent_of_journalist_donations_go_to_Democrat.

32 Guilluy, *Twilight of the Elites*, 35–37.

33 Kathleen McLaughlin, "The big journalism void: 'The real crisis is not technological, its geographical,'" *Guardian*, January 30, 2017, https://www.theguardian.com/media/2017/jan/30/the-big-journalism-void-the-real-crisis-is-not-technological-its-geographic.

34 Jennifer Kavanagh et al., *News in a Digital Age* (Santa Monica: Rand Corporation, 2019), https://www.rand.org/pubs/research_reports/RR2960.html; Kalev Leetaru, "A Small Number of Fact-Checkers Now Define Our Reality," *Real Clear Politics*, August 24, 2019, https://www.realclearpolitics.com/articles/2019/08/24/a_small_number_of_fact-checkers_now_define_our_reality_141087.html.

35 Jonathan Chait, "The Vast Left-Wing Conspiracy Is on Your Screen," *New York Magazine*, August 17, 2012, http://nymag.com/news/features/chait-liberal-movies-tv-2012-8/.

36 Jeremy Barr, "Top Hollywood Execs Give Overwhelmingly to Democrats for Midterms," *Hollywood Reporter*, October 12, 2018, https://www.hollywoodreporter.com/news/top-hollywood-execs-give-99-percent-political-donations-democrats-midterms-1151392; Joanna Piacenza, "Putting a Number on Hollywood's Perceived Liberalism," Morning Consult, March 1, 2018, https://morningconsult.com/2018/03/01/putting-number-hollywoods-perceived-liberalism/; Tom Jacobs, "Why Is Hollywood So Liberal?" *Pacific Standard*, May 14, 2019, https://psmag.com/news/why-is-hollywood-so-liberal.

37 Thomas Piketty, "Brahmin Left vs Merchant Right: Rising Inequality and the Changing Structure of Political Conflict (Evidence from France, Britain and the US, 1948–2017)," World Inequality Database, March 2018, http://piketty.pse.ens.fr/files/Piketty2018.pdf.

38 Mark Hemingway, "The Left Is Transforming into a Religion, Maybe a Bit Too Literally," *Washington Examiner*, March 28, 2017, https://www.weeklystandard.com/the-left-is-transforming-into-a-religion-maybe-a-bit-too-literally/article/2007416; Rob Henderson, "'Luxury Beliefs' are the latest status symbol for rich Americans," *New York Post*, August 17, 2019, https://nypost.com/2019/08/17/luxury-beliefs-are-the-latest-status-symbol-for-rich-americans/.

39 Matt Ridley, "Studying the Biases of Bureaucrats," *Wall Street Journal*, October 23, 2010, https://www.wsj.com/articles/SB10001424052702304410504575560323807741154.

40 Ernst Nolte, *Three Faces of Fascism*, trans. Leila Vennewitz (New York: New American Library, 1969), 57; Michael Grant, *The Fall of the Roman Empire* (New York: Collier, 1990), 92.

41 Friedrich Engels, "Socialism: Utopian and Scientific," in *The Essential Left: Marx, Engels, Lenin: Their Basic Teachings*, trans. Edward Aveling (New York: Barnes & Noble, 1961), 138–42.

42 Isaiah Berlin, *Karl Marx: His Life and Environment* (Oxford: Oxford University Press, 1963), 63, 244–45.

43 Volkogonov, *Autopsy for Empire*, 63, 75, 78; Figes, *A People's Tragedy*, 125, 127, 511, 551, 682; Masha Gessen, *The Future Is History: How Totalitarianism Reclaimed Russia* (New York: Riverhead Books, 2017), 38–39; Richard Pipes, *Russia under the Old Regime* (New York: Scribner, 1974), 161; Nicholas Riasanovsky, *A History of Russia* (New York: Oxford University Press, 1963), 521.

44 Richard Pipes, *Communism: A History* (New York: Modern Library, 2001), 44, 65, 66; Barbara Tuchman, *A Distant Mirror: The Calamitous 14th Century* (New York: Knopf, 1978), 17.

45 Pipes, *Communism*, 86; Vladislav Zuboc, *A Failed Empire: The Soviet Union in the Cold War from Stalin to Gorbachev* (Raleigh: University of North Carolina Press, 2007), 9; Riasanovsky, *A History of Russia*, 621.

46 William H. McNeill, *The Pursuit of Power: Technology, Armed Force, and Society since A.D. 1000* (Chicago: University of Chicago Press, 1982), 69; Cho-yun Hsu, "The Roles of the Literati and of Regionalism in the Fall of the Han Dynasty," in *The Collapse of Ancient States and Civilizations*, ed. Norman Yoffee and George L. Cowgill (Tucson: University of Arizona Press, 1998), 178.

47 James Hankins, "Reforming Elites the Confucian Way," *American Affairs Journal*, Summer 2017, https://americanaffairsjournal.org/2017/05/reforming-elites-confucian-way/; Barrington Moore, Jr., *Social Origins of Dictatorship and Democracy: Lord and Peasant in the Making of the Modern World* (Boston: Beacon, 1967), 163–64; Weber, *Economy and Society*, vol. 1: 1048; Tu Wei-ming, *Confucian Thought: Selfhood as Creative Transformation* (Albany, N.Y.: SUNY Press, 1985), 53.

48 Pipes, *Communism*, 129–31; Milovan Djilas, *The Unperfect Society: Beyond the New Class* (New York: Harcourt, 1969), 16.

49 Yang Jisheng, *Tombstone: The Great Chinese Famine, 1958–1962,* trans. Stacey Mosher and Guo Jian (New York: Farrar, Straus & Giroux, 2008), 254–55; Richard McGregor, *The Party: The Secret World of China's Communist Rulers* (New York: Harper, 2010), 15–19.

50 Jisheng, *Tombstone,* 261.

51 Karen Gilchrist, "Here are the 10 wealthiest people in China—a country leading the way for self-made billionaires," CNBC, February 22, 2018, https://www.cnbc.com/2018/02/20/self-made-billionaires-chinas-10-richest-billionaires.html.

52 He Huifeng, "In China, three in five men are dumped because they can't afford a flat, survey suggests," *South China Morning Post,* July 20, 2017, https://www.scmp.com/news/china/society/article/2103399/sixty-cent-chinese-men-dumped-because-cant-afford-flat-survey; Zhuang Pinghui, "First the diploma, then the date: how China's educated elite find love," *South China Morning Post,* September 10, 2017, https://www.scmp.com/news/china/society/article/2110442/first-diploma-then-date-how-chinas-educated-elites-find-love.

53 David S. G. Goodman, *Class in Contemporary China* (Cambridge: Polity Press, 2014), 156–57, 180–81.

54 Richard Bernstein, "How America's Ivory Towers Flunked at Chinese Democracy," *Real Clear Investigations,* March 29, 2018, https://www.realclearinvestigations.com/articles/2018/03/27/chinese_students_in_the_u.html.

55 Lily Kuo, "China bans 23m from buying travel tickets as part of 'social credit' system," *Guardian,* March 1, 2019, https://www.theguardian.com/world/2019/mar/01/china-bans-23m-discredited-citizens-from-buying-travel-tickets-social-credit-system; Jacob Siegel, "The Post-Liberal Politician," *Tablet,* April 16, 2019, https://www.tabletmag.com/jewish-news-and-politics/283055/the-post-liberal-politician.

56 Karel van Wolferen, *The Enigma of Japanese Power: People and Politics in a Stateless Nation* (New York: Vintage, 1990), 45, 114–24.

57 Julius Krein, "James Burnham's Managerial Elite," *American Affairs,* Spring 2017, https://americanaffairsjournal.org/2017/02/james-burnhams-managerial-elite/; Todd Gaziano and Tommy Berry, "Career Civil Servants Illegitimately Rule America," *Wall Street Journal,* February 28, 2018, https://www.wsj.com/articles/career-civil-servants-illegitimately-rule-america-1519862395.

58 Huxley, *Brave New World,* 260.

59 Yascha Mounk, "Americans Strongly Dislike PC Culture," *Atlantic,* October 10, 2018, https://www.theatlantic.com/ideas/archive/2018/10/large-majorities-dislike-political-correctness/572581/.

60 Peter Berkowitz, "'The Most Politically Intolerant Americans,'" *Real Clear Politics,* March 21, 2019, https://www.realclearpolitics.com/articles/2019/03/21/the_most_politically_intolerant_americans_139810.html; Amanda Ripley, Rekha Tenjarla, and Angela Y. He, "The Geography of Partisan Prejudice," *Atlantic,* March 4, 2019, https://www.theatlantic.com/politics/archive/2019/03/us-counties-vary-their-degree-partisan-prejudice/583072/.

61 Bell, *The Coming of Post-Industrial Society,* 33.

62   Toni Airaksinen, "Google's 'Bias Busting' spreads to college campuses," *Campus Reform*, June 29, 2018, https://www.campusreform.org/?ID=11080; Richard Feloni and Sherin Shibu, "Here's the presentation Google gives employees on how to spot unconscious bias at work," *Business Insider*, February 12, 2016, https://www.businessinsider.com/google-unconscious-bias-training -presentation-2015-12; University of California Office of the President, UC Managing Implicit Bias Series, https://www.ucop.edu/local-human-resources /your-career/uc-implicit-bias-series.html; John Daniel Davidson, "Google's Insane Campus Is What Happens When You Politicize Everything," *Federalist*, http://thefederalist.com/2018/05/03/googles-insane-campus-is-what-happens -when-you-politicize-everything/; Derrick Johnson, "Before the next videotaped Starbucks disaster, everyone should take implicit bias training," *USA Today*, May 10, 2018, https://www.usatoday.com/story/opinion/2018 /05/08/starbucks-naacp-implicit-bias-training-racism-column/587402002/; Ryan P. Williams, "Algorithms of Suppression," *American Mind*, May 6, 2019, https://americanmind.org/post/algorithms-of-suppression/.

63   Paul Mozur, "Inside China's Dystopian Dreams: A.I., Shame and Lots of Cameras," *New York Times*, July 8, 2018, https://www.nytimes.com/2018/07/08 /business/china-surveillance-technology.html; Javier C. Hernandez, "Mao 101: Inside a Chinese Classroom Training the Communists of Tomorrow," *New York Times*, June 28, 2018, https://www.nytimes.com/2018/06/28/world/asia /chinese-classrooms-education-communists.html; Chen Guangcheng, "Apple Can't Resist Playing by China's Rules," *New York Times*, January 23, 2018, https://www.nytimes.com/2018/01/23/opinion/apple-china-data.html; "Don't do evil at China's bidding, Google," *Washington Post*, August 5, 2018, https:// www.washingtonpost.com/opinions/dont-do-evil-at-chinas-bidding -google/2018/08/05/b3628598-9687-11e8-810c-5fa705927d54_story.html.

CHAPTER 8—THE CONTROL TOWER

1   Richard V. Reeves and Joanna Venator, "The Inheritance of Education," Brookings, October 27, 2014, https://www.brookings.edu/blog/social-mobility -memos/2014/10/27/the-inheritance-of-education/.

2   David S. G. Goodman, *Class in Contemporary China* (Cambridge: Polity Press, 2014), 157; Yuzhuo Cai, "Chinese higher education: The changes in the past two decades and reform tendencies up to 2020," in *China and Brazil: Challenges and Opportunities*, ed. L. d. C. Ferreira and J. A. G. Albuquerque (São Paulo: Unicamp & Annablume, 2013), 91–118.

3   William J. Dobson, "The East Is Crimson," *Slate*, May 23, 2012, http://www .slate.com/articles/news_and_politics/foreigners/2012/05/harvard_and_the _chinese_communist_party_top_chinese_officials_are_studying_at_elite_u_s _universities_in_large_numbers_.html; Jennifer Levitz, Steve Eder, and Jeremy Page, "Bo Xilai's Son Appears to Have Left Home Near Harvard," *Wall Street Journal*, April 16, 2012, https://www.wsj.com/articles/ SB10001424052702304818404577345680438913376.

4   Ben Wildavsky, *The Great Brain Race: How Global Universities Are Reshaping the World* (Princeton: Princeton University Press, 2010), 169.

5   "NYU president on global universities, 'idea capitals' and 'talent snowballs,'" *Times Higher Education*, May 22, 2013, https://www.timeshighereducation.com

/comment/opinion/nyu-president-on-global-universities-idea-capitals-and
-talent-snowballs/2004033.article.

6 Claudia Goldin and Lawrence F. Katz, "The Shaping of Higher Education:
The Formative Years in the United States, 1890 to 1940," National Bureau of
Economic Research, April 1998, https://www.nber.org/papers/w6537.pdf.

7 Daniel Bell, *The Coming of Post-Industrial Society* (New York: Basic Books,
1973), 217–22; Erin Duffin, "U.S. college enrollment statistics for public and
private colleges from 1965 to 2016 and projections up to 2028," Statista, August
9, 2019, https://www.statista.com/statistics/183995/us-college-enrollment-and
-projections-in-public-and-private-institutions/.

8 Robert Gordon, *The Rise and Fall of American Growth* (Princeton: Princeton
University Press, 2016), 513, 521.

9 Max Roser and Esteban Ortiz-Ospina, "Tertiary Education," Our World in
Data, 2019, https://ourworldindata.org/tertiary-education; Angel Calderon,
"The higher education landscape is changing fast," *University World News*,
June 22, 2018, http://www.universityworldnews.com/article.php?story
=2018062208555853.

10 Allen Guelzo, "College Is Trade School for the Elite," *Wall Street Journal*,
August 6, 2017, https://www.wsj.com/articles/college-is-trade-school-for-the
-elite-1502051874.

11 Charles Murray, *Coming Apart: The State of White America, 1960–2010* (New
York: Crown Forum, 2012), 54–56; Thomas Piketty, *Capital in the Twenty-First
Century*, trans. Arthur Goldhammer (Cambridge, Mass.: Belknap/Harvard,
2014), 447.

12 Daniel Markovits, "How Life Becomes an Endless, Terrible Competition,"
Atlantic, September 2019, https://www.theatlantic.com/magazine/archive
/2019/09/meritocracys-miserable-winners/594760/.

13 Matthew Stewart, "The 9.9 Percent Is the New American Aristocracy," *Atlantic*,
June 2018, https://www.theatlantic.com/magazine/archive/2018/06/the-birth
-of-a-new-american-aristocracy/559130/; Matthew Continetti, "Our Bankrupt
Elite," *Washington Free Beacon*, March 15, 2019, https://freebeacon.com
/columns/our-bankrupt-elite/.

14 Robert Reich, "The Ivy League is ripping off America!" *Salon*, October 16, 2014,
https://www.salon.com/2014/10/16/robert_reich_the_ivy_league_is_ripping
_off_america_partner/?utm_source=twitter&utm_medium=socialflow.

15 Arthur Herman, *The Idea of Decline in Western History* (New York: Free Press,
1997), 159.

16 "Obama's Love of Elites," *National Journal*, https://www.nationaljournal.com
/s/62836.

17 "America's Elite: An hereditary meritocracy," *Economist*, January 22, 2015,
https://www.economist.com/news/briefing/21640316-children-rich-and
-powerful-are-increasingly-well-suited-earning-wealth-and-power.

18 David Goodhart, *The Road to Somewhere: The Populist Revolt and the Future of
Politics* (London: C. Hurst & Co., 2017), 186–87.

19 Noah Rothman, "A Professor's Revolt," *Commentary*, May 11, 2018, https://
www.commentarymagazine.com/culture-civilization/education/college
-professors-revolt-administrative/.

20 Ken Jacobs, Ian Perry, and Jenifer MacGillvary, "The High Public Cost of Low Wages," UC Berkeley Center for Labor Research and Education, April 2015, http://laborcenter.berkeley.edu/pdf/2015/the-high-public-cost-of-low-wages .pdf; Alastair Gee, "Facing poverty, academics turn to sex work and sleeping in cars," *Guardian*, September 28, 2017, https://www.theguardian.com/us-news /2017/sep/28/adjunct-professors-homeless-sex-work-academia-poverty?CMP =share_btn_fb; Neil Gross, "Professors Behaving Badly," *New York Times*, September 30, 2017, https://www.nytimes.com/2017/09/30/opinion/sunday /adjunct-professors-politics.html.

21 John Bagnell Bury, *A History of Freedom of Thought* (Cambridge: The University Press, 1913), http://www.gutenberg.org/files/10684/10684-h/10684-h .htm.

22 James Westfall Thompson and Edgar Nathaniel Johnson, *An Introduction to Medieval Europe* (New York: Norton, 1937), 724; Norman F. Cantor, *Medieval History: The Life and Death of a Civilization* (New York: Macmillan, 1963), 373, 385, 459, 503–5; Barbara Tuchman, *A Distant Mirror: The Calamitous 14th Century* (New York: Knopf, 1978), 160, 319, 371.

23 Thompson and Johnson, *An Introduction to Medieval Europe*, 706–8.

24 Christopher Hibbert, *Cavaliers and Roundheads: The English Civil War, 1642–1649* (New York: Scribner, 1993), 68–69, 93; Jonathan I. Israel, *The Dutch Republic: Its Rise, Greatness, and Fall, 1477–1806* (Oxford: Clarendon Press, 1998), 899–900.

25 Pitirim Sorokin, *The Crisis of Our Age* (London: Oneworld Publication, 1992), 103.

26 Dahlia Remler, "Are 90% of academic papers really never cited? Reviewing the literature on academic citations," London School of Economics and Political Science, November 1, 2016, https://blogs.lse.ac.uk/impactofsocialsciences /2014/04/23/academic-papers-citation-rates-remler/.

27 Joseph Conley, "Just Another Piece of Quit Lit," *Chronicle*, March 8, 2018, https://www.chronicle.com/article/Just-Another-Piece-of-Quit-Lit/242756; Guelzo, "College Is Trade School for the Elite."

28 Vladislav Zubok, *A Failed Empire: The Soviet Union in the Cold War from Stalin to Gorbachev* (Chapel Hill: University of North Carolina Press, 2009), 166.

29 F. L. Carsten, *The Rise of Fascism* (Berkeley: University of California Press, 1967), 33.

30 Austin Williams, *The Enemies of Progress: The Dangers of Sustainability* (Exeter: Societas, 2008), 75.

31 Herman, *The Idea of Decline in Western History*, 299–302, 320–28; Herbert Marcuse, *One Dimensional Man* (Boston: Beacon, 1964), 7.

32 "The dramatic shift among college professors that's hurting students' education," *Washington Post*, January 11, 2016, https://www.washingtonpost. com/news/wonk/wp/2016/01/11/the-dramatic-shift-among-college-professors -thats-hurting-students-education; "Publications—The Faculty Survey," Higher Education Research Institute, https://heri.ucla.edu/publications-fac/.

33 Mitchell Langbert, "Homogeneous: The Political Affiliations of Elite Liberal Arts College Faculty," National Association of Scholars, Summer 2018, https:// www.nas.org/articles/homogenous_political_affiliations_of_elite_liberal.

34 Paul Caron, "BYU and Pepperdine Are the Most Ideologically Balanced Faculties Among the Top 50 Law Schools (2013)," TaxProf Blog, August 14, 2018, http://taxprof.typepad.com/taxprof_blog/2018/08/byu-and-pepperdine -are-the-most-ideologically-balanced-faculties-among-the-top-50-law -schools-2013.html; Toni Airaksinen, "Study: Profs Less Likely to Hire NRA Members, Republicans," *PJ Media*, August 9, 2018, https://pjmedia.com /trending/study-profs-less-likely-to-hire-nra-members-republicans/; Kathryn Hinderaker, "The assault on academic freedom at UCLA," *College Fix*, October 23, 2017, https://www.thecollegefix.com/assault-academic-freedom-ucla/; Nicolas Kristof, "A Confession of Liberal Intolerance," *New York Times*, May 7, 2016, https://www.nytimes.com/2016/05/08/opinion/sunday/a-confession-of -liberal-intolerance.html.

35 Noah Carl, "Lackademia: Why Do Academics Lean Left?" Adam Smith Institute, March 2, 2017, https://www.adamsmith.org/research/lackademia -why-do-academics-lean-left; Goodhart, *The Road to Somewhere*, 37.

36 M. R. Nakhaie and Barry D. Adam, "Political Affiliation of Canadian University Professors," *Canadian Journal of Sociology*, vol. 33:4 (2008), 873–98, https:// journals.library.ualberta.ca/cjs/index.php/CJS/article/viewFile/1036/3661; James Galbraith, "The Future of the Left in Europe?" *American Prospect*, August 17, 2016, http://prospect.org/article/future-left-europe.

37 Jonathan Kay, "A Black Eye for the Columbia Journalism Review," *Quillette*, June 18, 2019, https://quillette.com/2019/06/18/a-black-eye-for-the-columbia -journalism-review/.

38 Cass R. Sunstein, "The Problem With All Those Liberal Professors," Bloomberg, September 17, 2018, https://www.bloomberg.com/view/articles/2018-09-17 /colleges-have-way-too-many-liberal-professors; Chase Watkins, "Study finds 'ideological similarity, hostility, and discrimination' rampant in academic philosophy," *College Fix*, August 21, 2019, https://www.thecollegefix.com/study -finds-ideological-similarity-hostility-and-discrimination-rampant-in- academic-philosophy/.

39 Rex Murphy, "Laurier, trading 'free speech' for 'better speech,' proves unspeakably clueless still," *National Post*, August 3, 2018, https://nationalpost. com/opinion/rex-murphy-now-laurier-wants-to-ditch-free-speech-for-better -speech-can-we-converse.

40 Kate Hardiman, "Universities require scholars pledge commitment to diversity," *College Fix*, April 14, 2017, https://www.thecollegefix.com /universities-require-scholars-pledge-commitment-diversity/.

41 James Barrett, "University Panel: Is Intersectionality a Religion?" *Daily Wire*, March 5, 2018, https://www.dailywire.com/news/27825/watch-university -panel-intersectionality-religion-james-barrett.

42 Musa Al-Gharbi, "Academic and Political Elitism," *Inside Higher Ed*, August 27, 2019, https://www.insidehighered.com/views/2019/08/27/academe-should -avoid-politicizing-educational-attainment-opinion; Amanda Ripley, Rekha Tenjarla, and Angela Y. He, "The Geography of Partisan Prejudice," *Atlantic*, March 4, 2019, https://www.theatlantic.com/politics/archive/2019/03/us -counties-vary-their-degree-partisan-prejudice/583072/; Stav Atir, Emily Rosenzweig, and David Dunning, "When Knowledge Knows No Bounds:

Self-Perceived Expertise Predicts Claims of Impossible Knowledge," *Psychological Science*, vol. 26:8 (August 1, 2015), 1295–303, https://journals. sagepub.com/doi /abs/10.1177/0956797615588195.

43 Jane Jacobs, *Dark Ages Ahead* (New York: Random House, 2004), 43–46.

44 Scott Jaschik, "'Academically Adrift,'" *Inside Higher Ed*, January 18, 2011, https:// www.insidehighered.com/news/2011/01/18/academically-adrift.

45 Kate Davidson, "Employers Find 'Soft Skills' Like Critical Thinking in Short Supply," *Wall Street Journal*, August 30, 2016, https://www.wsj.com/articles /employers-find-soft-skills-like-critical-thinking-in-short-supply-1472549400.

46 Jacobs, *Dark Ages Ahead*, 7–9.

47 James Hannam, "Did Early Christians Destroy Pagan Literature?" *Medieval Science and Philosophy*, 2007, http://jameshannam.com/literature.htm.

48 Alison Flood, "Sharp decline in children reading for pleasure, survey finds," *Guardian*, January 9, 2015, https://www.theguardian.com/books/2015/jan/09 /decline-children-reading-pleasure-survey.

49 Charles Hymas, "Children's literacy levels fall as social media hits reading," *Telegraph*, August 20, 2018, https://www.telegraph.co.uk/news/2018/08/20 /childrens-literacy-levels-fall-social-media-hits-reading/.

50 John Tierney, "Reeducation Campus," *City Journal*, Summer 2018, https:// www.city-journal.org/first-year-experience-16032.html; John M. Ellis, "Higher Education's Deeper Sickness," *Wall Street Journal*, November 13, 2017, https:// www.wsj.com/articles/higher-educations-deeper-ailment-1510615185.

51 Ashley Thorne, "Why are American universities shying away from the classics?" *Guardian*, August 25, 2013, https://www.theguardian.com /commentisfree/2013/aug/25/american-universities-not-reading-classics; Irvin Weathersby, Jr., "The Case for Teaching Dead White Authors, Even During Black History Month," *Atlantic*, February 12, 2015, https://www.theatlantic.com /education/archive/2015/02/dead-white-authors-matter/385421/.

52 Cathy Young, "Half of college students aren't sure protecting free speech is important. That's bad news," *Los Angeles Times*, April 8, 2018, http://www .latimes.com/opinion/op-ed/la-oe-young-free-speech-on-campus-20180408 -story.html; Jacob Poushter, "40% of millennials OK with limiting speech offensive to minorities," Pew Research Center, November 20, 2015, http://www .pewresearch.org/fact-tank/2015/11/20/40-of-millennials-ok-with-limiting -speech-offensive-to-minorities/.

53 Gwynn Guilford, "Harvard research suggests an entire global generation has lost faith in democracy," *Quartz*, November 30, 2016, https://qz.com/848031 /harvard-research-suggests-that-an-entire-global-generation-has-lost-faith -in-democracy/; Andrew A. Michta, "Losing the Nation-State," *American Interest*, July 1, 2017, https://www.the-american-interest.com/2017/07/01 /losing-nation-state/.

CHAPTER 9—NEW RELIGIONS

1 Samuel P. Huntington, *The Clash of Civilizations and the Remaking of World Order* (New York: Simon & Schuster, 1996), 47.

2 William H. McNeill, *The Rise of the West: A History of the Human Community* (1963; Chicago: University of Chicago Press, 2009), 34–60, 351.

3 Jim Geraghty, "The Catholic Church Drives the Nail into Its Own Moral Authority," *National Review*, August 20, 2018, https://www.nationalreview.com/the-morning-jolt/the-catholic-church-drives-the-nail-into-its-own-moral-authority/; Harry Bruinius, "Amid Evangelical decline, growing split between young Christians and church elders," *Christian Science Monitor*, October 10, 2017, https://www.csmonitor.com/USA/Politics/2017/1010/Amid-Evangelical-decline-growing-split-between-young-Christians-and-church-elders; Damon Linker, "The dangers of the great American unchurching," *The Week*, September 8, 2017, http://theweek.com/articles/723203/dangers-great-american-unchurching.

4 Betsy Cooper et al., "Exodus: Why Americans are Leaving Religion—and Why They're Unlikely to Come Back," PRRI, September 22, 2016, https://www.prri.org/research/prri-rns-poll-nones-atheist-leaving-religion/; Robert Putnam, *Bowling Alone: The Collapse and Revival of American Community* (New York: Simon & Shuster, 2000), 65–69.

5 Oliver Smith, "Mapped: The World's most (and least) religious countries," *Telegraph*, January 14, 2018, https://www.telegraph.co.uk/travel/maps-and-graphics/most-religious-countries-in-the-world; Pew Research Center, "Young adults around the world as less religious by several measures," June 13, 2018, https://www.pewforum.org/2018/06/13/young-adults-around-the-world-are-less-religious-by-several-measures/.

6 David Campbell, John Green, and Alan Cooperman, "American Grace: How Religion Divides and Unites Us," Pew Research Center, December 16, 2010, http://www.pewforum.org/2010/12/16/american-grace-how-religion-divides-and-unites-us/.

7 Angie Thurston and Casper ter Kuile, "How We Gather," April 2015, https://caspertk.files.wordpress.com/2015/04/how-we-gather.pdf.

8 Ian Lovett, "Politics in the Pews: Anti-Trump Activism Is Reviving Protestant Churches—at a Cost," *Wall Street Journal*, May 4, 2018, https://www.wsj.com/articles/trump-in-the-pews-politics-is-convulsing-mainline-churches-1525445467; Raymond D. Aumack, "The Jesuits are Too Liberal," *America: The Jesuit Review*, May 24, 2004, https://www.americamagazine.org/issue/486/faith-focus/jesuits-are-too-liberal; "U.S. Jews Share Shuls Due to Low Attendance," *Haaretz*, November 5, 2013, https://www.haaretz.com/jewish/.premium-u-s-jews-share-shuls-due-to-low-attendance-1.5285750.

9 Tyler O'Neil, "Democrats Outnumber Republicans 70 to 1 in College Religion Departments, 10 to 1 Overall," *PJ Media*, May 4, 2018, https://pjmedia.com/lifestyle/democrats-outnumber-republicans-70-to-1-in-college-religion-departments-10-to-1-overall/.

10 Michael Lipka, "Mainline Protestants make up shrinking number of U.S. Adults," Pew Research Center, May 18, 2015, http://www.pewresearch.org/fact-tank/2015/05/18/mainline-protestants-make-up-shrinking-number-of-u-s-adults/.

11 Pew Research Center, "Religion in Latin America," November 13, 2014, http://www.pewforum.org/2014/11/13/religion-in-latin-america/.

12 Jared C. Wilson, "Traditionalism Is Winning," For the Church, August 2, 2015, https://ftc.co/resource-library/blog-entries/traditionalism-is-winning; Charles Colson, "How Christianity Is Growing Around the World," Christian Broadcasting Network, http://www1.cbn.com/how-christianity-growing -around-world.

13 "Islam poised to over take established Christianity in UK: report," *Express Tribune*, March 21, 2018, https://tribune.com.pk/story/1665803/9-islam-poised -overtake-established-christianity-uk-reports-guardian/.

14 Joel Garreau, "Environmentalism as Religion," *New Atlantis*, no. 28 (Summer 2010), 61–74, https://www.thenewatlantis.com/publications/environmentalism- as-religion; Mark J. Perry, "18 Spectacularly Wrong Predictions Made Around the Time of the First Earth Day in 1970. Expect More This Year," Foundation for Economic Education, April 22, 2018, https://fee.org/articles/18-spectacularly -wrong-predictions-made-around-the-time-of-the-first-earth-day-in-1970 -expect-more-this-year/; James Ridgeway, *The Politics of Ecology* (New York: Dutton, 1970), 195.

15 Garreau, "Environmentalism as Religion"; Thomas Robert Malthus, *An Essay on the Principle of Population* (New York: Norton, 2018), 42; David Adler, "Straight to Hell: Millenarianism and the Green New Deal," *Quillette*, May 21, 2019, https://quillette.com/2019/05/21/straight-to-hell-millenarianism-and -the-green-new-deal/.

16 Marc Bloch, *Feudal Society*, trans. L. A. Manyon (London: Routledge, 1961), 84; Johan Huizinga, *The Waning of the Middle Ages* (Garden City, N.Y.: Doubleday, 1954), 138; Barbara Tuchman, *A Distant Mirror: The Calamitous 14th Century* (New York: Knopf, 1978), 327.

17 Prof. Alexandratos, "Is human greed at the core of modern day environmental issues?" Environmental Science and Technology, MCH Seminar 3, Macaulay Honors College at CUNY, Fall 2016, https://eportfolios.macaulay.cuny.edu /est2016/2016/09/11/is-human-greed-at-the-core-of-modern-day -environmental-issues/; Rev. Peter Sawtell, "The top environmental problems are selfishness, greed, and apathy and resignation. We need spiritual and cultural transformation," Global Catholic Climate Movement, April 22, 2019, https://catholicclimatemovement.global/the-top-environmental-problems -are-selfishness-greed-and-apathy-and-resignation-we-need-spiritual-and -cultural-transformation/; Suzanne Goldenberg, "US cult of greed is now a global environmental threat, report warns," *Guardian*, January 12, 2010, https://www.theguardian.com/environment/2010/jan/12/climate-change-greed -environment-threat.

18 Norman Yoffee, "Orienting Collapse," in *The Collapse of Ancient States and Civilizations,* ed. Norman Yoffee and George L. Cowgill (Tucson: University of Arizona Press, 1991), 4–5.

19 Scott Whitlock, "Flashback: ABC's '08 Prediction: NYC Under Water from Climate Change by June 2015," Media Research Center, June 12, 2015, https:// www.newsbusters.org/blogs/scott-whitlock/2015/06/12/flashback-abcs-08 -prediction-nyc-under-water-climate-change-june.

20 Abe Greenwald, "When the Scientific Consensus Is Corrected by a Skeptic," *Commentary*, November 16, 2018, https://www.commentarymagazine.com

/culture-civilization/science/when-the-scientific-consensus-is-corrected-by-a
-skeptic/; Francis Menton, "How Do You Tell If the Earth's Climate System 'Is
Warming,'" Manhattan Contrarian, August 9, 2018, https://www
.manhattancontrarian.com/blog/2018-8-9-how-do-you-tell-if-the-earths
-climate-system-is-warming; Oren Cass, "Climate Song and Dance," *City
Journal*, November 10, 2017, https://www.city-journal.org/html/climate
-song-and-dance-15556.html; Oren Cass, "Doomsday Climate Scenarios Are a
Joke," *Wall Street Journal*, March 11, 2018, https://www.wsj.com/articles
/doomsday-climate-scenarios-are-a-joke-1520800377; "Don't Tell Anyone,
But We Just Had Two Years of Record-Breaking Global Cooling," Editorial,
Investor's Business Daily, May 16, 2018, https://www.investors.com/politics
/editorials/climate-change-global-warming-earth-cooling-media-bias/; Larry
Kummer, "Listening to climate doomsters makes our situation worse," Fabius
Maximus, June 24, 2019, https://fabiusmaximus.com/2019/06/24/climate
-doomsters/; Anthony Watts, "Terrifying predications about the melting North
Pole!" Watts Up With That?, https://wattsupwiththat.com/2019/04/30
/terrifying-predictions-about-the-melting-north-pole/.

21 Marian L. Tupy, "How Humanity Won the War on Famine," *Human Progress*,
August 16, 2018, https://humanprogress.org/article.php?p=1459.

22 Pierre Riché, *Daily Life in the World of Charlemagne*, trans. Jo Ann McNamara
(Philadelphia: University of Pennsylvania Press, 1978), 33; Tuchman, *A Distant
Mirror*, 28.

23 Blythe Copeland, "7 green philanthropists making a difference," Mother Nature
Network, January 11, 2013, https://www.mnn.com/leaderboard/stories/7-green-
philanthropists-making-a-difference; Tara Weiss, "The $3 Billion Man," *Forbes*,
November 28, 2006, https://www.forbes.com/2006/11/26/leadership-branson
-virgin-lead-citizen-cx_tw_1128branson.html#224723ce1fa5.

24 Robert Kirchhoeffer, "Granting Environmental Indulgences," *American
Spectator*, July 15, 2009, https://spectator.org/41248_granting-environmental
-indulgences/.

25 Rebecca Ratcliffe, "Record private jet flights into Davos as leaders arrive for
climate talk," *Guardian*, January 22, 2019, https://www.theguardian.com/global
-development/2019/jan/22/record-private-jet-flights-davos-leaders-climate
-talk; Alan Moore, "The Top 12 Celebrity Climate Hypocrites," Media Research
Center, March 1, 2016, https://www.mrctv.org/blog/top-12-climate-hypocrites;
Fraser Myers, "An establishment rebellion," *Spiked*, August 8, 2019, https://
www.spiked-online.com/2019/08/08/an-establishment-rebellion/.

26 Judith Curry, "The perils of 'near-tabloid science,'" Climate Etc., July 22, 2018,
https://judithcurry.com/2018/07/22/the-perils-of-near-tabloid-science
/#more-24240; Judith Curry, "Hearing on the Biodiversity Report," Climate
Etc., May 22, 2019, https://judithcurry.com/2019/05/22/hearing-on-the-un
-biodiversity-report/#more-24890; Judith Curry, "The latest travesty in
'consensus enforcement,'" Climate Etc., August 14, 2019, https://judithcurry
.com/2019/08/14/the-latest-travesty-in-consensus-enforcement; Roger Pielke,
Jr., "My Unhappy Life as a Climate Heretic," *Wall Street Journal*, December 2,
2016, https://www.wsj.com/articles/my-unhappy-life-as-a-climate-heretic
-1480723518/; David B. Rivkin, Jr. and Andrew M. Grossman, "Punishing

Climate-Change Skeptics," *Wall Street Journal*, March 23, 2016, https://www
.wsj.com/articles/punishing-climate-change-skeptics-1458772173.

27 Valerie Richardson, "Bill Nye, the science guy, is open to criminal charges
and jail time to climate change dissenters," *Washington Times*, April 14, 2016,
https://www.washingtontimes.com/news/2016/apr/14/bill-nye-open-criminal
-charges-jail-time-climate-c/; Mark Hemingway, "Senator: Use RICO Laws
to Prosecute Global Warming Skeptics," *Washington Examiner*, June 2, 2015,
https://www.weeklystandard.com/mark-hemingway/senator-use-rico-laws-to
-prosecute-global-warming-skeptics; Robert Bryce, "An Environmentalist Sues
over an Academic Disagreement," *National Review*, November 10, 2017, https://
www.nationalreview.com/2017/11/environmentalist-who-claimed-us-could
-run-renewables-sues-over-academic-disagreement/.

28 Steven Hayward, "Make Socialism Scientific Again," *Power Line*, August 9,
2018, https://www.powerlineblog.com/archives/2018/08/make-socialism-
scientific-again.php.

29 Steven Koonin, "A 'Red Team' Exercise Would Strengthen Climate Science,"
Wall Street Journal, April 20, 2017, https://www.wsj.com/articles/a-red-team
-exercise-would-strengthen-climate-science-1492728579.

30 Jaron Lanier, *Who Owns the Future?* (New York: Simon & Schuster, 2013),
325–26.

31 Wesley J. Smith, "Transhumanism: A Wail of Despair in the Night," *National
Review*, May 14, 2018, https://www.nationalreview.com/2018/05
/transhumanism-promise-immortality-glorified-body-ersatz-christian-hope/.

32 Dyllan Furness, "Technology makes our lives easier, but is it at the cost of our
humanity?" *Digital Trends*, April 28, 2018, https://www.digitaltrends.com
/cool-tech/re-engineer-humanity-evan-selinger-interview/.

33 Ashlee Vance, "Merely Human? That's So Yesterday," *New York Times*, June 12,
2010, https://www.nytimes.com/2010/06/13/business/13sing.html; "A Timeline
of Transhumanism," The Verge, https://www.theverge.com/a/transhumanism
-2015/history-of-transhumanism; Mark Piesing, "Silicon Valley's 'suicide pill'
for mankind," UnHerd, August 20, 2018, https://unherd.com/2018/12/silicon-
valleys-suicide-pill-mankind-2/; Michelle Quinn, "Silicon Valley's fascination
with a fountain of youth," *Mercury News*, August 24, 2016, https://www
.mercurynews.com/2016/08/09/silicon-valleys-fascination-with-a-fountain
-of-youth/; "Measuring deep-brain neurons' electrical signals at high speed
with light instead of electrodes," Kurzweilai, February 28, 2018, http://www
.kurzweilai.net/measuring-deep-brain-neurons-electrical-signals-at-high
-speed-with-light-instead-of-electrodes.

34 Antonio Regalado, "A startup is pitching a mind-uploading service that is '100
percent fatal,'" *MIT Technology Review*, March 13, 2018, https://www
.technologyreview.com/s/610456/a-startup-is-pitching-a-mind-uploading
-service-that-is-100-percent-fatal/.

35 Mark Harris, "God Is a Bot, and Anthony Levandowski Is His Messenger,"
Wired, September 27, 2017, https://www.wired.com/story/god-is-a-bot-and
-anthony-levandowski-is-his-messenger/.

36 Thomas Metzinger, "Silicon Valley evangelists sell an ancient dream of

immortality," *Financial Times,* August 20, 2017, https://www.ft.com/content /7a89c998-828d-11e7-94e2-c5b903247afd.

37 Georges Lefebvre, *The Coming of the French Revolution,* trans. R. R. Palmer (Princeton: Princeton University Press, 1947), 215.

38 Yuval Noah Harari, *Homo Deus: A Brief History of Tomorrow* (New York: HarperCollins, 2017), 44.

39 Tad Walch, "Mormon humanitarian donations quadruple in response to disasters," *Deseret News,* November 3, 2017, https://www.deseretnews.com /article/865692237/Mormon-humanitarian-donations-quadruple-in-response -to-disasters.html; Jill DiSanto, "Penn Research Shows that Mormons Are Generous and Active in Helping Others," *Penn Today,* April 17, 2012, https:// penntoday.upenn.edu/news/penn-research-shows-mormons-are-generous -and-active-helping-others; John Ellis, "The Best-Kept Secret in Disaster Relief: Southern Baptists," *PJ Media,* September 11, 2017, https://pjmedia.com/faith /2017/09/11/the-best-kept-secret-in-disaster-relief-southern-baptists/; "Evangelicals Give More to Charity, Study Finds," *Christian Headlines,* https:// www.christianheadlines.com/blog/evangelicals-give-more-to-charity-study -finds.html.

CHAPTER 10—THE RISE AND DECLINE OF UPWARD MOBILITY

1 J. P. V. D. Balsdon, *Romans and Aliens* (Chapel Hill: University of North Carolina Press, 1979), 167; DutchReview Crew, "Romans in Clogs: The Roman Empire in the Netherlands," *DutchReview,* June 13, 2014, https://dutchreview .com/latest/roman-empire-in-the-netherlands/; Jona Lendering, "The Batavian Revolt," *Ancient History Encyclopedia,* November 28, 2011, https://www.ancient .eu/article/286/the-batavian-revolt/.

2 Fernand Braudel, *The Perspective of the World,* vol. 3 of *Civilization and Capitalism, 15th–18th Century,* trans. Sian Reynolds (New York: Harper & Row, 1984), 98, 177–78.

3 Ibid., 178–84, 190–91; Jonathan Israel, *The Dutch Republic: Its Rise, Greatness, and Fall, 1477–1806* (New York: Oxford University Press, 1995), 905.

4 Immanuel Wallerstein, *The Modern World System: Capitalist Agriculture and the Origins of the European World Economy in the 16th Century* (New York: Academic Press, 1974), 208–9.

5 Philippe Ariès, *Centuries of Childhood: A Social History of Family Life,* trans. Robert Baldick (New York: Vintage, 1962), 375, 398; Simon Schama, *An Embarrassment of Riches: An Interpretation of Dutch Culture in the Golden Age* (New York: Vintage, 1997), 297; Israel, *The Dutch Republic,* 41, 80, 787.

6 Braudel, *The Perspective of the World,* 186–89; Bernard Lewis, *The Muslim Discovery of Europe* (New York: Norton, 1982), 112.

7 Braudel, *The Perspective of the World,* 177; Schama, *An Embarrassment of Riches,* 263.

8 Schama, *An Embarrassment of Riches,* 38–39; Braudel, *The Perspective of the World,* 177–78, 201; Israel, *The Dutch Republic,* 106; Andro Linklater, *Owning the Earth: The Transforming History of Land Ownership* (New York: Bloomsbury USA, 2013), 50.

9 Robert S. Lopez, *The Birth of Europe* (New York: M. Evans & Co., 1967), 21–23.

10 James Westfall Thompson and Edgar Nathaniel Johnson, *An Introduction to Medieval Europe* (New York: Norton, 1937), 349; Barbara Tuchman, *A Distant Mirror: The Calamitous 14th Century* (New York: Knopf, 1978), 135.

11 Lopez, *The Birth of Europe*, 171; Marc Bloch, *Feudal Society*, trans. L. A. Manyon (London: Routledge, 1961), 278; Frances and Joseph Gies, *Daily Life in Medieval Times* (New York: Barnes & Noble, 1969), 148–49; Norman F. Cantor, *Medieval History: The Life and Death of a Civilization* (New York: Macmillan, 1963), 277; Barrington Moore, Jr., *Social Origins of Dictatorship and Democracy: Lord and Peasant in the Making of the Modern World* (Boston: Beacon, 1967), 10.

12 William H. McNeill, *The Pursuit of Power: Technology, Armed Force, and Society since A.D. 1000* (Chicago: University of Chicago Press, 1984), 82–83, 117–19.

13 Christopher Hibbert, *Cavaliers and Roundheads: The English Civil War, 1642–1649* (New York: Scribner, 1993), 197, 247–48.

14 R. R. Palmer, *The World of the French Revolution* (New York: Harper & Row, 1971), 97.

15 Richard Reeves, "Capitalism used to promise a better future. Can it still do that?" *Guardian*, May 22, 2019, https://www.theguardian.com/commentisfree /2019/may/22/capitalism-broken-better-future-can-it-do-that.

16 Max Roser, "Economic Growth," Our World in Data, University of Oxford, https://ourworldindata.org/economic-growth.

17 Karl Marx, *Capital*, trans. Ben Fowkes (New York: Vintage, 1957), vol. 1: 914–15; Karl Marx and Friedrich Engels, "The Manifesto of the Communist Party," in *The Essential Left* (New York: Barnes & Noble, 1961), 15–17.

18 E. J. Hobsbawm, *The Age of Revolution* (New York: New American Library, 1962), 222.

19 Peter Lindert and Jeffrey Williamson, "Unequal gains: American growth and inequality since 1700," *Vox*, CEPR Policy Portal, June 16, 2016, https://voxeu .org/article/american-growth-and-inequality-1700.

20 Hans Rosling, "Good news at last: the world isn't as horrific as you think," *Guardian*, April 11, 2018, https://www.theguardian.com/world/commentisfree /2018/apr/11/good-news-at-last-the-world-isnt-as-horrific-as-you-think; Homi Kharas and Kristofer Hamel, "A global tipping point: Half the world is now middle class or wealthier," September 27, 2018, https://www.brookings.edu/blog /future-development/2018/09/27/a-global-tipping-point-half-the-world-is-now -middle-class-or-wealthier/?utm_campaign=Brookings%20Brief&utm _source=hs_email&utm_medium=email&tm_content=66298094.

21 Lindert and Williamson, "Unequal gains: American growth and inequality since 1700."

22 David DeGraw, "We're living in a system of new feudalism. Here's how to change it," *New Statesman*, October 31, 2013, http://www.newstatesman.com /2013/10/were-living-system-new-feudalism-heres-how-change-it.

23 Michael D. Carr and Emily E. Wiemers, "The decline in lifetime earnings mobility in the U.S.: Evidence from survey-linked administrative data," Equitable Growth, September 7, 2016, https://equitablegrowth.org/working

-papers/the-decline-in-lifetime-earnings-mobility-in-the-u-s-evidence-from
-survey-linked-administrative-data/.

24 Mona Chalabi, "The world's wealthy: where on earth are the richest 1%?"
    Guardian, October 9, 2013, https://www.theguardian.com/news/datablog/2013
    /oct/09/worlds-wealthy-where-russia-rich-list; Andrea Willige, "5 charts
    that show what is happening to the middle class around the world," World
    Economic Forum, January 12, 2017, https://www.weforum.org/agenda
    /2017/01/5-charts-which-show-what-is-happening-to-the-middle-class
    -around-the-world/.

25 Anna Ludwinek et al., *Social Mobility in the EU,* Eurofound, 2017, http://www
    .praxis.ee/wp-content/uploads/2014/11/Social-mobility-in-the-EU-2017.pdf;
    Adam O'Neal, "Why Bernie Sanders Is Wrong About Sweden," *Wall Street
    Journal*, August 23, 2019, https://www.wsj.com/articles/why-bernie-sanders
    -is-wrong-about-sweden-11566596536; Liz Alderman, "Europe's Middle Class Is
    Shrinking. Spain Bears Much of the Pain," *New York Times*, February 14, 2019,
    https://www.nytimes.com/2019/02/14/business/spain-europe-middle-class.
    html.

26 "Germany: the hidden divide in Europe's richest country," *Financial Times*,
    August 17, 2017, https://www.ft.com/content/db8e0b28-7ec3-11e7-9108
    -edda0bcbc928.

27 David Goodhart, *The Road to Somewhere: The New Tribes Shaping British
    Politics* (London: Penguin, 2017), 149–51, 183.

28 Yvonne Roberts, "Millennials are struggling. Is it the fault of the baby
    boomers?" *Guardian*, April 28, 2018, https://www.theguardian.com/society
    /2018/apr/29/millennials-struggling-is-it-fault-of-baby-boomers
    -intergenerational-fairness.

29 Willige, "5 charts that show what is happening to the middle class around the
    world"; Pew Research Center, "Wealth gap between middle-income and upper-
    income families reaches record high," December 9, 2015, http://www
    .pewsocialtrends.org/2015/12/09/5-wealth-gap-between-middle-income
    -and-upper-income-families-reaches-record-high/.

30 Alex Rowell, "New Census Data Show Household Incomes Are Rising Again,
    but Share Going to Middle Class Is at Record Low," Center for American
    Progress, September 12, 2017, https://www.americanprogress.org/issues
    /economy/news/2017/09/12/438778/new-census-data-show-household
    -incomes-rising-share-going-middle-class-record-low/.

31 Chad Stone, Danilo Trisi, Arloc Sherman, and Roderick Taylor, "A Guide to
    Statistics on Historical Trends in Income Inequality," Center on Budget and
    Policy Priorities, August 21, 2019, https://www.cbpp.org/research/poverty-and
    -inequality/a-guide-to-statistics-on-historical-trends-in-income-inequality.

32 Richard V. Reeves, *Dream Hoarders: How the American Upper Middle Class
    Is Leaving Everyone Else in the Dust, Why That Is a Problem, and What to Do
    About It* (Washington, D.C.: Brookings Institution Press, 2017), 23.

33 Les Leopold, "The Rich Have Gained $5.6 Trillion in the 'Recovery,' While the
    Rest of Us Have Lost $669 Billion," *Huffington Post*, December 6, 2017, https://
    www.huffingtonpost.com/les-leopold/the-rich-have-gained-56-t_b_3237528.
    html.

34 John Michaelson, "America's Lost Decade," *City Journal*, Winter 2018, https://www.city-journal.org/html/america%E2%80%99s-lost-decade-15653.html.

35 Jeffrey A. Winters, *Oligarchy* (Cambridge: Cambridge University Press, 2011), 226.

36 Matthew Stewart, "The 9.9 Percent Is the New American Aristocracy," *Atlantic*, June 2018, https://www.theatlantic.com/magazine/archive/2018/06/the-birth-of-a-new-american-aristocracy/559130/.

37 David Pilling, *Bending Adversity: Japan and the Art of Survival* (New York: Penguin, 2014), 121–22.

38 David S. G. Goodman, *Class in Contemporary China* (Cambridge: Polity Press, 2014), 45; Central Intelligence Agency, "Country Comparison: Distribution of Family Income—GINI Index," https://www.cia.gov/library/publications/the-world-factbook/rankorder/2172rank.html.

39 Thomas Piketty, Li Yang, and Gabriel Zuchman, "Capital Accumulation, Private Property and Rising Inequality in China," National Bureau of Economic Research, June 2017, https://www.nber.org/papers/w23368.

40 Salvatore Babones, "China's Middle Class Is Pulling Up the Ladder Behind Itself," *Foreign Policy*, February 1, 2018, https://foreignpolicy.com/2018/02/01/chinas-middle-class-is-pulling-up-the-ladder-behind-itself/.

41 Winters, *Oligarchy*, 78–90, 92; Montesquieu, *Considerations on the Causes of Rome's Greatness and Fall*, chap. 2 and 9, in *Selected Political Writings*, ed. and trans. Melvin Richter (Indianapolis: Hackett, 1990), 86–87, 99; Aristotle, *Politics*, trans. Benjamin Jowett, Bk. 3, http://classics.mit.edu/Aristotle/politics.3.three.html.

42 Michael Grant, *The Fall of the Roman Empire* (New York: Collier, 1990), 58–60, 72, 79; Edward Gibbon, *The History of the Decline and Fall of the Roman Empire* (New York: Modern Library, 1930), vol. 1: 1101–2; Thompson and Johnson, *An Introduction to Medieval Europe*, 13–15; Norman F. Cantor, *Medieval History: The Life and Death of a Civilization* (New York: Macmillan, 1963), 33.

43 Gies, *Daily Life in Medieval Times*, 24, 26–28; Lopez, *The Birth of Europe*, 170.

44 Cho-yun Hsu, "The Roles of the Literati and of Regionalism in the Fall of the Han Dynasty," in *The Collapse of Ancient States and Civilizations*, ed. Norman Yoffee and George L. Cowgill (Tucson: University of Arizona Press, 1988), 176–77; Charles O. Hucker, *China's Imperial Past: An Introduction to Chinese History and Culture* (Stanford: Stanford University Press, 1975), 52–53.

45 McNeill, *The Pursuit of Power*, 31–33.

46 Andrew R. Wilson, "Southern Trade and Northern Defense: Ming Mission to Manila," in *Chinese Diaspora Since Admiral Zheng He*, ed. Leo Suryadinata, (Singapore: Chinese Heritage Center, 2007), 99–111.

47 Hucker, *China's Imperial Past*, 10–11, 57, 84, 176.

48 McNeill, *The Pursuit of Power*, 28–48, 69.

49 Edward Luce, *In Spite of the Gods: The Rise of Modern India* (New York: Anchor Books, 2006), 71; Romila Thapar, *History of India*, vol. 1 (New York: Penguin, 1990), 77–78, 239; Moore, *Social Origins of Dictatorship and Democracy*, 317–19.

50 John Hale, *The Civilization of Europe in the Renaissance* (New York:

Touchstone, 1993), 389–90; J. H. Elliot, *Imperial Spain* (New York: St. Martin's, 1964), 88, 95, 115, 189–90.

51   David Rock, *Argentina, 1516–1987: From Spanish Colonization to Alfonsín* (Berkeley: University of California Press, 1985), xxi, xxiv, 177, 213; Robert D. Crasswaller, *Perón and the Enigmas of Argentina* (New York: Norton, 1987), 30; Braudel, *The Perspective of the World*, 400–8.

52   T. R. Fehrenbach, *Fire and Blood: A History of Mexico* (New York: Collier, 1973), 112, 203, 247, 256.

53   Elisa Wiener Bravo, "The concentration of land ownership in Latin America: An approach to current problems," International Land Coalition, January 2011, http://www.landcoalition.org/sites/default/files/documents/resources/LA _Regional_ENG_web_11.03.11.pdf; Oxfam, "Divide and Purchase: How land ownership is being concentrated in Colombia," https://www-cdn.oxfam.org /s3fs-public/file_attachments/rr-divide-and-purchase-land-concentration -colombia-270913-en_0.pdf.

54   Nathan Rosenberg and L. E. Birdzell, Jr., *How the West Grew Rich: The Economic Transformation of the Industrial World* (New York: Basic Books, 1986), 24; Edward B. Barbier, *Scarcities and Frontiers: How Economies Have Developed Through Natural Resource Exploitation* (Cambridge: Cambridge University Press, 2011), 407, 605.

55   Thompson and Johnson, *An Introduction to Medieval Europe*, 328.

56   Moore, *Social Origins of Dictatorship and Democracy*, 418.

57   Robert W. July, *A History of the African People* (New York: Scribner, 1970), 468–71.

58   McNeill, *The Pursuit of Power*, 259–60; Ian Buruma, *Inventing Japan: 1853–1964* (New York: Modern Library, 2004), 74.

CHAPTER 11—A LOST GENERATION?

1   Montesquieu, *The Spirit of the Laws*, chap. 5, "Education in a Republican Government," in *Selected Political Writings*, ed. and trans. Melvin Richter (Indianapolis: Hackett, 1990), 139.

2   NBC News/*Wall Street Journal* Survey, August 2014, https://online.wsj.com /public/resources/documents/WSJNBCpoll08062014.pdf.

3   Bruce Stokes, "Public divided on prospects for the next generation," Pew Research Center, June 5, 2017, http://www.pewglobal.org/2017/06/05/2-public -divided-on-prospects-for-the-next-generation/.

4   Raj Chetty et al., "The Fading American Dream: Trends in Absolute Income Mobility since 1940," National Bureau of Economic Research, December 2016, http://www.equality-of-opportunity.org/papers/abs_mobility_paper.pdf; Opportunity Insights, https://opportunityinsights.org/.

5   OECD, "Governments must act to help struggling middle class," April 10, 2019, https://www.oecd.org/newsroom/governments-must-act-to-help-struggling -middle-class.htm.

6   William R. Emmons, Ana H. Kent, and Lowell R. Ricketts, "A Lost Generation? Long-Lasting Wealth Impacts of the Great Recession on Young Families," in *The Demographics of Wealth, 2018 Series: How Education, Race and Birth Year Shape Financial Outcomes*, Center for Household Financial Stability, Federal

Reserve Bank of St. Louis, May 2018, https://www.stlouisfed.org/~/media/files /pdfs/hfs/essays/hfs_essay_2_2018.pdf?la=en.

7 Val Srinivas and Urval Goradia, "The future of wealth in the United States: Mapping trends in generational wealth," Deloitte Insights, November 10, 2015, https://www2.deloitte.com/insights/us/en/industry/investment-management /us-generational-wealth-trends.html.

8 Harry A. Patrinos, "50 Years of 'Returns to Education' studies," March 19, 2015, World Bank Blogs, http://blogs.worldbank.org/education/50-years-returns -education-studies; Peter Orszag, "Why Are So Many College Graduates Driving Taxis?" Bloomberg, June 26, 2013, https://www.bloomberg.com /opinion/articles/2013-06-25/why-are-so-many-college-graduates-driving -taxis-; Josh Mitchell, "College Still Pays Off, but Not for Everyone," *Wall Street Journal*, August 9, 2019, https://www.wsj.com/articles/college-still-pays-off-but -not-for-everyone-11565343000.

9 Emmons et al., "A Lost Generation?"

10 Sue Shellenberger, "The Most Anxious Generation Goes to Work," *Wall Street Journal*, May 9, 2019, https://www.wsj.com/articles/the-most-anxious -generation-goes-to-work-11557418951; Stef W. Kight, "Young Americans are embracing socialism," *Axios*, March 10, 2019, https://www.axios.com/exclusive -poll-young-americans-embracing-socialism-b051907a-87a8-4f61-9e6e -0db75f7edc4a.html.

11 Stokes, "Public divided on prospects for the next generation."

12 "India fares worst among developing countries in World Bank study on upward mobility," *Business Today*, June 5, 2018, https://www.businesstoday.in/current /world/india-developing-countries-world-bank-upward-mobility-study /story/278455.html.

13 Bruce Stokes and Kat Devlin, "Despite Rising Economic Confidence, Japanese See Best Days Behind Them and Say Children Face a Bleak Future," Pew Research Center, November 12, 2018, http://www.pewglobal.org/2018/11/12 /despite-rising-economic-confidence-japanese-see-best-days-behind-them -and-say-children-face-a-bleak-future/.

14 Robert Gordon, *The Rise and Fall of American Growth* (Princeton: Princeton University Press, 2016), 106.

15 Janet Adamy and Paul Overberg, "'Playing Catch-Up in the Game of Life.' Millennials Approach Middle Age in Crisis," *Wall Street Journal*, May 19, 2019, https://www.wsj.com/articles/playing-catch-up-in-the-game-of-life -millennials-approach-middle-age-in-crisis-11558290908.

16 John Daley and Brendan Coates, "Housing Affordability: Re-imagining the Australian Dream," Grattan Institute, March 2018, https://grattan.edu .au/wp-content/uploads/2018/03/901-Housing-affordability.pdf; Leith Van Onselen, "The sad death of Australian home ownership," MacroBusiness, August 7, 2018, https://www.macrobusiness.com.au/2018/08/sad-death -australian-home-ownership/; Nathan Stitt, "Renting for life is becoming Melbourne's new normal—but is the law keeping up?" ABC News, October 17, 2018, https://www.abc.net.au/news/2018-10-18/melbourne-renters-overtaking -home-ownership-are-laws-keeping-up/10375226.

17 Mark Keenan, "Revealed: the rental trap that aspiring homeowners fall into," *Independent*, June 5, 2017, https://www.independent.ie/business/personal

-finance/property-mortgages/revealed-the-rental-trap-that-aspiring
-homeowners-fall-into-35788771.html.

18 Yvonne Roberts, "Millennials are struggling. Is it the fault of the baby
boomers?" *Guardian*, April 29, 2018, https://www.theguardian.com/society
/2018/apr/29/millennials-struggling-is-it-fault-of-baby-boomers-
intergenerational-fairness; Lindsay Judge and Daniel Tomlinson, "Home
improvements: action to address the housing challenges faced by young
people," Resolution Foundation, April 17, 2018, https://www.
resolutionfoundation.org/publications/home-improvements-action-to
-address-the-housing-challenges-faced-by-young-people/.

19 Kamal Ahmed, "Up to a third of millennials 'face renting their entire life,'" BBC,
April 17, 2018, https://www.bbc.com/news/business-43788537.

20 Yuan Yang, "The quiet revolution: China's millennial backlash," *Financial
Times*, April 18, 2018, https://www.ft.com/content/dae2c548-4226-11e8-93cf
-67ac3a6482fd.

21 Andrea Willige, "5 charts which show what is happening to the middle class
around the world," World Economic Forum, January 12, 2017, https://www
.weforum.org/agenda/2017/01/5-charts-which-show-what-is-happening-to
-the-middle-class-around-the-world/.

22 Lisa Boone, "They don't own homes. They don't have kids. Why millennials are
plant addicts," *Los Angeles Times*, July 24, 2018, http://www.latimes.com/home
/la-hm-millennials-plant-parents-20180724-story.html.

23 Ryan Dezember and Laura Kusisto, "House Money: Wall Street Is Raising More
Cash Than Ever for Its Rental-Home Gambit," *Wall Street Journal*, July 9, 2018,
https://www.wsj.com/articles/house-money-wall-street-is-raising-more-cash
-than-ever-for-its-rental-home-gambit-1531128600.

24 Chris Salviati, "Student Debt and Millennial Homeownership," Apartment List,
January 25, 2018, https://www.apartmentlist.com/rentonomics/student-debt
-millennial-homeownership/; Valerie Bauerlein, "American Suburbs Swell Again
as a New Generation Escapes the City," *Wall Street Journal*, July 1, 2019, https://
www.wsj.com/articles/american-suburbs-swell-again-as-a-new-generation
-escapes-the-city-11561992889?mod=hp_lead_pos8; "5 Millennial Real Estate
Trends in 2019," *Realtor Magazine*, November 25, 2018, https://magazine.
realtor/daily-news/2018/11/29/5-millennial-real-estate-trends-in-2019; National
Association of Realtors, *Profile of Home Buyers and Sellers, 2016*, https://www
.nar.realtor/sites/default/files/reports/2016/2016-profile-of-home-buyers-and
-sellers-10-31-2016.pdf; Wendell Cox, "Suburban Nations: Canada, Australia
and the United States," *New Geography*, December 30, 2016, http://www
.newgeography.com/content/005495-suburban-nations-canada-australia-and
-united-states; Kris Hudson, "Generation Y Prefers Suburban Home Over City
Condo," *Wall Street Journal*, January 21, 2015, https://www.wsj.com/articles
/millennials-prefer-single-family-homes-in-the-suburbs-1421896797.

25 Dave Merrill and Lauren Leatherby, "Here's How America Uses Its Land,"
Bloomberg, July 31, 2018, https://www.bloomberg.com/graphics/2018-us
-land-use/; Wendell Cox, "Tearing Down American Dream Boundaries: An
Imperative," *New Geography*, November 26, 2016, http://www.newgeography.
com/content/005461-removing-american-dream-boundaries-an-imperative;

Carey L. Biron, "In U.S. first, Minneapolis rethinks housing density to make homes cheaper," Reuters, April 8, 2019,https://www.reuters.com/article/us-usa -housing-cities/in-us-first-minneapolis-rethinks-housing-density-to-make -homes-cheaper-idUSKCN1RK1DX; Leith van Onselen, "UK Moves to Reform Housing Disaster," *New Geography*, September 24, 2011, http://www .newgeography.com/content/002458-uk-moves-reform-planning-disaster; Wendell Cox, "The Cost of Smart Growth Revisited: A 40 Year Perspective," *New Geography*, July 7, 2011, http://www.newgeography.com/content/002324 -the-costs-smart-growth-revisited-a-40-year-perspective; Wendell Cox, "New Index Estimates New House Cost Impact of Land Regulation," *New Geography*, November 1, 2010, http://www.newgeography.com/content/001841-new-index -estimates-new-house-cost-impact-land-regulation.

26 Ross Kendall and Peter Tulip, "The Effect of Zoning on Housing Prices," Research Discussion Paper 2018-03 (March 2018), Economic Research Department, Reserve Bank of Australia, https://www.rba.gov.au/publications /rdp/2018/pdf/rdp2018-03.pdf.

27 Data from Wendell Cox, and from Estimated Urban Land Area: Selected Nations, Demographia, http://www.demographia.com/db-intlualand.htm.

28 James Heartfield, *Green Capitalism: Manufacturing Scarcity in an Age of Abundance* (London: Mute, 2008), 45–47.

29 Alexandra Stevenson and Jin Wu, "Tiny Apartments and Punishing Work Hours: The Economic Roots of Hong Kong's Protests," *New York Times*, July 22, 2019, https://www.nytimes.com/interactive/2019/07/22/world/asia/hong-kong -housing-inequality.html; Benjamin Haas, "My week in Lucky House: the horror of Hong Kong's coffin homes," *Guardian*, August 28, 2017, https://www .theguardian.com/world/2017/aug/29/hong-kong-coffin-homes-horror-my -week.

30 Ryan Kilpatrick, "Feudalism, not overpopulation or land shortage, is to blame for Hong Kong's housing problems," *Hong Kong Free Press*, June 2, 2018, https:// www.hongkongfp.com/2018/06/02/feudalism-not-overpopulation-land -shortage-blame-hong-kongs-housing-problems/.

31 Ben Bland, "Pressure to Spread the Wealth," *Financial Times*, May 11, 2018; https://www.nytimes.com/interactive/2019/07/22/world/asia/hong-kong -housing-inequality.html.

32 Bill Emmott, *The Sun Also Sets: The Limits to Japan's Economic Power* (New York: Times Books, 1989), 48–49, 79.

33 Emmons et al., "The Demographics of Wealth: How Education, Race and Birth Year Shape Financial Outcomes."

34 Edward N. Wolff, "The Asset Price Meltdown and the Wealth of the Middle Class," National Bureau of Economic Research, November 2012, http://www .nber.org/papers/w18559.pdf?new_window=1; American Community Survey data from Wendell Cox, www.demographia.com; Jonathan Eggleston and Donald Hays, "Gaps in the Wealth of Americans by Household Type," U.S. Census Bureau, August 2, 2019, https://www.census.gov/library/stories/2019 /08/gaps-in-wealth-americans-by-household-type.html.

35 Thomas Piketty, *Capital in the Twenty-First Century*, trans. Arthur Goldhammer (Cambridge, Mass.: Belknap/Harvard, 2014), 107, 538–43.

36 Gillian B. White, "Millennials Who Are Thriving Financially Have One Thing in Common," *Atlantic*, July 15, 2015, https://www.theatlantic.com/business /archive/2015/07/millennials-with-rich-parents/398501/.

37 Wojciech Kopczuk and Joseph P. Lupton, "To Leave or Not to Leave: The Distribution of Bequest Motives," National Bureau of Economic Research, November 2005, https://www.nber.org/papers/w11767.pdf; Suzanne Woolley, "Rich Kids Are Counting On Inheritance to Pay for Retirement," Bloomberg, June 7, 2018, https://www.bloomberg.com/news/articles/2018-06-07/rich-kids -are-counting-on-inheritance-to-pay-for-retirement.

38 Claire Thompson, "Millennial medium chill: What the screwed generation can teach us about happiness," *Grist*, April 30, 2013, https://grist.org/living /millennial-medium-chill/; Lisa Hymas, "Say it loud—I'm childfree and I'm proud," *Grist*, March 31, 2010, https://grist.org/article/2010-03-30-gink -manifesto-say-it-loud-im-childfree-and-im-proud/.

39 Dezember and Kusisto, "House Money: Wall Street Is Raising More Cash Than Ever for Its Rental-Home Gambit"; Piketty, *Capital in the Twenty-First Century*, 534–37.

40 Gaspard Koenig, "We Are All Digital Serfs But the Time is Ripe for Revolution," *Irish Examiner*, July 24, 2018, https://www.irishexaminer.com/ breakingnews/views/analysis/we-are-all-digital-serfs-but-the-time-is-ripe -for-revolution-857216.html.

CHAPTER 12—CULTURE AND CAPITALISM

1 Pierre Riché, *Daily Life in the World of Charlemagne*, trans. Jo Ann McNamara (Philadelphia: University of Pennsylvania Press, 1978), 133.

2 David S. G. Goodman, *Class in Contemporary China* (Cambridge: Polity Press, 2014), 86, 89.

3 Fernand Braudel, *The Perspective of the World*, vol. 3 of *Civilization and Capitalism, 15th–18th Century*, trans. Sian Reynolds (New York: Harper & Row, 1984), 205.

4 Scott Kerwin, "Are the wealthiest Americans Republicans, or are they Democrats?" *Quora*, February 7, 2017, https://www.quora.com/Are-the -wealthiest-Americans-Republicans-or-Democrats; Greg Ferenstein, "How Silicon Valley Is Overhauling the Democratic Party (in 11 charts)," *Medium*, November 11, 2015, https://medium.com/the-ferenstein-wire/what-the -democratic-party-will-look-like-when-silicon-valley-takes-over-in-9-charts -904cd0cd6feb; Katelyn Carelle, "90 percent of political donations from Google-related companies go to Democrats: Study," *Washington Examiner*, September 7, 2018, https://www.washingtonexaminer.com/policy/technology /90-percent-of-political-donations-from-google-related-companies-go-to -democrats-study; John Hinderaker, "It's Official: Google Is a Democratic Party Front," *Power Line*, September 12, 2018, https://www.powerlineblog.com /archives/2018/09/its-official-google-is-a-democratic-party-front.php; Cecilia Kang and Juliet Eilperin, "Why Silicon Valley is the new revolving door for Obama staffers," *Washington Post*, February 28, 2015, https://www .washingtonpost.com/business/economy/as-obama-nears-close-of-his-tenure -commitment-to-silicon-valley-is-clear/2015/02/27/3bee8088-bc8e-11e4-bdfa

-b8e8f594e6ee_story.html?utm_term=.bb4a8855a73a; Irina Ivanova, "Wall Street's campaign contributions are flowing mostly to Democrats," CBS News, October 31, 2018, https://www.cbsnews.com/news/wall-street-political -campaign-contibutions-flowing-mostly-to-democratic-candidates-for -congress/.

5 Thomas Piketty, "Brahmin Left vs Merchant Right: Rising Inequality and the Changing Structure of Political Conflict (Evidence from France, Britain and the US, 1948–2017)," World Inequality Database, March 2018, http://piketty.pse .ens.fr/files/Piketty2018.pdf.

6 Alvin Toffler, *Future Shock* (New York: Random House, 1970), 452.

7 John Benjamin, "Business Class," *New Republic*, May 14, 2018, https:// newrepublic.com/article/148368/ideology-business-school; John Gray, "The problem of hyper-liberalism," *TLS*, March 30, 2018, https://www.the-tls.co.uk /articles/public/john-gray-hyper-liberalism-liberty/; Angelo Codevilla, "America's Ruling Class," *American Spectator*, July 16, 2010, https://spectator .org/americas-ruling-class/; Jeremy Au and Rafael Rivera, "HBS Election Poll," *Harbus*, October 18, 2016, http://www.harbus.org/2016/hbs-election-poll/.

8 Nick Dedeke, "Is Corporate Vigilantism a Threat to Democracy?" *Real Clear Politics*, May 4, 2019, https://www.realclearpolitics.com/articles/2019/05/04 /is_corporate_vigilantism_a_threat_to_democracy_140218.html; Harlan Loeb, "CEO Activism: Taking Risks to Build Trust," Edelman, July 24, 2018, https:// www.edelman.com/post/ceo-activism-taking-risks-to-build-trust; Jill Priluck, "America's corporate activism: the rise of the CEO as social justice warrior," *Guardian*, July 2, 2019, https://www.theguardian.com/commentisfree/2019 /jul/01/americas-corporate-activism-the-rise-of-the-ceo-as-social-justice -warrior.

9 Anna Kambhampaty, "Selling social movements: 5 brands using politics in their ad campaigns—for better and for worse," CNBC, August 11, 2017, https:// www.cnbc.com/2017/08/11/selling-social-movements-five-brands-using -politics-in-their-ads.html; Toby Young, "The woke corporation: how campus madness entered the workplace," *Spectator*, March 7, 2019, https://spectator. us/woke-corporation-campus-madness/; Dave Gershgorn, "Microsoft staff are openly questioning the value of diversity," *Quartz*, April 19, 2019, https:// qz.com/1598345/microsoft-staff-are-openly-questioning-the-value-of-diversity /; Nikasha Tiku, "Survey Finds Conservatives Feel Out of Place in Silicon Valley," *Wired*, February 2, 2018, https://www.wired.com/story/survey-finds -conservatives-feel-out-of-place-in-silicon-valley/; Alan Murray, "America's CEOs Seek a New Purpose for the Corporation," *Fortune*, August 19, 2019, https://fortune.com/longform/business-roundtable-ceos-corporations -purpose/.

10 Paul Caron, "Lawyer Presidential Campaign Contributions: 97% ro Clinton, 3% to Trump," TaxProf Blog, January 20, 2017, http://taxprof.typepad.com /taxprof_blog/2017/01/lawyer-presidential-campaign-contributions-97-to -clinton-3-to-trump.html; Andy Kiersz and Hunter Walker, "These Charts Show the Political Bias of Workers in Each Profession," *Business Insider*, November 3, 2014, https://amp.businessinsider.com/charts-show-the-political -bias-of-each-profession-2014-11?__twitter_impression=true.

11 Fred Siegel, *The Revolt Against the Masses: How Liberalism Has Undermined the Middle Class* (New York: Encounter, 2015), xv.

12 Dennis Meadows et al., *Limits to Growth* (New York: Signet, 1972), 120–21, 170–71.

13 Spencer Walrath, "Rockefellers Use New Front Group to Advance Climate Liability Campaign," Energy In Depth, September 28, 2018, https://eidclimate. org/rockefellers-use-new-front-group-to-advance-climate-liability-campaign/; Rupert Darwall, "Democrats' dark money and the climate industrial complex," *Washington Examiner*, May 18, 2018, https://www.washingtonexaminer.com /opinion/op-eds/democrats-dark-money-and-the-climate-industrial-complex; David Friedman and Jennifer Hernandez, *California Environmental Quality Act, Greenhouse Gas Regulation, and Climate Change*, Chapman University, 2015, https://www.chapman.edu/wilkinson/_files/ghg-fn.pdf; David Callahan, *Fortunes of Change: The Rise of the Liberal Rich and the Remaking of America* (New York: Wiley, 2010), 57–82; Rupert Darwall, "A Veneer of Certainty Stoking Climate Alarm," Competitive Enterprise Institute, November 27, 2017, https://cei.org/content/stoking-climate-action.

14 Anand Giridharadas, *Winners Take All: The Elite Charade of Changing the World* (New York: Knopf, 2018), 7.

15 James Heartfield, *Green Capitalism: Manufacturing Scarcity in an Age of Abundance* (London: Mute, 2008), 21–22.

16 Ibid., 10, 28; Michael Wirth, "The Tragic Cost of Energy Poverty," *Real Clear Politics*, June 26, 2018, https://www.realclearpolitics.com/articles/2018/06/26 /the_tragic_cost_of_energy_poverty_137345.html.

17 Max Roser and Esteban Ortiz-Ospina, "Literacy," Our World in Data, https:// ourworldindata.org/literacy.

18 Benjamin Franklin, *The Autobiography of Benjamin Franklin* (New Haven: Yale University Press, 1964), 130–31.

19 Siegel, *The Revolt Against the Masses*, 112–15.

20 Nina Metz, "Hollywood's sweeping generalizations about 'Mainstream America' are getting it wrong," *Chicago Tribune*, May 24, 2018, https://www .chicagotribune.com/entertainment/tv/ct-ent-inclusion-minorities-0529-story .html; Jason Guerrasio, "The last 16 best-picture Oscar winners show how out of touch Hollywood's biggest night is with general audiences," *Business Insider*, February 25, 2019, https://www.businessinsider.com/best-picture-oscar- winners-compared-to-yearly-box-office-winners-2018-3; Raquel Laneri, "The Oscars' new 'popular film' award proves it's out of touch and elitist," *New York Post*, August 9, 2018, https://nypost.com/2018/08/09/the-oscars-new-popular -film-award-proves-its-out-of-touch-and-elitist/; Chris Lee, "Why the Academy Keeps Giving Oscars to Movies No One Sees," *Fortune*, February 29, 2016, http://fortune.com/2016/02/29/spotlight-oscars-movies-box-office/.

21 The Numbers, "All Time Worldwide Box Office for Super Hero Movies," https://www.the-numbers.com/box-office-records/worldwide/all-movies /creative-types/super-hero; Erin Free, "The Age of Heroes: Why Are Superhero Movies So Popular?" *Film Ink*, March 19, 2016, https://www.filmink.com.au /the-age-of-heroes-why-are-superhero-movies-so-popular/; Dave Gonzales, "Hollywood loves white guys, but its real superhero audience will surprise you,"

Guardian, July 29, 2014, https://www.theguardian.com/commentisfree/2014/jul/29/hollywood-superhero-audience-box-office-comic-con.

22 Bentley University, "The PreparedU Project: An In-Depth Look at Millennial Preparedness for Today's Workforce," 2014, https://www.slideshare.net/BentleyU/prepared-u-project-on-millennial-preparedness; Robert Schooley, "Why Are Soft Skills Missing in Today's Applicants?" Murray State University, 2017, https://digitalcommons.murraystate.edu/cgi/viewcontent.cgi?referer=https://www.google.com/&httpsredir=1&article=1038&context=etd.

23 Jean M. Twenge, "Have Smartphones Destroyed a Generation?" *Atlantic*, September 2017, https://www.theatlantic.com/magazine/archive/2017/09/has-the-smartphone-destroyed-a-generation/534198/; Sara G. Miller, "Too Much Social Media Use Linked to Feelings of Isolation," Live Science, March 6, 2017, http://www.livescience.com/58121-social-media-use-perceived-isolation.html.

24 Cision, "Are Declining Attention Spans Killing Your Content Marketing Strategy?" January 22, 2018, https://www.cision.com/us/2018/01/declining-attention-killing-content-marketing-strategy/.

25 Glenn Harlan Reynolds, "Social media firms want us addicted to approval. So much for Wifi making us smarter," *USA Today*, April 1, 2018, https://www.usatoday.com/story/opinion/2018/04/01/social-media-business-model-addicts-us-approval-not-information-column/476719002/.

26 "These Tech Insiders Are Shielding Their Children From the Technology They Work With," Science Alert, March 31, 2018, https://www.sciencealert.com/tech-insiders-are-shielding-their-children-from-the-tech-they-work-with; Tim Hains, "Former Facebook Exec: Social Media Is Ripping Our Social Fabric Apart," *Real Clear Politics*, December 11, 2017, https://www.realclearpolitics.com/video/2017/12/11/fmr_facebook_exec_social_media_is_ripping_our_social_fabric_apart.html.

27 Barbara Tuchman, *A Distant Mirror: The Calamitous 14th Century* (New York: Knopf, 1978), 49–50; Frances and Joseph Gies, *Daily Life in Medieval Times* (New York: Barnes & Noble, 1969), 179; Fernand Braudel, *The Structures of Everyday Life*, vol. 1 of *Civilization and Capitalism, 15th–18th Century*, trans. Sian Reynolds (Berkeley: University of California Press, 1992), 74.

28 Norman F. Cantor, *Medieval History: The Life and Death of a Civilization* (New York: Macmillan, 1963), 111; Michael Grant, *The Fall of the Roman Empire* (New York: Collier, 1990), 150; Katherine Lynch, *Individuals, Families, and Communities in Europe: The Urban Foundations of Western Society* (Cambridge: Cambridge University Press, 2003), 8.

29 James Westfall Thompson and Edgar Nathaniel Johnson, *An Introduction to Medieval Europe* (New York: Norton, 1937), 596; Nathan Rosenberg and L E. Birdzell, Jr., *How the West Got Rich: The Economic Transformation of the Industrial World* (New York: Basic Books, 1987), 140; Steven Ozment, *When Fathers Ruled: Family Life in Reformation Europe* (Cambridge, Mass.: Harvard University Press, 1983), 40–41, 99, 152–53; John Hale, *The Civilization of Europe in the Renaissance* (New York: Harper, 1993), 438–50; Philippe Ariès, *Centuries of Childhood: A Social History of Family Life*, trans. Robert Baldick (New York: Vintage, 1962), 398.

30   Simon Schama, *An Embarrassment of Riches: An Interpretation of Dutch Culture in the Golden Age* (New York: Vintage, 1997), 481–85; Ariès, *Centuries of Childhood*, 351–53.

31   Kay S. Hymowitz, *Marriage and Caste in America* (Chicago: Ivan R. Dee, 2006), 35.

32   Tova Cohen, "Israel has the highest birth rate in the developed world, and that's becoming a problem," *Business Insider*, September 25, 2015, https://www .businessinsider.com/israel-has-the-highest-birth-rate-in-the-developed -world-and-thats-becoming-a-problem-2015-9; Richard V. Reeves, *Dream Hoarders: How the American Upper Middle Class Is Leaving Everyone Else in the Dust, Why That Is a Problem, and What to Do About It* (Washington, D.C.: Brookings Institution Press, 2018), 28.

33   Sarah Knapton, "Soaring house prices reduce number of babies born in England," *Telegraph*, April 12, 2017, https://www.telegraph.co.uk/science/2017 /04/12/soaring-house-prices-reduce-number-babies-born-england/; Sarah O'Grady, "British birth rate at record low and women opt out raising a family," *Express*, November 25, 2017, https://www.express.co.uk/life-style/health /884120/office-national-statistics-ons-united-kingdom-birth-rate-women -family-children.

34   Jennifer A. Holland, "Love, marriage, then the baby carriage? Marriage timing and childbearing in Sweden," *Demographic Research*, vol. 29:11 (August 2013), 275–306, https://www.demographic-research.org/volumes/vol29/11/29-11.pdf; Andrew Cherlin, "Marriage Has Become a Trophy," *Atlantic*, March 20, 2018, https://www.theatlantic.com/family/archive/2018/03/incredible-everlasting -institution-marriage/555320/.

35   Lyman Stone, "The Decline of American Motherhood," *Atlantic*, May 13, 2018, https://www.theatlantic.com/family/archive/2018/05/mothers-day-decline -motherhood/560198/.

36   Claire Cain Miller, "Americans are having fewer babies. They told us why," *New York Times*, July 5, 2018, https://www.nytimes.com/2018/07/05/upshot /americans-are-having-fewer-babies-they-told-us-why.html; Elizabeth Bauer, "What's Next for the Fertility Rate? (Part 2)," *Forbes*, May 19, 2018, https://www .forbes.com/sites/ebauer/2018/05/19/whats-next-for-the-fertility-rate-part -2/#736c4b7a2e72; Dave Baldwin, "It Cost $31,000 More to Raise a Kid Today Than in 1960. Where's all the extra money going?" Fatherly, August 13, 2018, https://www.fatherly.com/love-money/why-cost-raising-kids-skyrocketed -since-1960/; Heidi Steinour, "Baby bust: 5 Charts show how expensive it is to have kids in the US today," *The Conversation*, March 28, 2018, https:// theconversation.com/baby-bust-5-charts-show-how-expensive-it-is-to-have -kids-in-the-us-today-91532; Lauren Alix Brown, "When will America wise up to the truth about why women aren't having children?" *Quartz*, July 7, 2018, https://qz.com/1323241/young-americans-arent-having-children-for-a-variety -of-reasons-beyond-the-economy/.

37   Jacqueline Howard, "The costs of child care around the world," CNN, April 25, 2018, https://www.cnn.com/2018/04/25/health/child-care-parenting -explainer-intl/index.html; Charlie Weston, "Cost of raising a child from birth to college is €100,000," *Independent*, July 17, 2015, https://www.independent.ie

/life/family/cost-of-raising-a-child-from-birth-to-college-is-100000-31383511.html.

38 "Are we facing a future without families?" *Maclean's*, December 4, 2012, https://www.macleans.ca/politics/are-we-facing-a-future-without-families/.

39 Alvin Toffler, *Future Shock* (New York: Random House, 1970), 238–51.

40 Tim Henderson, "Growing Number of People Living Solo Can Pose Challenges," Pew Charitable Trust, September 11, 2014, https://www.pewtrusts.org/en/research-and-analysis/blogs/stateline/2014/09/11/growing-number-of-people-living-solo-can-pose-challenges; Steven Kurutz, "One Is the Quirkiest Number," *New York Times*, February 22, 2012, https://www.nytimes.com/2012/02/23/garden/the-freedom-and-perils-of-living-alone.html; Ashley Fetters, "Living alone and liking it," *Curbed*, June 20, 2018, https://www.curbed.com/2018/6/20/17479740/living-alone-tips-women-advice.

41 He Wei, "The rise of solo living," *China Daily*, July 28, 2017, http://usa.chinadaily.com.cn/china/2017-07/28/content_30286948.htm.

42 "Going it alone: Solo dwellers will account for 40% of Japan's households by 2040, forecast says," *Japan Times*, January 13, 2018, https://www.japantimes.co.jp/news/2018/01/13/national/social-issues/going-alone-solo-dwellers-will-account-40-japans-households-2040-forecast-says/.

43 Norimitsu Onishi, "A Generation in Japan Faces a Lonely Death," *New York Times*, November 30, 2017, https://www.nytimes.com/2017/11/30/world/asia/japan-lonely-deaths-the-end.html.

44 Seymour Martin Lipset and Gabriel Salman Lenz, "Corruption, Culture and Markets," in *Culture Matters*, ed. Lawrence E. Harrison and Samuel P. Harrington (New York: Basic Books, 2001), 119–21.

45 Daniel Bell, *The Coming of Post-Industrial Society* (New York: Basic Books, 1973), 478–80.

46 David Pilling, *Bending Adversity: Japan and the Art of Survival* (New York: Penguin, 2014), 175.

47 Greg Wilford, "Young Japanese people are not having sex," *Independent*, July 8, 2017, https://www.independent.co.uk/news/world/asia/japan-sex-problem-demographic-time-bomb-birth-rates-sex-robots-fertility-crisis-virgins-romance-porn-a7831041.html.

CHAPTER 13—BEYOND THE RING ROAD

1 Li Sun, *Rural Migration and Policy Intervention in China* (Singapore: Palgrave, 2019), 2–4; David S. G. Goodman, *Class in Contemporary China* (Cambridge: Polity Press, 2014), 161–62.

2 "Foxconn admits schoolchildren in China factory worked overnight to build Amazon's Alexa devices, blaming 'lax oversight' by local management," *South China Morning Post*, August 10, 2019, https://www.scmp.com/news/china/article/3022237/foxconn-admits-schoolchildren-china-factory-worked-overnight-build.

3 Li Sun, *Rural Migration and Policy Intervention in China*, 3–4; Goodman, *Class in Contemporary China*, 124; Jamie Condliffe, "Foxconn Is Under Scrutiny for Worker Conditions. It's Not the First Time," *New York Times*, June 11, 2018,

https://www.nytimes.com/2018/06/11/business/dealbook/foxconn-worker
-conditions.html.

4   Alemayedu Bishaw and Kirby G. Posey, "A Comparison of Rural and Urban
America: Household Income and Poverty," U.S. Census Bureau, December 8,
2016, https://www.census.gov/newsroom/blogs/random-samplings/2016/12/a
_comparison_of_rura.html; Goodman, *Class in Contemporary China*, 140; Nan
Chen, "China's Missing Middle Class," Foreign Policy in Focus, May 24, 2012,
https://fpif.org/chinas_missing_middle_class/.

5   "Shanghai to cap population at 25 million to battle 'big city disease,'" NBC
News, December 26, 2017, https://www.nbcnews.com/news/world/shanghai
-cap-population-25-million-battle-big-city-disease-n832591; Eva Dou and
Dominique Fong, "Homeward Bound: Beijing Boots Migrant Workers to Trim
Its Population," *Wall Street Journal*, November 29, 2017, https://www.wsj.com/
articles/beijing-evictions-of-migrant-workers-sparks-outrage-1511962464;
Salvatore Babones, "China's Middle Class Is Pulling Up the Ladder Behind
Itself," *Foreign Policy*, February 1, 2018, https://foreignpolicy.com/2018/02/01
/chinas-middle-class-is-pulling-up-the-ladder-behind-itself/; Eva Dou, "Rare
Protests in Beijing Condemn Forced Evictions," *Wall Street Journal*, December
10, 2017, https://www.wsj.com/articles/rare-protests-in-beijing-condemn
-forced-evictions-1512915082; Viola Zhou and Zhuang Pinghui, "Migrant
workers take to streets of Beijing to protest against forced evictions," *South
China Morning Post*, December 10, 2017, https://www.scmp.com/news/china
/policies-politics/article/2123714/migrant-workers-take-streets-beijing
-protest-against.

6   Goodman, *Class in Contemporary China*, 6, 35, 42, 98.

7   John Sudworth, "Counting the cost of China's left-behind children," BBC, April
12, 2016, https://www.bbc.com/news/world-asia-china-35994481; Lijia Zhang,
"The Orphans of China's Economic Miracle," *New York Times*, March 27, 2018,
https://www.nytimes.com/2018/03/27/opinion/china-left-behind-children
.html?ribbon-ad-idx=2&rref=opinion.

8   Joe Zhang, "As China grows, equal opportunity and social mobility are fast
becoming a cruel life," *South China Morning Post*, July 7, 2017, http://www
.scmp.com/comment/insight-opinion/article/2101654/china-grows-equal
-opportunity-and-social-mobility-are-fast.

9   Nan Chen, "China's Missing Middle Class."

10 Loukas Karabarbounis and Brent Neiman, "The Global Decline of the Labor
Share," National Bureau of Economic Research, June 2013, http://www.nber
.org/papers/w19136.pdf.

11 Norman F. Cantor, *Medieval History: The Life and Death of a Civilization*
(New York: Macmillan, 1963), 33; Michael Grant, *The Fall of the Roman
Empire* (New York: Collier, 1990), 59–60, 72, 79.

12 Marc Bloch, *Feudal Society*, trans. L. A. Manyon (London: Routledge, 1961),
265.

13 Mark Cartwright, "Serf," *Ancient History Encyclopedia*, December 4, 2018,
https://www.ancient.eu/Serf/.

14 Ibid.

15 Edward Barbier, *Scarcities and Frontiers: How Economies Have Developed Through Natural Resource Exploitation* (Cambridge: Cambridge University Press, 2011), 84–91, 156, 176; Jeffrey A. Winters, *Oligarchy* (Cambridge: Cambridge University Press, 2011), 28–29.

16 Fernand Braudel, *The Structures of Everyday Life*, vol. 1 of *Civilization and Capitalism* (New York: Harper & Row, 1982), 187, 283–84.

17 Ernst Nolte, *Three Faces of Fascism*, trans. Leila Vennewitz (New York: New American Library, 1969), 374, 365–74.

18 Mao Tse-tung, *The Chinese Revolution and the Chinese Communist Party*, December 1939, https://www.marxists.org/reference/archive/mao/selected -works/volume-2/mswv2_23.htm; Andro Linklater, *Owning the Earth: The Transforming History of Land Ownership* (New York: Bloomsbury USA, 2013), 152–53; Barbier, *Scarcity and Frontiers*, 230.

19 Phillip A. M. Taylor, *The Industrial Revolution in Britain: Triumph or Disaster?* (Boston: D. C. Heath, 1958), 40; E. J. Hobsbawm, *The Age of Revolution* (New York: New American Library, 1962), 64.

20 Arnold Toynbee, *The Industrial Revolution* (Boston: Beacon, 1956), 25–26, 30–31, 41, 60.

21 Alexis de Tocqueville, "On the Middle Class and the People," in *Tocqueville and Beaumont on Social Reform*, ed. and trans. Seymour Drescher (New York: Harper, 1968), 175–77.

22 Alexis de Tocqueville, "Letters on Conditions in France," in *Tocqueville and Beaumont on Social Reform*, 192.

23 Harvey Mitchell and Peter N. Stearns, *Workers and Protests: The European Labor Movement, the Working Classes, and the Origins of Social Democracy* (Ithaca, N.Y.: Peacock, 1971), 25–27; Asa Briggs, *Victorian People: A Reassessment of Persons and Themes, 1851–1867* (Chicago: University of Chicago Press, 1955), 2.

24 John Lewis Gaddis, *The Cold War: A New History* (New York: Penguin, 2006), 86; Isaiah Berlin, *Karl Marx: His Life and Environment* (London: Oxford University Press, 1996), 224.

25 Charles A. Beard and Mary R. Beard, *The Rise of American Civilization* (New York: Macmillan, 1930), vol. 1: 341–44.

26 Arthur M. Schlesinger, *The Age of Jackson* (New York: Book Find Club, 1945), 57–58, 339, 346, 353.

27 Beard, *The Rise of American Civilization*, vol. 2: 383–84.

28 William LeFevre, "The Treaty of Detroit," Seeking Michigan, August 23, 2011, http://seekingmichigan.org/look/2011/08/23/treaty-of-detroit.

29 Abigail Thernstrom and Stephan Thernstrom, "Black Progress: How far we've come, and how far we have to go," Brookings, March 1, 1998, https://www .brookings.edu/articles/black-progress-how-far-weve-come-and-how-far-we -have-to-go/.

30 John Kenneth Galbraith, *The Affluent Society* (New York: Mentor, 1958), 75.

31 John Kenneth Galbraith, *The New Industrial State* (Princeton: Princeton University Press, 2007), 363, 441.

32   Max Green, *Epitaph for American Labor: How Union Leaders Lost Touch with America* (Washington: AEI, 1996), 19.

33   Matthew Stewart, "The 9.9 Percent Is the New American Aristocracy," *Atlantic*, June 2018, https://www.theatlantic.com/magazine/archive/2018/06/the-birth-of-a-new-american-aristocracy/559130/; Timothy Taylor, "Unions in Decline: Some International Comparisons," Conversable Economist, June 20, 2017, http://conversableeconomist.blogspot.com/2017/06/unions-in-decline-some-international.html.

34   David E. Noble, *Forces of Production: A Social History of Industrial Automation* (New York: Knopf, 1984), 249; Robert Gordon, *The Rise and Fall of American Growth* (Princeton: Princeton University Press, 2016), 499; Economic Policy Institute, "The growing trade deficit with China has led to a loss of 3.4 million U.S. jobs between 2001 and 2017," October 23, 2018, https://www.epi.org/press/the-growing-trade-deficit-with-china-has-led-to-a-loss-of-3-4-million-u-s-jobs-between-2001-and-2017/.

35   David Goodhart, *The Road to Somewhere: The New Tribes Shaping British Politics* (London: Penguin, 2017), 151.

36   Sherry Linkon and John Russo, "Economic Nationalism and the Half-Life of Deindustrialization," *Working-Class Perspectives*, October 30, 2017, https://workingclassstudies.wordpress.com/2017/10/30/economic-nationalism-and-the-half-life-of-deindustrialization/.

37   Alan B. Krueger, "The Rise and Consequences of Inequality," Council of Economic Advisors, January 12, 2012, https://milescorak.files.wordpress.com/2012/01/speech-2012_01_12_final_web-1.pdf.

38   Fatih Guvenen et al., "Lifetime Incomes in the United States Over Six Decades," National Bureau of Economic Research, April 2017, https://www.nber.org/papers/w23371.pdf.

39   Phillip Inman, "Social mobility in richest countries 'has stalled since 1990,'" *Guardian*, June 15, 2018, https://www.theguardian.com/society/2018/jun/15/social-mobility-in-richest-countries-has-stalled-since-1990s; Miles Corak, "Inequality from Generation to Generation: The United States in Comparison," in *The Economics of Inequality, Poverty, and Discrimination in the 21st Century*, ed. Robert Rycroft (Santa Barbara: ABC-CLIO, 2013); Metin Feyyaz, "Turkey's Defiant Working Class: From Offense to Defense," *International Viewpoint*, November 22, 2018, http://www.internationalviewpoint.org/spip.php?article5795.

40   Alan Berube, "Middle-skilled workers still making up for lost ground on earnings," Brookings, October 19, 2016, https://www.brookings.edu/blog/the-avenue/2016/10/19/middle-skilled-workers-still-making-up-for-lost-ground-on-earnings/; Tavia Grant, "The continuing decline of the 'middle-skill' worker," *Globe and Mail*, June 3, 2013, https://www.theglobeandmail.com/report-on-business/economy/jobs/the-continuing-decline-of-the-middle-skill-worker/article12303799/.

41   Enrique Fernandez-Macias, "Job Polarisation in Europe: Are Mid-Skilled Jobs Disappearing?" Social Europe, July 30, 2015, https://www.socialeurope.eu/job-polarisation-in-europe-are-mid-skilled-jobs-disappearing; Margo Hoftijzer and Lucas Gortazar, *Skills and Europe's Labor Market*, World Bank

Report on the European Union, World Bank Group, 2018, http://pubdocs. worldbank.org/en/115971529687983521/EU-GU-Skills-and-Labor-Markets -final-5-29-2018.pdf; Christophe Guilluy, *Twilight of the Elites: Prosperity, the Periphery, and the Future of France*, trans. Malcolm Debevoise (New Haven: Yale University Press, 2019), 14.

42 Goodhart, *The Road to Somewhere*, 151.

43 Rajan Menon, "The United States Has a National-Security Problem—and It's Not What You Think," *Nation*, July 16, 2018, https://www.thenation.com/article /united-states-national-security-problem-not-think/; Guilluy, *Twilight of the Elites*, 56, 71.

44 Neha Thirani Bagri, "In the great robot job takeover, women are less likely to suffer than men," *Quartz*, March 28, 2017, https://qz.com/943978/in-the-great -robot-job-takeover-women-are-less-likely-to-suffer-than-men-a- pricewaterhousecoopers-study-suggests/; Natalie Kitroeff, "Robots could replace 1.7 million American truckers in the next decade," *Los Angeles Times*, September 25, 2016, http://www.latimes.com/projects/la-fi-automated-trucks -labor-20160924/.

45 Kourtney Adams, "Bureau of Labor Statistics projects major loss of middle -class jobs by 2024," WIFR, March 22, 2018, http://www.wifr.com/content /news/Bureau-of-Labor-Statistics-projects-the-loss-of-tens-of-thousands-of -middle-class-jobs-by-2024-477101543.html.

CHAPTER 14—THE FUTURE OF THE WORKING CLASS

1 "Apple says illegal student labor discovered at iPhone X plant," Reuters, November 22, 2107, https://uk.reuters.com/article/us-apple-foxconn-labour /apple-says-illegal-student-labor-discovered-at-iphone-x-plant- idUKKBN1DM1LA; Neil Irwin, "To Understand Rising Inequality, Consider the Janitors at Two Top Companies, Then and Now," *New York Times*, September 3, 2017, https://www.nytimes.com/2017/09/03/upshot/to-understand -rising-inequality-consider-the-janitors-at-two-top-companies-then-and-now. html.

2 Bryan Menegus, "Elon Musk Responds to Claims of Low Pay, Injuries, and Anti-Union Policies at Tesla Plant," Gizmodo, September 2, 2017, https:// gizmodo.com/elon-musk-responds-to-claims-of-low-pay-injuries-and-a -1792190512; "Analysis of Tesla Injury Rates: 2014 to 2017," Work Safe, May 24, 2017, https://worksafe.typepad.com/files/worksafe_tesla5_24.pdf; Will Evans and Alyssa Jeong Perry, "Tesla says its factory is safer. But it left injuries off the books," *Mercury News*, https://www.mercurynews.com/2018/06/01/elon-musk -and-unions-congressman-asks-tesla-ceo-to-stop-threats/.

3 Josh Eidelson, "Tesla Workers Claim Racial Bias and Abuse at Electric Car Factory," Bloomberg, April 12, 2018, https://www.bloomberg.com/news/ features/2018-04-12/tesla-workers-claim-racial-bias-and-abuse-at-electric-car -factory; Caroline O'Donavon, "At Tesla's Factory, Building the Car of the Future Has Painful and Permanent Consequences for Some Workers," *Buzzfeed*, February 4, 2018, https://www.buzzfeed.com/carolineodonovan /tesla-fremont-factory-injuries?utm_term=.jf1qexXmj#.iajjZb6x8; Julie Carrie Wong, "Tesla factory workers reveal pain, injury and stress: 'Everything feels like the future but us,'" *Guardian*, May 18, 2017, https://www.theguardian.com

/technology/2017/may/18/tesla-workers-factory-conditions-elon-musk;
https://www.revealnews.org/article/tesla-says-its-factory-is-safer-but-it-left
-injuries-off-the-books/.

4 Macrotrends, "Amazon: Number of Employees 2006–2019," https://www
.macrotrends.net/stocks/charts/AMZN/amazon/number-of-employees.

5 Stacy Mitchell and Olivia LaVecchia, "Report: Amazon's Stranglehold: How
the Company's Tightening Grip on the Economy Is Stifling Competition,
Eroding Jobs, and Threatening Communities," Institute for Local Self-Reliance,
November 29, 2016, https://ilsr.org/amazon-stranglehold/; "What Amazon
does to wages," *Economist*, January 20, 2018, https://www.economist.com
/united-states/2018/01/20/what-amazon-does-to-wages; Luke Barnes, "A large
number of Amazon workers rely on food stamps for assistance," *Think Progress*,
April 20, 2018, https://thinkprogress.org/amazon-workers-rely-on-food-stamps
-24ab86dd6495/; Joseph Pisani, "Amazon's $15 an hour a win? Not so, some
workers say," AP News, October 4, 2018, https://www.apnews.com/8e60d4d9e1
b74171a34d3196081910d1.

6 Julia Glum, "The Median Amazon Employee's Salary Is $28,000. Jeff Bezos
Makes More Than That in 10 Seconds," *Money*, May 2, 2018, http://time.com
/money/5262923/amazon-employee-median-salary-jeff-bezos/.

7 Chris Pollard, "Rushed Amazon warehouse staff pee into bottles as they're
afraid of 'time-wasting,'" *Sun*, April 15, 2018, https://www.thesun.co.uk/news
/6055021/rushed-amazon-warehouse-staff-time-wasting/; Ceylan Yeginsu, "If
Workers Slack Off, the Wristband Will Know. (And Amazon Has a Patent for
It)," *New York Times*, February 1, 2018, https://www.nytimes.com/2018/02/01
/technology/amazon-wristband-tracking-privacy.html?smid=tw
-nytimesworld&smtyp=cur; Olivia Solon, "Amazon patents wristband that
tracks warehouse workers' movements," *Guardian*, February 1, 2018, https://
www.theguardian.com/technology/2018/jan/31/amazon-warehouse
-wristband-tracking; Alan Boyle, "Amazon wins a pair of patents for wireless
wristbands that track warehouse workers," *Geek Wire*, January 30, 2018, https://
www.geekwire.com/2018/amazon-wins-patents-wireless-wristbands-track
-warehouse-workers/; Natasha Bernal, "Amazon's warehouse computer
system tracked and fired hundreds of workers," *Telegraph*, April 26, 2019,
https://www.telegraph.co.uk/technology/2019/04/26/amazons-warehouse
-computer-system-tracked-fired-hundreds-workers/.

8 David Goldman, "Why Apple will never bring manufacturing jobs back to the
U.S.," CNN Business, October 17, 2012, https://money.cnn.com/2012/10/17
/technology/apple-china-jobs/; "China tech factory conditions fuel suicides,"
France 24, November 14, 2018, https://www.france24.com/en/20181114-china
-tech-factory-conditions-fuel-suicides-study.

9 Guy Standing, "Meet the precariat, the new global class fuelling the rise of
populism," World Economic Forum, November 9, 2016, https://www.weforum
.org/agenda/2016/11/precariat-global-class-rise-of-populism/.

10 Sarah Jaffe, "The New Working Class," *New Republic*, February 22, 2018, https://
newrepublic.com/article/146904/new-working-class; U.S. Bureau of Labor
Statistics, "Employment by major industry sector," https://www.bls.gov/emp
/tables/employment-by-major-industry-sector.htm; U.S. Bureau of Labor

Statistics, "Home Health Aides and Personal Care Aides," https://www.bls.gov /ooh/healthcare/home-health-aides-and-personal-care-aides.htm.

11 Bradley Hardy and James P. Ziliak, "Decomposing Trends in Income Volatility: The 'Wide Ride' at the Top and Bottom," *Economic Inquiry*, January 2014, http://www.bradleyhardy.com/wp-content/uploads/2016/09/Hardy-Ziliak -2014-Final-EI.pdf.

12 Tavia Grant, "The continuing decline of the 'middle-skill' worker," *Globe and Mail*, June 3, 2013, https://www.theglobeandmail.com/report-on-business /economy/jobs/the-continuing-decline-of-the-middle-skill-worker/article 12303799/.

13 "Independent Work: Choice, Necessity, and the Gig Economy," McKinsey & Company, October 2016, https://www.mckinsey.com/~/media/McKinsey /Featured%20Insights/Employment%20and%20Growth/Independent%20 work%20Choice%20necessity%20and%20the%20gig%20economy/Independent -Work-Choice-necessity-and-the-gig-economy-Executive-Summary.ashx.

14 Annie Lowrey, "What the Gig Economy Looks Like Around the World," *Atlantic*, April 13, 2017, https://www.theatlantic.com/business/archive/2017/04 /gig-economy-global/522954/.

15 Alana Samuels, "The Mystery of Why Japanese People Are Having So Few Babies," *Atlantic*, July 20, 2017, https://www.theatlantic.com/business/archive /2017/07/japan-mystery-low-birth-rate/534291/.

16 Alison Griswold, "People are joining the gig economy because of a powerful myth," *Quartz*, May 31, 2018, https://qz.com/1293741/people-join-the-gig -economy-to-be-their-own-boss-but-the-algorithm-is-really-in-charge.

17 Nathan Heller, "Is the Gig Economy Working?" *New Yorker*, May 8, 2017, https://www.newyorker.com/magazine/2017/05/15/is-the-gig-economy -working; Jeff Daniels, "Nearly half of California's gig economy workers struggling with poverty, new survey says," CNBC, August 28, 2018, https:// www.cnbc.com/2018/08/28/about-half-of-californias-gig-economy-workers -struggling-with-poverty.html; Leonid Bershidsky, "Gig-Economy Workers Are the Modern Proletariat," Bloomberg, September 25, 2018, https://www .bloomberg.com/opinion/articles/2018-09-25/gig-economy-workers-are-last -of-marx-s-oppressed-proletarians.

18 Kate Aronoff, "How the On-Demand Economy Enables the Cycle of Racial Labor Discrimination," *Color Lines*, July 5, 2017, https://www.colorlines.com /articles/how-demand-economy-enables-cycle-racial-labor-discrimination; Robert Reich, "The Share-the-Scraps Economy," February 2, 2015, https:// robertreich.org/post/109894095095.

19 Charles Murray, *Coming Apart: The State of White America, 1960–2010* (New York: Crown Forum, 2012), 125–27; Maria Koulogou, "The New Inequality; The Decline of the Working Class Family," *Quillette*, June 13, 2019, https://quillette. com/2019/06/13/the-new-inequality-the-decline-of-the-working-class-family/.

20 E. J. Hobsbawm, *The Age of Revolution, 1789–1848* (New York: New American Library, 1962), 241; Friedrich Engels, *The Condition of the Working Class in England* (London: Penguin, 2009), 144.

21 Isabel V. Sawhill, "Inequality and social mobility: Be afraid," Brookings, May 27,

2015, https://www.brookings.edu/blog/social-mobility-memos/2015/05/27/inequality-and-social-mobility-be-afraid/; Motoko Rich et al., "Money, Race and Success; How Your School District Compares," *New York Times*, April 29, 2015, https://www.nytimes.com/interactive/2016/04/29/upshot/money-race-and-success-how-your-school-district-compares.html?_r=1; Raj Chetty and Nathaniel Hendren, "The Impacts of Neighborhoods on Intergenerational Mobility: Childhood Exposure Effects and County-Level Estimates," Harvard University and NBER, May 2015, https://scholar.harvard.edu/files/hendren/files/nbhds_paper.pdf; Stephanie Coontz, "How unmarried Americans are changing everything," CNN, September 22, 2017, http://www.cnn.com/2017/09/21/opinions/how-unmarried-americans-are-changing-the-game-coontz/index.html; Kay S. Hymowitz, *Marriage and Caste in America* (Chicago: Ivan R. Dee, 2006), 6–7, 22–23; Murray, *Coming Apart*, 164–65.

22   David Autor et al., "When Work Disappears: Manufacturing Decline and the Falling Marriage-Market Value of Men," University of Massachusetts, July 2017, http://www.umass.edu/preferen/You%20Must%20Read%20This/Autor-Dorn-Hanson-MarriageMarket.pdf.

23   Matthew Stewart, "The 9.9 Percent Is the New American Aristocracy," *Atlantic*, June 2018, https://www.theatlantic.com/magazine/archive/2018/06/the-birth-of-a-new-american-aristocracy/559130/; Anne Case and Sir Angus Deaton, "Mortality and morbidity in the 21st century," Brookings, March 23, 2017, https://www.brookings.edu/bpea-articles/mortality-and-morbidity-in-the-21st-century/.

24   Severin Carrell, "Scotland records highest level of drugs deaths in Europe," *Guardian*, July 3, 2018, https://www.theguardian.com/society/2018/jul/03/scotland-records-highest-level-of-drugs-deaths-in-europe.

25   Lee Chang-gon, "Economic crises the biggest threat to South Korean families," *Hankyoreh*, March 21, 2017, http://english.hani.co.kr/arti/english_edition/e_national/787399.html.

26   Kristin Celello and Hanan Kholoussy, "Domestic Tensions, National Anxieties: Global Perspectives on Marriage, Crisis, and Nation," Oxford Scholarship Online, March 2016, http://www.oxfordscholarship.com/view/10.1093/acprof:oso/9780199856749.001.0001/acprof-9780199856749-chapter-12.

27   Andrew Jacobs and Adam Century, "As China Ages, Beijing Turns to Morality Tales to Spur Filial Devotion," *New York Times*, September 6, 2012.

28   Li Sun, *Rural Urban Migration and Policy Intervention in China* (Singapore: Palgrave, 2019), 31–33, 105, 133, 158; Andrew Browne, "The Underclass That Threatens Xi's 'China Dream,'" *Wall Street Journal*, December 5, 2017, https://www.wsj.com/articles/the-underclass-that-threatens-xis-china-dream-1512470693?mod=itp&mod=djemITP_h.

29   Ferdinand Lundberg, *The Rich and the Super-Rich: A Study in the Power of Money Today* (New York: Lyle Stuart, 1968), 919; Eugene V. Schneider, "The Sociology of C. Wright Mills," in *C. Wright Mills*, ed. Stanley Aronowitz (New York: SAGE Publications, 2004), 20.

30   David Goodhart, *The Road to Somewhere: The New Tribes Shaping British Politics* (London: Penguin, 2017), 75; Thomas Piketty, "Brahmin Left vs Merchant Right: Rising Inequality and the Changing Structure of Political

Conflict," World Inequality Database, March 2018, http://piketty.pse.ens.fr
/files/Piketty2018.pdf; Mark Rolfe, "Identity crisis: who does the Australian
Labor Party represent?" *The Conversation*, April 16, 2014, https://
theconversation.com/identity-crisis-who-does-the-australian-labor-party
-represent-25374; Morris P. Fiorina, "The Revolt of the Masses," Hoover
Institution, January 11, 2018, https://www.hoover.org/research/revolt-masses;
Tim Pearce, "Union Members Have Traditionally Supported Democrats, but
This Poll Shows a Dramatic Shift," *Daily Caller*, October 16, 2018, https://
dailycaller.com/2018/10/16/union-members-republican-democrat/; Frank
Furedi, "Who will speak for the European working class?" *Spiked*, June 1, 2018,
https://www.spiked-online.com/2018/06/01/who-will-speak-for-the-european
-working-class/.

31　Bo Rothstein, "The Long Affair Between the Working Class and the Intellectual
Cultural Left Is Over," Social Europe, February 10, 2017, https://www
.socialeurope.eu/long-affair-working-class-intellectual-cultural-left.

32　Jan Rovny, "What happened to Europe's left?" London School of Economics
and Political Science, February 20, 2018, http://blogs.lse.ac.uk/europpblog
/2018/02/20/what-happened-to-europes-left/; Philip Manow et al., *Welfare
Democracies and Party Politics* (Oxford: Oxford University Press, 2018), https://
global.oup.com/academic/product/welfare-democracies-and-party-politics
-9780198807971?q=palier+manow&lang=en&cc=nl; Herbert Kitschelt,
"Diversification and Reconfiguration of Party Systems in Postindustrial
Democracies," *Europäische Politik*, March 2004, http://library.fes.de/pdf-files
/id/02608.pdf.

33　"'Labour will be in serious peril if it loses its working-class voters,'" *Spiked*,
July 19, 2019, https://www.spiked-online.com/2019/07/19/labour-will-be-in
-serious-peril-if-it-loses-its-working-class-voters/.

34　Rupert Darwall, "Behind the Green New Deal: An elite war on the working
class," *New York Post*, March 26, 2019, https://nypost.com/2019/03/26/behind
-the-green-new-deal-an-elite-war-on-the-working-class/; David Friedman
and Jennifer Hernandez, *California, Greenhouse Gas Regulation, and Climate
Change*, Center for Demographics and Policy, Chapman University, http://
www.newgeography.com/files/California%20GHG%20Regulation%20Final
.pdf.

35　Timothy Puko, "The Big Name in Coal's Resurgence: China," *Wall Street
Journal*, August 27, 2017, https://www.wsj.com/articles/the-big-name-in-coals
-resurgence-china-1503835205; Fernand Braudel, *The Structures of Everyday
Life*, vol. 1 of *Civilization and Capitalism* (New York: Harper & Row, 1982), 369.

36　Robert Bryce, "How to Lower U.S. Living Standards," *Wall Street Journal*,
September 21, 2015, https://www.wsj.com/articles/how-to-lower-u-s-living
-standards-1442876463; EU Energy Poverty Observatory, "Energy Poverty in
Germany—Highlights of a Beginning Debate," European Commission, July 9,
2014, https://www.energypoverty.eu/news/energy-poverty-germany-highlights
-beginning-debate; EU Energy Poverty Observatory, "Measure Energy Poverty
in Greece," European Commission, 2016, https://www.energypoverty.eu
/publication/measuring-energy-poverty-greece.

37　Austin Williams, *The Enemies of Progress: The Dangers of Sustainability* (Exeter:
Societas, 2008), 20–22, 25; Mariah Haas, "Google summit on climate change

attended by stars in private jets, mega yachts slammed as 'hypocritical,'" Fox News, August 2, 2019, https://www.foxnews.com/entertainment/google -summit-attended-by-hollywood-stars-slammed-as-hypocritical.

38 Christopher Caldwell, "Europe is a continent in crisis—where lo-vis people now wear hi-vis jackets," *Spectator*, January 3, 2019, https://spectator.us /europe-continent-high-vis-jackets/; Christophe Guilluy, *Twilight of the Elites: Prosperity, the Periphery, and the Future of France*, trans. Malcolm Debevoise (New Haven: Yale University Press, 2019), 50.

39 Didier Eribon, *Returning to Reims,* trans. Michael Lucey (South Pasadena: Semiotext/MIT Press, 2013), 29–30, 128.

40 Pawel Zerka, "Europe's underestimated young voters," European Council on Foreign Relations, May 2, 2019, https://www.ecfr.eu/article/commentary _europes_underestimated_young_voters_elections; Lori Hinnant, "Europe's far-right parties hunt down the youth vote," AP News, May 16, 2019, https:// www.apnews.com/7f177b0cf15b4e87a53fe4382d6884ca.

41 Michael Hobbes, "Turns Out White Millennials Are Just as Conservative as Their Parents," *Huffington Post*, June 2, 2019, https://www.huffpost.com/entry /turns-out-white-millennials-are-just-as-conservative-as-their-parents_n_5ce8 56fee4b0512156f16939; Chris Kahn, "Democrats lose ground with millennials," Reuters, April 30, 2018, https://www.reuters.com/article/us-usa-election -millennials/exclusive-democrats-lose-ground-with-millennials-reuters-ipsos -poll-idUSKBN1I10YH.

42 Alexis de Tocqueville, "Gale of Revolution in the Air," January 29, 1848, Speech Vault, http://www.speeches-usa.com/Transcripts/alexis_deTocqueville-gale .html.

CHAPTER 15—PEASANT REBELLIONS

1 Christopher Caldwell, "Sending Jobs Overseas," *Claremont Review of Books*, Spring 2017, http://www.claremont.org/crb/article/sending-jobs-overseas/# .WRfoXNzmbGE.twitter.

2 Adele M. Stan, "Trump and the Rise of 21st Century Fascism," *American Prospect*, August 27, 2018, http://prospect.org/article/trump-and-rise-21st -century-fascism.

3 Wolfgang Streeck, *How Will Capitalism End? Essays on a Failing System* (Brooklyn: Verso, 2016), 67; Anand Giridharadas, "After the Financial Crisis, Wall Street Turned to Charity—and Avoided Justice," *New Yorker*, September 15, 2018, https://www.newyorker.com/news/news-desk/after-the-financial-crisis -wall-street-turned-to-charityand-avoided-justice.

4 Dani Rodrik, "Populism and the economics of globalization," *Journal of International Business Policy*, 2018, https://drodrik.scholar.harvard.edu/files /dani-rodrik/files/populism_and_the_economics_of_globalization.pdf.

5 Pierre Riché, *Daily Life in the World of Charlemagne*, trans. Jo Ann McNamara (Philadelphia: University of Pennsylvania Press, 1978), 67–68, 211–12; Frances and Joseph Gies, *Daily Life in Medieval Times* (New York: Barnes & Noble, 1969), 128; Norman F. Cantor, *Medieval History: The Life and Death of a Civilization* (New York: Macmillan, 1963), 87, 540; James Westfall Thompson and Edgar Nathaniel Johnson, *An Introduction to Medieval Europe* (New York: Norton, 1937), 290–91.

6 Mark Cartwright, "Serf," *Ancient History Encyclopedia*, December 4, 2018, https://www.ancient.eu/Serf/.

7 Barbara Tuchman, *A Distant Mirror: The Calamitous 14th Century* (New York: Knopf, 1978), 176–82.

8 "Tyler, Watt," *The Columbia Encyclopedia*, 6th ed., ed. Paul Lagassé (Columbia University Press, 2000).

9 Tuchman, *A Distant Mirror*, 372–96; William H. McNeill, *The Rise of the West: A History of the Human Community* (Chicago: University of Chicago Press, 1992), 556; Immanuel Wallerstein, *The Modern World System: Capitalist Agriculture and the Origins of the European World Economy in the 16th Century* (New York: Academic Press, 1974), 24.

10 J. C. Davis, *Oliver Cromwell* (London: Arnold, 2001), 194–95.

11 Karel van Wolferen, *The Enigma of Japanese Power: People and Politics in a Stateless Nation* (New York: Vintage, 1990), 261.

12 T. R. Fehrenbach, *Fire and Blood: A History of Mexico* (New York: Collier, 1973), 255, 270, 305, 542–44, 591; Robert McCaa, "Missing millions: the human cost of the Mexican Revolution," University of Minnesota Population Center, 2001, http://users.pop.umn.edu/~rmccaa/missmill/mxrev.htm.

13 Nicholas Riasanovsky, *A History of Russia* (New York: Oxford University Press, 1963), 287–89, 410; Richard Pipes, *Russian Under the Old Regime* (New York: Penguin, 1974), 155, 169–70; Orlando Figes, *A People's Tragedy: The Russian Revolution, 1891–1924* (New York: Penguin, 1996), 754–75, 764.

14 "Taiping Rebellion," *History*, February 22, 2018, updated August 21, 2018, https://www.history.com/topics/china/taiping-rebellion.

15 Kenneth Scott LaTourette, *The Chinese: Their History and Culture* (New York: Macmillan, 1967), 284–86, 292–94.

16 United Nations, "International Migration Report," 2017, http://www.un.org/en /development/desa/population/migration/publications/migrationreport/docs /MigrationReport2017_Highlights.pdf.

17 Betsy McKay and Gabriele Steinhauser, "Extreme Poverty Concentrates in Sub-Saharan Africa," *Wall Street Journal*, September 18, 2018, https://www.wsj.com /articles/extreme-poverty-concentrates-in-sub-saharan-africa-1537243201.

18 Charlotte Werther, "Rebranding Britain: Cool Britannia, the Millennium Dome and the 2012 Olympics," *Moderna språk*, 2011, http://ojs.ub.gu.se/ojs/index.php /modernasprak/article/viewFile/664/616.

19 "Number of migrants in Germany hits record high," Reuters, April 12, 2018, https://uk.reuters.com/article/uk-germany-immigration/number-of-migrants -in-germany-hits-record-high-idUKKBN1HJ2BQ; Krishnadev Calamur, "Migration Is Down, Crime Is Low, but Merkel Is in Trouble," *Atlantic*, June 18, 2018, https://www.theatlantic.com/international/archive/2018/06/germany -migration-politics/563051/; Project 28, "Immigration," 2017, Századvég Foundation, http://project28.eu/migrants-2017/.

20 Jacob Poushter, "European opinions of the refugee crisis in 5 charts," Pew Research Center, September 16, 2016, https://www.pewresearch.org /fact-tank/2016/09/16/european-opinions-of-the-refugee-crisis-in-5-charts/.

21 Phillip Connor and Jens Manuel Krogstad, "Many worldwide oppose more migration—both into and out of their countries," Pew Research Center,

December 10, 2018, https://www.pewresearch.org/fact-tank/2018/12/10/many
-worldwide-oppose-more-migration-both-into-and-out-of-their-countries/.

22 Elena Cavallone, "The Netherlands tougher on migration after granting asylum
to Armenian family," *Euro News*, February 25, 2019, https://www.euronews.com
/2019/02/25/the-netherlands-tougher-on-migration-after-granting-asylum
-to-armenian-family; Nikolaj Nielsen, "France tightens immigration law,
sparking division," *EU Observer*, April 23, 2018, https://euobserver.com
/migration/141661; Richard Orange, "Mette Frederiksen: the anti-immigration
left leader set to win power in Denmark," *Guardian*, May 11, 2019, https://www.
theguardian.com/world/2019/may/11/denmark-election-matte-frederiksen
-leftwing-immigration; Asylum Information Database, "Germany: A
Controversial Law Package Passes the Parliament," June 14, 2019, https://www.
asylumineurope.org/news/14-06-2019/germany-controversial-law-package
-passes-parliament-1; "Slovakia drops in press freedom ranking," *Slovak
Spectator*, April 25, 2018, https://spectator.sme.sk/c/20812144/reporters
-without-borders-issues-report-slovakia-worsened-in-chart.html.

23 Paulina Neuding, "Sweden's violent reality is undoing a peaceful self-image,"
Politico, April 17, 2018, https://www.politico.eu/article/sweden-bombings
-grenade-attacks-violent-reality-undoing-peaceful-self-image-law-and-order/;
"Teens roam streets with rifles as crime swamps Sweden," *Times* (UK), January
21, 2018, https://www.thetimes.co.uk/article/teens-roam-streets-with-rifles-as
-crime-swamps-sweden-q83g055k9.

24 "On the run everywhere," *Washington Times*, March 21, 2018, https://www
.washingtontimes.com/news/2018/mar/21/editorial-the-reign-of-the-elites
-is-crumbling-in-/; Christophe Guilluy, *Twilight of the Elites: Prosperity, the
Periphery, and the Future of France*, trans. Malcolm Debevoise (New Haven:
Yale University Press, 2019), 24.

25 "The far right's new fascination with the Middle Ages," *Economist*, January 2,
2017, https://www.economist.com/blogs/democracyinamerica/2017/01
/medieval-memes.

26 Guilluy, *Twilight of the Elites*, 43.

27 Neil Munro, "Billionaire Steve Case says immigrants will offset middle class job
losses," *Daily Caller*, December 5, 2013, https://dailycaller.com/2013/12/05
/billionaire-steve-case-says-immigrants-will-offset-middle-class-job-losses/.

28 Alex Pfeiffer, "Bill Kristol Says 'Lazy' White Working Class Should Be Replaced
by 'New Americans,'" *Daily Caller*, February 8, 2017, https://dailycaller.com
/2017/02/08/bill-kristol-says-lazy-white-working-class-should-be-replaced
-by-new-americans/.

29 Geoff Colvin, "Donald Trump's Immigration Ban Ushers In a New Era of CEO
Activism," *Fortune*, February 7, 2017, http://fortune.com/2017/02/07/donald
-trumps-immigration-ban-ushers-in-a-new-era-of-ceo-activism/.

30 Douglas Murray, *The Strange Death of Europe: Immigration, Identity, Islam*
(London: Bloomsbury, 2017), 99, 226.

31 Giles Kepel, remarks at the Tocqueville Conversations, Château de Tocqueville,
Normandy, France, June 7–8, 2018.

32 Goodhart, *The Road to Somewhere*, 3–4, 100; "The Brexit Index: a who's who
of Remain and Leave supporters," Populus, https://www.populus.co.uk/

insights/2016/05/the-brexit-index-a-whos-who-of-remain-and-leave
-supporters/; House of Commons Library, "General Election 2019: Results
and Analysis," Number CBP 8749, 28 January 2020.

33 Peter Foster, "Denmark's EU referendum is a blow to David Cameron,"
    Telegraph, December 4, 2015, https://www.telegraph.co.uk/news/worldnews
    /europe/denmark/12032958/Denmarks-EU-referendum-is-a-blow-to-David
    -Cameron.html; "Dutch referendum voters overwhelmingly reject closer EU
    links to Ukraine," *Guardian*, April 7, 2016, https://www.theguardian.com
    /world/2016/apr/06/dutch-voters-reject-closer-eu-links-to-ukraine-in-
    referendum; Nick Gutteridge, "European Superstate to be unveiled: EU nations
    'to be morphed into one' post-Brexit," *Express*, June 29, 2016, https://www
    .express.co.uk/news/politics/683739/EU-referendum-German-French
    -European-superstate-Brexit; Project 28, "Handling the Immigration Crisis,"
    Századvég Foundation, http://project28.eu/.

34 Matthew Karnitschnig, "Cologne puts Germany's 'lying press' on defensive,"
    Politico, January 25, 2016, https://www.politico.eu/article/cologne-puts
    -germany-lying-media-press-on-defensive-migration-refugees-attacks-sex
    -assault-nye/; Robert Spencer, "Google manipulates Search Results to Conceal
    Criticism of Islam and Jihad," *PJ Media*, August 2, 2017, https://pjmedia.com/
    homeland-security/2017/08/02/google-manipulates-search-results-to-conceal
    -criticism-of-islam-and-jihad/; "Rome opens its gates to the modern
    barbarians," *Financial Times*, May 15, 2018, https://www.ft.com/content
    /6348cc64-5764-11e8-b8b2-d6ceb45fa9d0.

35 Goodhart, *The Road to Somewhere*, 14.

36 Robert Samuelson, "The Middle Class Rocks—Again," *Real Clear Politics*,
    September 18, 2017, https://www.realclearpolitics.com/articles/2017/09/18/the
    _middle_class_rocks-again_135014.html; Nate Silver, "Silver Bulletpoints:
    The Union Vote Could Swing the Election," FiveThirtyEight, May 2, 2019,
    https://fivethirtyeight.com/features/silver-bulletpoints-the-union-vote
    -could-swing-the-election/.

37 Richard Florida, "Why Is Your State Red or Blue? Look to the Dominant
    Occupational Class," City Lab, November 28, 2018, https://www.citylab.com/
    life/2018/11/state-voting-patterns-occupational-class-data-politics/575047/.

38 John Daniel Davidson, "Trump is no fascist. He is a champion for the forgotten
    millions," *Guardian*, February 5, 2017, https://www.theguardian.com
    /commentisfree/2017/feb/05/trump-not-fascist-champion-for-forgotten
    -millions.

39 Salena Zito and Brad Todd, T*he Great Revolt: Inside the Populist Coalition
    Reshaping American Politics* (New York: Crown Forum, 2018), 20, 234, 239,
    252–53.

40 James Traub, "It's Time for the Elites to Rise Up Against the Ignorant Masses,"
    Foreign Policy, June 28, 2016, https://foreignpolicy.com/2016/06/28/its-time-for
    -the-elites-to-rise-up-against-ignorant-masses-trump-2016-brexit/.

41 Goodhart, *The Road to Somewhere*, 91; Morris P. Fiorina, "The Revolt of the
    Masses," Hoover Institution, January 11, 2018, https://www.hoover.org/research
    /revolt-masses.

42   Eric D. Weitz, *Weimar Germany: Promise and Tragedy* (Princeton: Princeton University Press, 2007), 137–38, 348.

43   John McCormick, "Americans Blame Wall Street for Making American Dream Harder to Achieve," Bloomberg, March 6, 2019, https://www.bloomberg.com /news/articles/2019-03-06/wall-street-blamed-for-making-american-dream -harder-to-achieve?srnd=premium.

44   "Socialism 'More Popular Than Capitalism' With Brits, Germans, US Youth," *Sputnik News*, February 24, 2016, https://sputniknews.com/europe/2016022410 35283984-socialism-popularity-britain-germany/.

45   Marco Damiani, "The transformation of Jean-Luc Mélenchon: From radical outsider to populist leader," London School of Economics and Political Science, April 22, 2017, http://blogs.lse.ac.uk/europpblog/2017/04/22/the-transformation -of-jean-luc-melenchon/.

46   Lucy Pasha-Robinson, "Election 2017: 61.5 per cent of under-40s voted for Labour, new poll finds," *Independent*, June 14, 2017, https://www.independent. co.uk/news/uk/politics/election-2017-labour-youth-vote-under-40s-jeremy -corbyn-yougov-poll-a7789151.html; Jim Edwards, "Bernie Sanders and the youth vote: Stats and history suggest he may doom the Democrats," *Business Insider*, March 4, 2020, https://www.businessinsider.com/how-bernie-sanders -reliance-on-youth-vote-could-doom-democrats-2020-3.

47   Ben Knight, "Why the German urban middle class is going Green," *New Statesman*, July 17, 2019, https://www.newstatesman.com/culture /observations/2019/07/why-german-urban-middle-class-going-green.

48   Sohrab Ahmari, "Making the World Safe for Communism—Again," *Commentary*, October 18, 2017, https://www.commentarymagazine.com /politics-ideas/making-the-world-safe-for-communism-again/.

49   "More young people voted for Bernie Sanders than Trump and Clinton combined," *Washington Post*, June 20, 2016, https://www.washingtonpost.com /news/the-fix/wp/2016/06/20/more-young-people-voted-for-bernie-sanders -than-trump-and-clinton-combined-by-a-lot/?utm_term=.60f572274c06.

50   Joel Kotkin, "Moderation's Limits," *City Journal*, March 6, 2020, https://www .city-journal.org/biden-victories-democrats-leftist-future.

51   Victims of Communism Memorial Foundation, 2019 Annual Poll, https://www .victimsofcommunism.org/2019-annual-poll; Jade Scipioni, "Half of millennials would give up their rights to get out of debt," *New York Post*, September 14, 2017, https://nypost.com/2017/09/14/half-of-millennials-would-give-up-their -rights-to-get-out-of-debt/; Clay Routledge, "Why Are Millennials Wary of Freedom?" *New York Times*, October 14, 2017, https://www.nytimes.com/2017 /10/14/opinion/sunday/millennials-freedom-fear.html.

52   Ronald Brownstein, "Millennials to pass baby boomers as largest voter-eligible age group and what it means," CNN, July 25, 2017, https://www.cnn.com/2017 /07/25/politics/brownstein-millennials-largest-voter-group-baby-boomers/ index.html.

53   Li Sun, *Rural Urban Migration and Policy Intervention in China* (Singapore: Palgrave, 2019), 133; Zhiming Cheng, Haining Wang, and Russell Smyth, "Happiness and job satisfaction in urban China: A comparative study of two

generations of migrants and urban locals," *Urban Studies,* vol. 51:10 (November 2013), 2160–84.

54 Rob Schmitz, "In China, The Communist Party's Latest, Unlikely Target: Young Marxists," NPR, November 21, 2018, https://www.npr.org/2018/11/21 /669509554/in-china-the-communist-partys-latest-unlikely-target-young -marxists?fbclid=IwAR2Qubw2ENnDLE_G1GHwGwsDaOUtwmBfR ZalygyhQmO-Au7xAAd28CLXGwc; "Officials in Beijing worry about Marx- loving students," *Economist,* September 27, 2018, https://www.economist.com /china/2018/09/27/officials-in-beijing-worry-about-marx-loving-students.

55 Guy Standing, "A 'Precariat Charter' is required to combat the inequalities and insecurities produced by global capitalism," London School of Economics and Political Science, May 5, 2014, http://blogs.lse.ac.uk/europpblog/2014/05/05 /a-precariat-charter-is-required-to-combat-the-inequalities-and-insecurities -produced-by-global-capitalism/; Aaron M. Renn, "Post-Work Won't Work," *City Journal,* August 4, 2017, https://www.city-journal.org/html/post-work -wont-work-15383.html.

56 Wendell Berry, *What Are People For?* (New York: Northpoint, 1990), 125.

CHAPTER 16—THE NEW GATED CITY

1 Richard Florida, "How and Why American Cities Are Coming Back," City Lab, May 17, 2012, https://www.citylab.com/life/2012/05/how-and-why-american -cities-are-coming-back/2015/; Lauren Nolan, "A Deepening Divide: Income Inequality Grows Spatially in Chicago," Voorhees Center for Neighborhood and Community Improvement, March 11, 2015, https://voorheescenter. wordpress.com/2015/03/11/a-deepening-divide-income-inequality-grows -spatially-in-chicago/; Aaron M. Renn, "Caterpillar's HQ Move to Chicago Shows America's Double Divide," Urbanophile, January 31, 2017, http://www .urbanophile.com/2017/01/31/caterpillars-hq-move-to-chicago-shows-americas -double-divide/.

2 Shane Hedmon. "The U.S. Cities with the Most Active Tower Cranes," Construction Junkie, July 23, 2018, https://www.constructionjunkie.com/blog /2018/7/23/the-us-cities-with-the-most-active-tower-cranes.

3 Walter E. Williams, "Enough's Enough," *Town Hall,* August 15, 2018, https:// townhall.com/columnists/walterewilliams/2018/08/15/enoughs-enough -n2509315; William Hageman, "Chicago Is a Rat's Kind of Town," *Chicago Tribune,* October 17, 2014, https://www.chicagotribune.com/lifestyles /ct-chicago-americas-rattiest-city-20141017-story.html.

4 Francesca Mirabile and Daniel Nass, "What's the Homicide Capital of America? Murder Rates in U.S. Cities, Ranked," *The Trace,* April 26, 2018, https://www.thetrace.org/2018/04/highest-murder-rates-us-cities-list/; Max Rust, Scott Calvert, and Shibani Mahtani, "Murder in America: What Makes Cities More Dangerous," *Wall Street Journal,* December 26, 2017, https://www. wsj.com/articles/murder-in-america-what-makes-cities-more-dangerous -1514293200; Heather Mac Donald, "In Denial About Crime," *City Journal,* Winter 2016, https://www.city-journal.org/html/denial-about-crime-14118. html.

5 William Cronon, *Nature's Metropolis: Chicago and the Great West* (New York: Norton, 1991), 4.

6 Pete Saunders, "More on Bifurcating Chicago and Detroit," *New Geography*, May 29, 2018, http://www.newgeography.com/content/005988-more -bifurcating-chicago-and-detroit.

7 Cronon, *Nature's Metropolis*, 283, 311; Alana Samuels, "Chicago's Awful Divide," *Atlantic*, March 28, 2018, https://www.theatlantic.com/business/archive /2018/03/chicago-segregation-poverty/556649/; Center for Opportunity Urbanism, *Beyond Gentrification: Towards More Equitable Urban Growth*, https://opportunityurbanism.org/wp-content/uploads/2019/01/Toward-More -Equitable-Urban-Growth.pdf.

8 Linda Lutton, "The Middle Class Is Shrinking Everywhere—In Chicago It's Almost Gone," WBEZ 91.5 Chicago, February 18, 2019, https://www.wbez.org /shows/wbez-news/the-middle-class-is-shrinking-everywhere-in-chicago-its -almost-gone/e63cb407-5d1e-41b1-9124-a717d4fb1b0b; Jessica Kursman and Nick Zettel, "Who Can Live in Chicago," Voorhees Center, June 6, 2018, https:// voorheescenter.wordpress.com/2018/06/06/who-can-live-in-chicago-part-i/.

9 Samuels, "Chicago's Awful Divide"; Teresa L. Cordova and Matthew D. Wilson, "Abandoned in Their Neighborhoods: Youth Joblessness amidst the Flight of Industry and Opportunity," Great Cities Institute, January 29, 2017, https:// greatcities.uic.edu/2017/01/29/abandoned-in-their-neighborhoods-youth -joblessness-amidst-the-flight-of-industry-and-opportunity/; Manny Ramos, "Cook County's black population continues to decline," *Chicago Sun Times*, June 20, 2018, https://chicago.suntimes.com/news/cook-county-black -population-continues-to-decline-census-data/.

10 Patrick Sisson, "How a 'reverse Great Migration' is reshaping U.S. Cities," *Curbed*, July 31, 2018, https://www.curbed.com/2018/7/31/17632092/black -chicago-neighborhood-great-migration.

11 Aaron M. Renn, "How Richard Longworth Predicted 20 Years Ago That Globalization Would Cause a Social Crisis," Urbanophile, February 12, 2017, https://www.urbanophile.com/2017/02/12/how-richard-longworth-predicted -20-years-ago-that-globalization-would-cause-a-social-crisis/.

12 Edward Gibbon, *The History of the Decline and Fall of the Roman Empire* (New York: Modern Library, 1931), vol. 1: 1102–3, 1107, 1302–3; Peter Heather, *Empires and Barbarians: The Fall of Rome and the Birth of Europe* (Oxford: Oxford University Press, 2010), 279.

13 Gibbon, *The History of the Decline and Fall of the Roman Empire*, vol. 1: 976; vol. 2: 55; Michael Grant, *The Fall of the Roman Empire* (New York: Collier, 1990), 164; Henri Pirenne, *Mohammed and Charlemagne* (Mineola, N.Y.: Dover, 2001), 169–70.

14 Norman F. Cantor, *Medieval History: The Life and Death of a Civilization* (New York: Macmillan, 1963), 178, 278, 399; Frances and Joseph Gies, *Daily Life in Medieval Times* (New York: Barnes & Noble: 1969), 229; Vito Fumagalli, *Landscapes of Fear: Perceptions of Nature and City in the Middle Ages*, trans. Shayne Mitchell (Cambridge: Polity Press, 1994), 68.

15 Heng Chye Kiang, *Cities of Aristocrats and Bureaucrats: The Development of Medieval Chinese Cityscapes* (Honolulu: University of Hawaii Press, 1999), 1–3.

16 Stewart H. Holbrook, *The Age of the Moguls: The Story of the Robber Barons and the Great Tycoons* (New York: Doubleday, 1954), 131; Charles A. Beard and Mary R. Beard, *The Rise of American Civilization* (New York: Macmillan, 1930), vol. 2: 385.

17 James Cherowbrier, "Leading billionaire cities in Europe in 2014 and 2016, by billionaire population," Statista, March 2017, https://www.statista.com/statistics/434709/leading-bilionaire-cities-europe/; WealthX, "The WealthX Billionaire Census 2018," May 15, 2018, https://www.wealthx.com/report/the-wealth-x-billionaire-census-2018/; Stratfor, "Mapping the World's Wealthiest Cities," February 22, 2018, https://worldview.stratfor.com/article/mapping-worlds-wealthiest-cities.

18 Daniel W. Drezner, "'Connectography' by Parag Khanna," *New York Times*, May 1, 2016, https://www.nytimes.com/2016/05/01/books/review/connectography-by-parag-khanna.html?_r=0; Simon Curtis, "What Comes After the End of the Global City?" De Gruyter Conversations, April 17, 2018, https://blog.degruyter.com/what-comes-after-the-end-of-the-global-city/; Joseph Gyourko et al., "Superstar Cities," National Bureau of Economic Research, July 2006, https://www.nber.org/papers/w12355.

19 Wendell Cox, "Paris, London Lead European Metropolitan Areas: Latest Data," *New Geography*, July 10, 2019, http://www.newgeography.com/content/006349-paris-london-lead-european-metropolitan-areas-latest-data; Christophe Guilluy, *Twilight of the Elites: Prosperity, the Periphery, and the Future of France*, trans. Malcolm Debevoise (New Haven: Yale University Press, 2019), 85; Wendell Cox, "The Long Term: Metro America Goes From 82% to 86% Suburban since 1990," *New Geography*, June 11, 2014, http://www.newgeography.com/content/004361-the-long-term-metro-america-goes-from-82-86-suburban-since-1990.

20 Fred Siegel and Harry Siegel, "Can Bloomberg's 'Luxury' City Survive?" *Wall Street Journal*, October 15, 2009, https://www.wsj.com/articles/SB10001424052748704107204574472892886003298; "Bloomberg: Would Be 'Godsend' If More Billionaires Moved to NYC," NBC New York, September 20, 2013, https://www.nbcnewyork.com/news/local/Mayor-Bloomberg-Billionaires-Rich-Poor-Income-Gap--224592951.html.

21 William A. Galston, "Why Cities Boom While Towns Struggle," *Wall Street Journal*, March 13, 2018, https://www.wsj.com/articles/why-cities-boom-while-towns-struggle-1520983492?mod=ITP_opinion_0&tesla=y; Will Wilkinson, "A Tale of Two Moralities, Part One: Regional Inequality and Moral Polarization," Niskanen Center, January 19, 2017, https://niskanencenter.org/blog/tale-two-moralities-part-one-regional-inequality-moral-polarization/.

22 Richard Florida, "How Your Social Class Affects Where You'll Move," City Lab, April 4, 2018, https://www.citylab.com/equity/2018/04/how-your-social-class-affects-where-youll-move/557060/; Conor Dougherty and Andrew Burton, "A 2:15 Alarm, 2 Trains and a Bus Get Her to Work by 7 A.M.," *New York Times*, August 17, 2017, https://www.nytimes.com/2017/08/17/business/economy/san-francisco-commute.html.

23 Data derived from the American Community Survey 2012–2016 by Wendell Cox, www.demographia.com.

24 Chad Shearer and Alan Berube, "The Surprisingly Short List of Metro Areas Achieving Inclusive Economic Growth," Brookings, April 27, 2017, https://www .brookings.edu/blog/the-avenue/2017/04/27/the-surprisingly-short-list-of-u-s -metro-areas-achieving-inclusive-economic-growth/; Kevin Baker, "The Death of a Once Great City," *Harper's*, July 2018, https://harpers.org/archive/2018/07 /the-death-of-new-york-city-gentrification/?ex_cid=SigDig.

25 Francesco Andreoli and Eugenio Peluso, "So close yet so unequal: Reconsidering spatial inequality in U.S. cities," Dipartimento di Economia e Finanza, February 2017, https://dipartimenti.unicatt.it/economia-finanza -def055.pdf.

26 Rakesh Kochhar, "The American middle class is stable in size, but losing ground financially to upper-income families," Pew Research Center, September 6, 2018, https://www.pewresearch.org/fact-tank/2018/09/06/the-american -middle-class-is-stable-in-size-but-losing-ground-financially-to-upper -income-families/; Wendell Cox, "2018 COU Standard of Living Index," Center for Opportunity Urbanism, December 2018, https://opportunityurbanism.org /wp-content/uploads/2018/12/2018-COU-Standard-of-Living-Index.pdf.

27 Nathaniel Baum-Snow and Ronni Pavan, "Inequality and City Size," *Review of Economics and Statistics*, vol. 95:5 (December 2013), 1535–48; https://www.ncbi .nlm.nih.gov/pmc/articles/PMC4063360/; Enrico Moretti, "America's Great Divergence," *Salon*, May 20, 2012, https://www.salon.com/2012/05/20/america _resegregated/; James Parrott, "As Income Gap Widens, New York Grows Apart," *Gotham Gazette*, January 18, 2011, http://www.gothamgazette.com /index.php/economy/683-as-incomes-gap-widens-new-york-grows-apart.

28 Amy Liu, "The Urgency to Achieve an Inclusive Economy in the Bay Area," Brookings, June 7, 2018, https://www.brookings.edu/research/the-urgency -to-achieve-an-inclusive-economy-in-the-bay-area/.

29 Thomas Fuller, "San Francisco's Homeless Crisis Tests Mayoral Candidates' Liberal Ideals," *New York Times*, May 30, 2018, https://www.nytimes.com /2018/05/30/us/san-francisco-mayoral-election-homeless.html; Bigad Shaban, "Survey of Downtown San Francisco Reveals Trash on Every Block, 303 Piles of Feces and 100 Drug Needles," NBC Bay Area, February 2, 2018, https:// www.nbcbayarea.com/news/local/Diseased-Streets-472430013.html; Alexis C. Madrigal, "Who's Really Buying Property in San Francisco?" *Atlantic*, April 19, 2019, https://www.theatlantic.com/technology/archive/2019/04/san-francisco -city-apps-built-or-destroyed/587389/; Dave Clark, "San Francisco's Black population is less than 5 percent, exodus has been steady," KTVU, November 24, 2016, http://www.ktvu.com/news/san-franciscos-black-population-is-less -than-5-percent-exodus-has-been-steady.

30 Kathleen Maclay, "More gentrification, displacement in Bay Area forecast," *Berkeley News*, August 24, 2015, https://news.berkeley.edu/2015/08/24/more- gentrification-displacement-in-bay-area-forecast/; Sam Levin, "'Largest-ever' Silicon Valley eviction to displace hundreds of tenants," *Guardian*, July 7, 2016, https://www.theguardian.com/technology/2016/jul/07/silicon-valley-largest -eviction-rent-controlled-tenants-income-inequality; Rong-Gong Lin II and Gale Holland, "Silicon Valley homeless no longer welcome in 'the Jungle,'" *Los Angeles Times*, December 3, 2014, https://www.latimes.com/local/california /la-me-silicon-valley-homeless-20141204-story.html.

31 John Barber, "Toronto Divided: A tale of three cities," *Globe and Mail,* December 20, 2007, https://www.theglobeandmail.com/news/national/toronto -divided-a-tale-of-3-cities/article18151444/.

32 Kat Hanna and Nicolas Bosetti, "Inside Out: The New Geography of Wealth and Poverty in London," Centre for London, December 2015, https://www .centreforlondon.org/wp-content/uploads/2016/08/CFLJ3887-Inside-out -inequality_12.125_WEB.pdf; Rupert Neate, "Rich overseas parents buy £2bn of property to get top school places," *Guardian,* September 5, 2018, https://www .theguardian.com/uk-news/2018/sep/05/wealthy-overseas-parents-london -property-private-school-places.

33 David Goodhart, *The Road to Somewhere: The New Tribes Shaping British Politics* (London: Penguin, 2017), 135–39.

34 Sako Musterd et al., "Socioeconomic segregation in European capital cities. Increasing separation between poor and rich," *Urban Geography,* vol. 38:7 (2017), 1062–83, https://www.tandfonline.com/doi/full/10.1080/02723638.201 6.1228371; Richard Florida, "Economic Segregation and Inequality in Europe's Cities," City Lab, November 16, 2015, https://www.citylab.com/life/2015/11 /economic-segregation-and-inequality-in-europes-cities/415920/.

35 Guilluy, *Twilight of the Elites,* 38.

36 David Ottewell, "Which are the most foreigner-dominated places in Europe? (And only one of them is in the UK)," *Mirror,* June 7, 2016, https://www.mirror. co.uk/news/uk-news/most-foreigner-dominated-places-europe-8133284.

37 "Indicators of Immigrant Integration 2015," OECD, 2015, https://www.oecd -ilibrary.org/sites/6673aaf3-en/index.html?itemId=/content/component /6673aaf3-en; Trading Economics, "GDP Annual Growth Rate/Europe," https:// tradingeconomics.com/country-list/gdp-annual-growth-rate?continent =europe.

38 Kim Willsher, "Paris, city of romance, rues new image as the dirty man of Europe," *Observer,* September 22, 21019, https://www.theguardian.com /world/2019/sep/22/paris-dirty-image-litter-dog-mess; Angela Giuffrida, "Romans revolt as tourists turn their noses up at city's decay," *Guardian,* April 26, 2019, https://www.theguardian.com/world/2019/apr/26/romans-revolt-as- tourists-turn-their-noses-up-at-citys-decay; Michael Colborne, "The European Capital with a Swastika Epidemic," *Haaretz,* November 1, 2018, https://www. haaretz.com/world-news/europe/.premium.MAGAZINE-the-european -capital-with-a-swastika-epidemic-1.6613202; Kenan Malik, "The Failure of Multiculturalism," *Foreign Affairs,* March/April 2015, https://www .foreignaffairs.com/articles/western-europe/2015-02-18/failure-multiculturalism; Joel Kotkin, "Europe's Fading Cosmopolitan Dream," *City Journal,* August 12, 2019, https://www.city-journal.org/europe-multiculturalism.

39 "Austrian govt calls for 'restrictive asylum policy' amid growing foreign crime rate," RT, January 10, 2018, https://www.rt.com/news/415527-austria-foreign- crime-rate/; "Terrorisme, criminalité et immigration en Suède: les chiffres versus ce que dit Trump," RTBF, February 20, 2017, https://www.rtbf.be/info /monde/detail_terrorisme-criminalite-et-immigration-en-suede-les-chiffres -versus-ce-que-dit-trump?id=9535270; "Reality Check: Are migrants driving crime in Germany?" BBC, September 13, 2018, https://www.bbc.com/news /world-europe-45419466.

40 Raheem Kassam, "Trump Is Right: Sadiq Khan Is a Stone Cold Loser," *Human Events*, June 3, 2019, https://humanevents.com/2019/06/03/trump-is-right -sadiq-khan-is-a-stone-cold-loser/; Justin Fox, "Why London Has More Crime Than New York," Bloomberg, June 19, 2018, https://www.bloomberg.com /opinion/articles/2018-06-19/why-london-has-more-crime-than-new-york.

41 Center for Opportunity Urbanism, *Beyond Gentrification: Towards More Equitable Growth*, January 2019, https://opportunityurbanism.org/wp-content /uploads/2019/01/Toward-More-Equitable-Urban-Growth.pdf.

42 Jane Jacobs, *Dark Age Ahead* (New York: Random House, 2005), 37.

43 Aaron M. Renn, "Caterpillar's HQ Move to Chicago Shows America's Double Divide," Urbanophile, January 31, 2017, http://www.urbanophile.com/2017 /01/31/caterpillars-hq-move-to-chicago-shows-americas-double-divide/; Emily Badger, "What Happens When the Richest U.S. Cities Turn to the World?" *New York Times*, December 22, 2017, https://www.nytimes.com/2017/12/22/upshot /the-great-disconnect-megacities-go-global-but-lose-local-links.html.

44 Aaron M. Renn, "Population Transformation in Pittsburgh and Chicago," *New Geography*, April 13, 2018, http://www.newgeography.com/content/005937 -population-transformation-pittsburgh-and-chicago.

45 UCL Urban Laboratory, "How Ruth Glass shaped the way we approach our cities," University College London, January 13, 2015, http://www.ucl.ac.uk /urbanlab/news/ruth-glass-seminar.

46 Karen J. Gibson, "Bleeding Albina: A History of Community Disinvestment," *Transforming Anthropology*, vol. 15:1, (2007), 3–25, http://kingneighborhood. org/wp-content/uploads/2015/03/BLEEDING-ALBINA_-A-HISTORY-OF -COMMUNITY-DISINVESTMENT-1940%E2%80%932000.pdf; NYU Furman Center, "Focus on Gentrification," June 9, 2016, http://furmancenter.org/files /sotc/Part_1_Gentrification_SOCin2015_9JUNE2016.pdf; Jonathan Wynn and Andrew Deener, "Gentrification? Bring It," *The Conversation*, October 11, 2017, https://theconversation.com/gentrification-bring-it-82107.

47 Kevin Baker, "The Death of a Once Great City," *Harper's*, July 2018, https:// harpers.org/archive/2018/07/the-death-of-new-york-city-gentrification/; Theodore Dalrymple, "The Architect as Totalitarian," *City Journal*, Autumn 2009, https://www.city-journal.org/html/architect-totalitarian-13246.html; Claire Berlinski, "The Architectural Sacking of Paris," *City Journal*, Winter 2018, https://www.city-journal.org/html/architectural-sacking-paris-15655. html.

48 James Heartfield, "London's Social Cleansing," *New Geography*, May 13, 2012, http://www.newgeography.com/content/002824-london%E2%80 %99s-social-cleansing.

49 Ibid.; Sara Malm, "Is buying a house just a pipe dream? Concrete tubes just over eight feet wide, with a bench that turns into a bed, could be your solution," *Daily Mail*, January 15, 2018, http://www.dailymail.co.uk/news/article- 5271411/8ft-concrete-tubes-solution-housing-crisis.html; James Heartfield, "Britain's Housing Crisis: The Places People Live," *New Geography*, January 28, 2013, http://www.newgeography.com/content/003432-britains-housing-crisis -the-places-people-live.

50 Maggie Shen King, *An Excess Male* (New York: Harper, 2017), 11.

51 Richard Florida, *The Rise of the Creative Class* (New York: Basic Books, 2002).

52 Office of the New York Comptroller Scott M. Stringer, "New York City's Millennials in Recession and Recovery," April 2016, https://comptroller.nyc. gov/wp-content/uploads/documents/NYC_Millennials_In_Recession_and _Recovery.PDF; Corinne Lestch, "NYC affordable housing is vanishing as rents skyrocket, incomes decline: report," *New York Daily News*, April 23, 2014, https://www.nydailynews.com/new-york/nyc-rents-soar-incomes-decline -article-1.1765445; Patrick Clark, "The Exact Moment Big Cities Got Too Expensive for Millennials," Bloomberg, July 15, 2015, https://www.bloomberg .com/news/articles/2015-07-15/the-exact-moment-big-cities-got-too-expensive -for-millennials?utm_source=Mic+Check&utm_campaign=2b200dd408 -Thursday_July_167_15_2015&utm_medium=email&utm_term=0_51f2320b33 -2b200dd408-285306781.

53 Katy Murphy, "The California Dream is tough to afford if you're under 40," *Mercury News*, February 21, 2018, https://www.mercurynews.com/2018/02/18 /the-california-dream-is-tough-to-afford-if-youre-under-40/; Joel Kotkin and Wendell Cox, "Fading Promise: Millennial Prospects in the Golden State," Center for Demographics and Policy, May 5, 2017, http:// centerforcaliforniarealestate.org/publications/Kotkin-Fading-Dream -printable.pdf.

54 Center for Opportunity Urbanism, *Beyond Gentrification.*

55 John Aidan Byrne, "The Exodus of New York City's endangered middle class," *New York Post*, December 22, 2018, https://nypost.com/2018/12/22/the-exodus -of-new-york-citys-endangered-middle-class/; Jane Jacobs, *The Death and Life of Great American Cities* (New York: Vintage, 1962), 282.

56 National Urban Coalition, *Displacement: City Neighborhoods in Transition*, Washington, D.C., 1978.

57 Kristian Behrens and Frederic Robert-Nicoud, "Urbanization Makes the World More Unequal," *VoxEU*, July 24, 2014, https://voxeu.org/article/inequality -big-cities.

58 Richard Florida, "Mapping the New Urban Crisis," City Lab, April 13, 2017, https://www.citylab.com/equity/2017/04/new-urban-crisis-index/521037/; Patrick Sharkey, "Rich Neighborhood, Poor Neighborhood: How Segregation Threatens Social Mobility," Brookings, December 5, 2013, https://www .brookings.edu/blog/social-mobility-memos/2013/12/05/rich-neighborhood -poor-neighborhood-how-segregation-threatens-social-mobility/.

59 Helen Raleigh, "Gentrification Provokes a Coffee Clash in Denver's Five Points," *Wall Street Journal*, December 22, 2017, https://www.wsj.com/articles /gentrification-provokes-a-coffee-clash-in-denvers-five-points-1513983831; Cameron McWhirter, "Atlanta's Growing Pains Are Getting Worse," *Wall Street Journal*, August 31, 2018, https://www.wsj.com/articles/atlantas-growing-pains -are-getting-worse-1535707800; Richard Campanella, "Gentrification and Its Discontents: Notes From New Orleans," *New Geography*, February 28, 2013, http://www.newgeography.com/content/003526-gentrification-and-its- discontents-notes-new-orleans; "Google abandons Berlin base after two years of resistance," *Guardian*, October 24, 2018, https://www.theguardian.com/ technology/2018/oct/24/google-abandons

-berlin-base-after-two-years-of-resistance; Chantal Braganza, "Why opponents of gentrification have taken to the streets of Hamilton," TVO, April 5, 2018, https://tvo.org/article/current-affairs/why-opponents-of-gentrification-have -taken-to-the-streets-of-hamilton; David Streitfeld, "Protesters Block Google Buses in San Francisco, Citing 'Techsploitation,'" *New York Times*, May 31, 2018, https://www.nytimes.com/2018/05/31/us/google-bus-protest.html?emc=edit _ca_20180601&nl=california-today&nlid=8514846720180601&te=1.

60 Alene Tchekmedyian and Joseph Serna, "'I think it's arson': Developer suspects political motives as officials probe latest Bay Area fire," *Los Angeles Times*, July 10, 2017, https://www.latimes.com/local/lanow/la-me-ln-oakland-construction- fires-20170710-story.html; "Is Boyle Heights Coffee Shop Vandalism An Anti- Gentrification Message?" CBS Los Angeles, July 19, 2017, https://losangeles. cbslocal.com/2017/07/19/boyle-heights-vandalism-gentrification/.

61 Rakesh Kochhar, "The American middle class is stable in size, but losing ground financially to upper-income families," Pew Research Center, September 6, 2018, http://www.pewresearch.org/fact-tank/2018/09/06/the-american -middle-class-is-stable-in-size-but-losing-ground-financially-to-upper -income-families/.

CHAPTER 17—THE SOUL OF THE NEO-FEUDAL CITY

1 Fernand Braudel, *The Perspective of the World*, vol. 3 of *Civilization and Capitalism, 15th–18th Century*, trans. Sian Reynolds (New York: Harper & Row, 1984), 30.

2 Jason Long, "Rural-Urban Migration and Socioeconomic Mobility in Victorian Britain," 2002, Semantic Scholar, https://pdfs.semanticscholar.org/c433/83f5019 375b2ed737cec87fb764a0cf86920.pdf.

3 Christopher Rugaber, "Urban Middle Class Hollowing into Haves and Have -Nots, Pew Says," *Christian Science Monitor*, May 11, 2016, https://www .csmonitor.com/USA/Society/2016/0511/Urban-middle-class-hollowing-into -haves-and-have-nots-Pew-says.

4 Jed Kolko, "The Jobs Priced Out of Expensive Metros," Indeed Hiring Lab, May 17, 2018, https://www.hiringlab.org/2018/05/17/jobs-priced-expensive -metros/; Jana Kasperkevic, "These blue collar workers are getting priced out of the cities that need them," Marketplace, April 13, 2017, https://www .marketplace.org/2017/04/13/wealth-poverty/these-blue-collar-workers-are- getting-priced-out-cities-need-them; Aaron M. Renn, "The Lifeblood of Cities," *City Journal*, January 9, 2018, https://www.city-journal.org/html /lifeblood-cities-15639.html; Harrison Jacobs, "Incredible Maps Show How Working-Class Neighborhoods Are Disappearing From American Cities," *Business Insider*, September 30, 2014, http://www.businessinsider.com/working -class-neighborhoods-are-disappearing-from-american-cities-2014-9.

5 Emily Badger and Quoctrung Bai, "What if Cities Are No Longer the Land of Opportunity for Low-Skilled Workers?" *New York Times*, January 11, 2019, https://www.nytimes.com/2019/01/11/upshot/big-cities-low-skilled-workers -wages.html.

6 Gabriela Inchauste, *Living and Leaving: Housing, Mobility, and Welfare in the European Union*, World Bank Report on the European Union, World Bank Group, 2018, http://pubdocs.worldbank.org/en/507021541611553122

/Living-Leaving-web.pdf; William A. Galston, "Why Cities Boom While Towns Struggle," *Wall Street Journal*, March 13, 2018, https://www.wsj.com/articles/ why-cities-boom-while-towns-struggle-1520983492?mod=ITP_opinion _0&tesla=y.

7   Jan Woronoff, *Japan: The Coming Social Crisis* (Tokyo: Lotus Press, 1984), 312; Alex Martin, "Japan's Glut of Abandoned Homes: Hard to sell but bargains when opportunity knocks," *Japan Times*, December 26, 2017, https://www .japantimes.co.jp/news/2017/12/26/national/japans-glut-abandoned-homes -hard-sell-bargains-opportunity-knocks/#.W_Ap7OhKiUk; Jonathan Soble, "A Sprawl of Ghost Homes in Aging Tokyo Suburbs," *New York Times*, August 24, 2015, https://www.nytimes.com/2015/08/24/world/a-sprawl-of-abandoned -homes-in-tokyo-suburbs.html; Hiroko Tabuchi, "For Some in Japan, Home Is a Tiny Plastic Bunk," *New York Times*, January 1, 2010, http://www.nytimes .com/2010/01/02/business/global/02capsule.html.

8   Nate Berg, "Why China's Urbanization Isn't Creating a Middle Class," City Lab, February 29, 2012, https://www.citylab.com/life/2012/02/why-chinas -urbanization-isnt-creating-middle-class/1357/; "City Chickens and Country Eggs," *Economist*, August 4, 2013, https://www-economist-com.stanford.idm .oclc.org/analects/2013/08/04/city-chickens-and-country-eggs; Eva Dou and Dominique Fong, "Homeward Bound: Beijing Boots Migrant Workers to Trim Its Population," *Wall Street Journal*, November 29, 2017, https://www.wsj.com /articles/beijing-evictions-of-migrant-workers-sparks-outrage-1511962464.

9   Kai-Fu Lee, *AI Superpowers: China, Silicon Valley, and the New World Order* (Boston: Houghton Mifflin, 2018), 141; Hao Jingfang, "Folding Beijing," in *Invisible Planets: Contemporary Chinese Science Fiction in Translation*, trans. Ken Liu (New York: Tor, 2016), 221–62.

10   Richard Florida, "The Problem of Urbanization Without Economic Growth," City Lab, June 12 2015, https://www.citylab.com/life/2015/06/the-problem-of -urbanization-without-economic-growth/395648/; Richard Florida, "When Urbanization Doesn't Help," City Lab, June 22, 2016, https://www.citylab. com/equity/2016/06/disparities-of-urbanization-global-china-india/487625/; Susanne Frick, and Andres Rodriguez-Pose, "Big or Small Cities: On City Size and Economic Growth," *VoxEU*, October 20, 2017, https://voxeu.org/article /city-size-and-economic-growth.

11   Ivette Saldaña, "Estados del norte, los mas atractivos para la IED," *El Financiero*, April 7, 2008, http://biblioteca.iiec.unam.mx/index. php?option=com_content&task=view&id=1733&Itemid=146; "As Inequality Grows in Mexico, So Does Social Polarization," *World Politics Review*, January 19, 2017, https://www.worldpoliticsreview.com/trend-lines/20957/as-inequality -grows-in-mexico-so-does-social-polarization; Unequal Scenes, "Mexico City," https://unequalscenes.com/mexico-city-df.

12   M. S. Deshmukh, "Conditions of Slum Population of Major Sub-Urban Wards of Mumbai in Maharashtra," *Voice of Research*, vol. 2:2 (September 2013), 34–40, https://pdfs.semanticscholar.org/12a5/695be9318ee233fe025cc476eddc bc0580d3.pdf; Chittaranjan Tembhekar, "Mumbaikers die younger than other Indians," *Times of India*, November 3, 2009, https://timesofindia.indiatimes. com/india/Mumbaikars-die-younger-than-other-Indians-Study/articleshow /5190726.cms; R. N. Sharma, "The Housing Market in Mumbai Metropolis

and Its Relevance to the Average Citizen," in *Indian Cities in Transition*, ed. Annapurna Shaw (Chennai: Orient Longman, 2006), 284–85; Mira Advani, interview with author.

13　Michael Waldrep, "The Contemporary City at its Limits: Santa Fe, Mexico City," *National Geographic*, May 14, 2015, https://blog.nationalgeographic. org/2015/05/14/the-contemporary-city-at-its-limits-santa-fe-mexico-city/.

14　Rajiv Desai, "Incredible India Indeed," *Times of India*, November 6, 2009. https://timesofindia.indiatimes.com/edit-page/Incredible-India-Indeed /articleshow/5232986.cms.

15　John Sutherland, "The ideas interview: Saskia Sassen," *Guardian*, July 4, 2006, https://www.theguardian.com/world/2006/jul/04/globalisation.comment.

16　R. M. Sharma, interview with author, 2009.

17　Tomas Frejka, review of *Work: Ultra-Low Fertility in Pacific Asia: Trends, Causes and Policy Issues* by Gavin Jones et al., *Population and Development Review*, vol. 35:2 (2009), 423–25, https://www.jstor.org/stable/25487674; Joel Kotkin, "The Rise of Post-Familiaism: Humanity's Future?" Civil Service College Singapore and Chapman University, 2012, https://www.chapman. edu/wilkinson/_files/the-rise-of-post-familialism.pdf; Ali Modarres and Joel Kotkin, "The Childless City," *City Journal*, Summer 2013, https://www.city -journal.org/html/childless-city-13577.html.

18　Joel Kotkin and Wendell Cox, "America's Future Depends on the Bedroom, Not the Border," *New Geography*, April 22, 2019, http://www.newgeography.com /content/006282-america-s-future-depends-bedroom-not-border.

19　Derek Thompson, "The Future of the City Is Childless," *Atlantic*, July 18, 2019, https://www.theatlantic.com/ideas/archive/2019/07/where-have-all-the -children-gone/594133/.

20　NYU Furman Center, "Report Analyzes New York City's Gentrifying Neighborhoods and Finds Dramatic Demographic Shifts," *The Stoop*, May 9, 2016,.http://furmancenter.org/thestoop/entry/new-report-analyzes-new-york -citys-gentrifying-neighborhoods-and-finds-dram; Joel Kotkin, "America's Future Cities: Where the Youth Population Is Booming," *New Geography*, February 6, 2014, http://www.newgeography.com/content/004169-americas -future-cities-where-the-youth-population-is-booming.

21　Steve LeVine, "1 Big Thing: the great family exodus," *Axios*, January 25, 2019, https://www.axios.com/newsletters/axios-future-ddfc78e8-78ec-4285-87ab -f10565b42249.html.

22　Elizabeth Cheung, "Financial burdens, cramped living quarters and less sex: are these the reasons so many Hong Kong women are undecided about having children?" *South China Morning Post*, December 5, 2018, https://www.scmp. com/news/hong-kong/health-environment/article/2176389/financial-burdens -cramped-living-quarters-and-less.

23　"China's Birth Rates Reportedly Fell in Several Regions in 2018," CNBC, March 21, 2019, https://www.cnbc.com/2019/03/22/chinas-birth-rates-reportedly-fell -in-several-regions-in-2018.html; Sutirtho Patranobis, "Shanghai, Beijing have lowest fertility rates in the world," *Hindustan Times*, May 1, 2012, https://www .hindustantimes.com/world/shanghai-beijing-have-lowest-fertility-rates-in -the-world/story-cT8E4o0YxhFeXcgiydBX9O.html; Stuart Basten and

Quanbao Jiang, "Fertility in China: An Uncertain Future," *Population Studies*, vol. 69, Supp. 1 (April 30, 2015), S95–S105, https://www.ncbi.nlm.nih.gov/pmc/articles/PMC4440625/.

24 Greg Wilford, "Young Japanese people are not having sex," *Independent*, July 8, 2017, https://www.independent.co.uk/news/world/asia/japan-sex-problem-demographic-time-bomb-birth-rates-sex-robots-fertility-crisis-virgins-romance-porn-a7831041.html; Claire Aird, "Young Single People in Japan Aren't Having Sex and the Reason Is Proving Fatal," SBS, September 26, 2018, https://www.sbs.com.au/news/the-feed/young-single-people-in-japan-aren-t-having-sex-and-the-reason-is-proving-fatal.

25 Rachel Blundy, "Losing sex appeal? The future of Hong Kong's red light districts," *South China Morning Post*, December 3, 2016, https://www.scmp.com/news/hong-kong/economy/article/2051238/losing-sex-appeal-future-hong-kongs-red-light-districts.

26 Sui-Lee Wee, "In China, an Education in Dating," *New York Times*, November 18, 2017, https://www.nytimes.com/2017/11/18/business/china-dating-schools.html; Sui-Lee Wee, "In China, a School Trains Boys to Be 'Real Men,'" *New York Times*, November 23, 2018, https://www.nytimes.com/2018/11/23/business/china-boys-men-school.html; Interview with author.

27 John Dale Glover, "Xi's China Dreams Will Not Age Well," *Real Clear World*, November 9, 2017, https://www.realclearworld.com/articles/2017/11/09/xis_china_dreams_will_not_age_well_112625.html; Desmond Ng and Tan Jia Ning, "These are the leftover men of China, who just want to get married," CNA, July 3, 2018, https://www.channelnewsasia.com/news/cnainsider/leftover-men-china-get-married-gender-imbalance-one-child-policy-10485358; Qian Jinghua and Fan Yiying, "It's Complicated: Chinese Millennials and Marriage," *Sixth Tone*, August 4, 2018, http://www.sixthtone.com/news/1002717/its-complicated-chinese-millennials-and-marriage; Simon Denyer and Annie Gowen, "Too many men: China and India battle with the consequences of gender imbalance," *South China Morning Post*, April 24, 2018, https://www.scmp.com/magazines/post-magazine/long-reads/article/2142658/too-many-men-china-and-india-battle-consequences.

28 H. G. Wells, *Anticipations of the Reaction of Mechanical and Scientific Progress Upon Human Life and Thought* (Mineola, N.Y.: Dover Books, 1999), 31–32.

29 Joel Kotkin, *The City: A Global History* (New York: Modern Library, 2005), 114–16; Friedrich Engels, *The Condition of the Working Class in England* (London: Penguin, 2009), 31.

30 Frank Lloyd Wright, *The Living City* (New York: New American Library, 1958), 87.

31 R. K. Webb, *Modern England: From the Eighteenth Century to the Present* (New York: Dodd, Mead & Co., 1971), 576–77; Benjamin M. Friedman, *The Moral Consequences of Economic Growth* (New York: Knopf, 2005), 20, 63.

32 Mark Clapson, "Community and Association in Milton Keynes since 1970," in *The Best Laid Plans: Milton Keynes since 1967*, ed. Mark Clapson, Mervyn Dobbin, and Peter Waterman (Luton, UK: Luton University Press, 1998), 101–6; James Heartfield, *Let's Build: Why we need five hundred million new homes in the next ten years* (London: Audacity, 2006), 65; Karl Sharro, "Density Versus

Sprawl," in *The Future of Community (Reports of a Death Greatly Exaggerated)*, ed. Dave Clements et al. (London: Pluto Press, 2008), 67; John Boorman, *Adventures of a Suburban Boy* (London: Faber & Faber, 2003), n.p.

33 Wendell Cox, "Suburban Nations: Canada, Australia, and the United States," *New Geography*, December 30, 2016, http://www.newgeography.com/content /005495-suburban-nations-canada-australia-and-united-states.

34 Lawrence Yun et al., "2016 Profile of Home Buyers and Sellers," National Association of Realtors, October 31, 2016, https://www.nar.realtor/sites/ default/files/reports/2016/2016-profile-of-home-buyers-and-sellers-10-31 -2016.pdf; Joel Kotkin, "California Wages War on Single-Family Homes," *New Geography*, July 26, 2011, http://www.newgeography.com/content /002357-california-wages-war-on-single-family-homes.

35 Wendell Cox, "New York, Los Angeles, and Chicago Metro Areas All Lose Population," *New Geography*, April 19, 2019, http://www.newgeography.com /content/006280-new-york-los-angeles-and-chicago-metro-areas-all-lose -population.

36 Stephen Lacey, "Big smoke, bush or the 'burbs?" *Sidney Morning Herald*, June 27, 2013.

37 Shireen Khalil, "Australia needs to manage high density to be a successful global city, experts say," News.com.au, October 16, 2018, https://www.news .com.au/finance/real-estate/australia-needs-to-manage-high-density-to-be -a-successful-global-city-experts-say/news-story/2c9d0411daec4c9cf5eeebc009 ad24ba; Tony Rescei, "Predictable Punditry Down Under," *New Geography*, July 27, 2012, http://www.newgeography.com/content/002980-predictable-punditry -down-under; Urban Taskforce Australia, "Greater Sydney Plan sets direction but more advocacy for urban density needed," March 19, 2018, https://www .urbantaskforce.com.au/greater-sydney-plan-sets-direction-but-more -advocacy-for-urban-density-needed/.

38 Lester Black, "It's Official: Single Family Zoning Is Making Our City's Neighborhoods More White," *The Stranger*, December 4, 2018, https://www .thestranger.com/slog/2018/12/04/36711378/its-official-single-family-zoning -is-making-our-city-more-white; Henry Grabar, "Minneapolis confronts its history of housing segregation," *Slate*, December 7, 2018, https://slate.com /business/2018/12/minneapolis-single-family-zoning-housing-racism.html.

39 Victoria Fierce, "Why Building Housing Near Mass Transit Promotes Collectivism," *East Bay Express*, April 9, 2018, https://www.eastbayexpress.com /SevenDays/archives/2018/04/09/opinion-why-building-housing-near-mass -transit-promotes-collectivism.

40 Alicia Kurimska, "Looking Back: The Ideal Communist City," *New Geography*, January 19, 2015, http://www.newgeography.com/content/004830-looking -back-the-ideal-communist-city.

41 Robert Bruegmann, "The Anti-Suburban Crusade," in *Infinite Suburbia*, ed. Alan Berger and Joel Kotkin (New York: Princeton Architectural Press, 2018), 27–36.

CHAPTER 18—THE TOTALITARIAN URBAN FUTURE

1 Kevin Carty, "Tech Giants Are the Robber Barons of Our Time," *New York*

Post, February 3, 2018, https://nypost.com/2018/02/03/big-techs-monopolistic
-rule-is-hiding-in-plain-sight/.

2 Henry Grabar, "Building Googletown," *Slate*, October 25, 2017, https://slate.
com/technology/2017/10/sidewalk-labs-quayside-development-in-toronto
-is-googles-first-shot-at-building-a-city.html; Sophie Davies, "WiFi but No
Water: Can Smart Tech Help a City's Poor?" Reuters, January 4, 2018, https://
www.reuters.com/article/us-global-cities-tech-inequality/wi-fi-but-no-water
-can-smart-tech-help-a-citys-poor-idUSKBN1EU0JF.

3 William Mitchell, *City of Bits: Space, Place, and the Infobahn* (Cambridge,
Mass.: MIT Press, 1999), 50.

4 Luke Stangel, "Sam Altman wants Silicon Valley to sign on to a core set of
common values," *Silicon Valley Business Journal*, April 19, 2017, https://www
.bizjournals.com/sanjose/news/2017/04/19/sam-altman-donald-trump-silicon
-valley.html.

5 Jane Wakefield, "Tomorrow's Cities—nightmare vision of the future?" BBC,
February 22, 2017, https://www.bbc.com/news/technology-37384152.

6 Greg Ferenstein, "Silicon Valley's political endgame, summarized in 12 visuals,"
Medium, November 5, 2015, https://medium.com/the-ferenstein-wire/silicon
-valley-s-political-endgame-summarized-1f395785f3c1.

7 Geoff Nesnow, "73 Mind-blowing Implications of Driverless Cars and Trucks,"
Medium, February 9, 2018, https://medium.com/@DonotInnovate/73-mind
-blowing-implications-of-a-driverless-future-58d23d1f338d; Steve Andriole,
"Already Too Big to Fail—The Digital Oligarchy Is Alive, Well (& Growing),"
Forbes, July 29, 2017, https://www.forbes.com/sites/steveandriole/2017/07/29
/already-too-big-to-fail-the-digital-oligarchy-is-alive-well-growing
/#71125b7667f5.

8 Marisa Kendall, "Tech execs back California bill that aims to build more
housing near transit," *Mercury News*, January 25, 2018, https://www
.mercurynews.com/2018/01/24/tech-execs-back-bill-that-aims-to-build
-more-housing-near-transit/.

9 Ferenstein, "Silicon Valley's political endgame, summarized in 12 visuals."

10 Nellie Bowles, "Dorm Living for Professionals Comes for San Francisco," *New
York Times*, March 4, 2018, https://www.nytimes.com/2018/03/04/technology
/dorm-living-grown-ups-san-francisco.html; Emmie Martin, "Facebook and
Google are both building more affordable housing in Silicon Valley," CNBC,
July 10, 2017, https://www.cnbc.com/2017/07/07/facebook-and-google-are
-building-affordable-housing-in-silicon-valley.html; Avery Hartmans,
"Facebook is building a village that will include housing, a grocery store and a
hotel," *Business Insider*, July 7, 2017, https://www.businessinsider.com
/facebook-building-employee-housing-silicon-valley-headquarters-2017-7.

11 Ben Tarnoff, "Tech's push to teach coding isn't about kids' success—it's about
cutting wages," *Guardian*, September 21, 2017, https://www.theguardian.com
/technology/2017/sep/21/coding-education-teaching-silicon-valley-wages.

12 Gerard C. S. Mildner, "Density at Any Cost," *Center for Real Estate Quarterly
Report*, vol. 8:4 (Fall 2014), 3–23, https://www.pdx.edu/sba/sites/www.pdx.edu.
sba/files/01%20UGR%20-%20Mildner.pdf; Joel Kotkin, "U.S. Cities Have a Glut
of High-Rises and Still Lack Affordable Housing," *New Geography*, September

3, 2017, http://www.newgeography.com/content/005732-us-cities-have-a-glut -of-high-rises-and-still-lack-affordable-housing.

13 Erika Riggs, "Mark Zuckerberg spends $30 million on four homes to ensure privacy," NBC News, October 12, 2013, https://www.nbcnews.com/business /real-estate/mark-zuckerberg-spends-30-million-four-homes-ensure-privacy -f8C11379396; Melia Robinson, "We scouted the homes of the top tech executives, and they all live in this San Francisco suburb for the 1%," *Business Insider*, October 7, 2017, https://www.businessinsider.com/homes-of-tech-ceos -in-atherton-silicon-valley-2017-10; Meredith Bauer, "8 Amazing Homes of Silicon Valley's Tech Elite," The Street, May 23, 2015, https://www.thestreet.com /story/13160991/1/8-amazing-homes-of-silicon-valleys-tech-elite.html#3.

14 Veena Dubal, "Google as a landlord? A looming feudal nightmare," *Guardian*, July 11, 2019, https://www.theguardian.com/commentisfree/2019/jul/11/google -as-a-landlord-a-looming-feudal-nightmare?CMP=Share_iOSApp_Other.

15 Michele Lent Hirsch, "America's Company Towns, Then and Now," *Smithsonian*, September 4, 2015, https://www.smithsonianmag.com/travel /americas-company-towns-then-and-now-180956382/.

16 Andrew S. Ross, "In Silicon Valley, Age Can Be a Curse," *SFGate*, August 20, 2013, https://www.sfgate.com/business/bottomline/article/In-Silicon-Valley -age-can-be-a-curse-4742365.php.

17 Susan Crawford, "Beware of Google's Intentions," *Wired*, February 1, 2018, https://www.wired.com/story/sidewalk-labs-toronto-google-risks/; Sidewalk Toronto, "Toronto Tomorrow," https://sidewalktoronto.ca/#documents; Vipal Monga, "Toronto Officials Question Alphabet Unit's Ambitions for 'Smart City,'" *Wall Street Journal*, June 24, 2019, https://www.wsj.com/articles /toronto-officials-question-alphabet-units-ambitions-for-smart-city -11561412851.

18 "Sidewalk Labs's vision and your data privacy: A guide to the saga on Toronto's waterfront," *Globe and Mail*, June 24, 2019, https://www.theglobeandmail.com /canada/toronto/article-sidewalk-labs-quayside-toronto-waterfront-explainer/.

19 Crawford, "Beware of Google's Intentions."

20 "Albert Gidari," Center for Internet and Society, Stanford Law School, http:// cyberlaw.stanford.edu/about/people/albert-gidari.

21 Yulia Gorbunova, "Online and On All Fronts," Human Rights Watch, July 18, 2017, https://www.hrw.org/report/2017/07/18/online-and-all-fronts/russias -assault-freedom-expression; Leopord Hakizimana and Dr. Wilson Kipruto Cheruiyot, "The Use of an Intelligent Surveillance System in Developing Countries—Rwanda," *International Journal of Advanced Research in Computer Science and Software Engineering*, vol. 6:8 (August 2016), 162–68, https://www. researchgate.net/publication/317011846_The_Use_of_an_Intelligent _Surveillance_System_in_Developing_Countries-Rwanda.

22 Kai-Fu Lee, *AI Superpowers: China, Silicon Valley, and the New World Order* (Boston: Houghton Mifflin, 2018), 17, 83.

23 Ibid., 53.

24 Alexandra Ma, "China has started ranking citizens with a creepy 'social credit' system—here's what you can do wrong, and the embarrassing, demeaning ways

they can punish you," *Business Insider*, October 29, 2018, https://www
.businessinsider.com/china-social-credit-system-punishments-and-rewards
-explained-2018-4#a-prototype-blacklist-already-exists-and-has-been-used
-to-punish-people-8; Jeremy Page and Eva Dou, "In Sign of Resistance, Chinese
Balk at Using Apps to Snitch on Neighbors," *Wall Street Journal*, December 29,
2017, https://www.wsj.com/articles/in-sign-of-resistance-chinese-balk-at
-using-apps-to-snitch-on-neighbors-1514566110.

25 Christina Larson, "Who needs democracy when you have data?" *MIT
Technology Review*, August 20, 2018, https://www.technologyreview.com/s
/611815/who-needs-democracy-when-you-have-data/?utm.

26 Maggie Shen King, *An Excess Male* (New York: Harper, 2017), 393–84.

27 Tom Phillips, "China testing facial-recognition surveillance system in
Xinjiang—report," *Guardian*, January 18, 2018, https://www.theguardian.com
/world/2018/jan/18/china-testing-facial-recognition-surveillance-system-in
-xinjiang-report?CMP=share_btn_tw; "The Guardian view on surveillance
in China: Big Brother is watching," Editorial, *Guardian*, December 28, 2017,
https://www.theguardian.com/commentisfree/2017/dec/28/the-guardian-view
-on-surveillance-in-china-big-brother-is-watching; Megha Rajagopalan, "This
Is What a 21st-Century Police State Really Looks Like," *Buzzfeed*, October 17,
2017, https://www.buzzfeednews.com/article/meghara/the-police-state-of
-the-future-is-already-here#.kaqZrDywkR; Chris Buckley et al., "How China
Turned a City Into a Prison," *New York Times*, April 4, 2019, https://www
.nytimes.com/interactive/2019/04/04/world/asia/xinjiang-china-surveillance
-prison.html; Benjamin Haas, "Chinese authorities collecting DNA from all
residents of Xinjiang," *Guardian*, December 13, 2017, https://www.theguardian
.com/world/2017/dec/13/chinese-authorities-collecting-dna-residents-xinjiang;
Tom Phillips, "China orders GPS tracking of every car in troubled region,"
Guardian, February 21, 2017, https://www.theguardian.com/world/2017/feb
/21/china-orders-gps-tracking-of-every-car-in-troubled-region.

28 Josh Chin and Liza Lin, "China's All-Seeing Surveillance State Is Reading Its
Citizens' Faces," *Wall Street Journal*, June 26, 2017, https://www.wsj.com
/articles/the-all-seeing-surveillance-state-feared-in-the-west-is-a-reality-in
-china-1498493020; "Next-Level Surveillance: China Embraces Facial
Recognition," *Wall Street Journal*, June 26, 2017, https://www.wsj.com/video
/next-level-surveillance-china-embraces-facial-recognition/9ED95BFA-76EF
-48DA-A56B-50126AFDDA1C.html.

29 Stephen Chan, "'Forget the Facebook leak': China is mining data directly from
workers' brains on an industrial scale," *South China Morning Post*, May 2, 2018,
http://www.scmp.com/news/china/society/article/2143899/forget-facebook
-leak-china-mining-data-directly-workers-brains.

30 Richard Florida, "When Urbanization Doesn't Help," City Lab, June 22, 2016,
https://www.citylab.com/equity/2016/06/disparities-of-urbanization-global
-china-india/487625/.

31 Daniel Lyon, "Surveillance, Power, and Everyday Life," *Oxford Handbook of
Information and Communication Technologies*, https://panoptykon.org/sites
/default/files/FeedsEnclosure-oxford_handbook_3.pdf.

32 David Byrne, "Eliminating the Human," *Technology Review*, August 15, 2017, https://www.technologyreview.com/s/608580/eliminating-the-human/.

33 Peter Swire, "Should the Leading Online Tech Companies Be Regulated as Public Utilities?" *Lawfare*, August 2, 2017, https://www.lawfareblog.com /should-leading-online-tech-companies-be-regulated-public-utilities; Alex Shepard, "The Myth of Big Tech's Comeuppance," *New Republic*, December 29, 2017, https://newrepublic.com/article/146437/myth-big-techs-comeuppance.

34 Erin Griffith, "Facebook's Future Rests on Knowing You Even Better," *Wired*, February 1, 2019, https://www.wired.com/story/facebooks-future-rests-on -knowing-you-even-better/.

CHAPTER 19—THE TECHNOLOGICAL CHALLENGE

1 Andro Linklater, *Owning the Earth: The Transforming History of Land Ownership* (New York: Bloomsbury USA, 2013), 281; Jeffrey A. Winters, *Oligarchy* (Cambridge: Cambridge University Press, 2011), 5.

2 Sarah Jones, "Lessons From the Gilded Age," *New Republic*, June 13, 2018, https://newrepublic.com/article/149005/lessons-gilded-age; Fergus M. Bordewich, "How the Gilded Age Got That Way," *Wall Street Journal*, August 25, 2017, https://www.wsj.com/articles/how-the-gilded-age-got-that-way -1503683705.

3 Richard V. Reeves, *Dream Hoarders: How the American Upper Middle Class Is Leaving Everyone Else in the Dust, Why That Is a Problem, and What to Do About It* (Washington, D.C.: Brookings Institution Press, 2018), 8.

4 Satyajit Das, "Despite appearances, the idea of social progress is a myth," *Independent*, July 30, 2017, https://www.independent.co.uk/voices/despite -appearances-the-idea-of-social-progress-is-a-myth-a7867371.html.

5 H. G. Wells, *Anticipations of the Reaction of Mechanical and Scientific Progress Upon Human Life and Support* (Mineola, N.Y.: Dover Publications, 1999), 99; Fred Siegel, *The Revolt Against the Masses: How Liberalism Has Undermined the Middle Class* (New York: Encounter, 2015), 7, 43.

6 Ned Levin et al., "China Tightens Restrictions on Messaging Apps," *Wall Street Journal*, August 7, 2014, https://www.wsj.com/articles/china-issues-new -restrictions-on-messaging-apps-1407405666; Maya Wang, "China's Chilling 'Social Credit' Blacklist," *Wall Street Journal*, December 11, 2017, https://www .wsj.com/articles/chinas-chilling-social-credit-blacklist-1513036054.

7 Arjun Kharpal, "A.I. is in a 'golden age' and solving problems that were once in the realm of sci-fi, Jeff Bezos says," CNBC, May 8, 2017, https://www.cnbc .com/2017/05/08/amazon-jeff-bezos-artificial-intelligence-ai-golden-age.html; Michael Knox Beran, "The Narrowing of the Elite: Part One," *National Review*, September 19, 2018, https://www.nationalreview.com/2018/09/educated-elites -faith-in-salvation-through-technology/.

8 Jill Priluck, "America's corporate activism: the rise of the CEO as social justice warrior," *Guardian*, July 2, 2019, https://www.theguardian.com /commentisfree/2019/jul/01/americas-corporate-activism-the-rise-of-the-ceo -as-social-justice-warrior.

9 Irving Kristol, "Is Technology a Threat to Liberal Society?" *Public Interest*,

Spring 2001, https://www.nationalaffairs.com/storage/app/uploads/public /58e/1a4/fad/58e1a4fad2bd7881345590.pdf.

10   Judea Pearl and Dana Mackenzie, "AI Can't Reason Why," *Wall Street Journal*, May 18, 2018, https://www.wsj.com/articles/ai-cant-reason-why-1526657442.

11   "The Immortalist: Uploading the Mind to a Computer," BBC, March 14, 2016, https://www.bbc.com/news/magazine-35786771.

12   Stanley Bing, *The Immortal Life* (New York: Simon & Schuster, 2017), 142–43.

13   Polina Aronson and Judith Duportail, "The quantified heart," *Aeon*, July 12, 2018, https://aeon.co/essays/can-emotion-regulating-tech-translate-across -cultures; Gale M. Lucas, "It's only a computer: Virtual humans increase willingness to disclose," *Computers in Human Behavior*, vol. 37 (August 2014), 94–100, https://www.sciencedirect.com/science/article/pii/S0747563214002647.

14   Polina Aronson, "Romantic regimes," *Aeon*, October 22, 2015, https://aeon.co /essays/russia-against-the-western-way-of-love.

15   David Crotty, "Algorithms Are Opinions Embedded in Code," Scholarly Kitchen, January 19, 2018, https://scholarlykitchen.sspnet.org/2018/01/19 /algorithms-opinions-embedded-code/.

16   Jean M. Twenge, "Have Smartphones Destroyed a Generation?" *Atlantic*, September 2017, https://www.theatlantic.com/magazine/archive/2017/09/has -the-smartphone-destroyed-a-generation/534198/; Rhitu Chatterjee, "Americans Are a Lonely Lot, And Young People Bear the Heaviest Burden," NPR, May 1, 2018, https://www.npr.org/sections/health-shots/2018/05/01 /606588504/americans-are-a-lonely-lot-and-young-people-bear-the-heaviest -burden.

17   Michelle N. Meyer, "Everything You Need to Know About Facebook's Controversial Emotion Experiment," *Wired*, June 30, 2014, https://www.wired .com/2014/06/everything-you-need-to-know-about-facebooks-manipulative -experiment/; Roger McNamee, "I invested early in Google and Facebook. Now they terrify me," *USA Today*, August 10, 2017, https://www.usatoday.com/story /opinion/2017/08/08/my-google-and-facebook-investments-made-fortune-but -now-they-menace/543755001/.

18   Nellie Bowles, "A Dark Consensus About Screens and Kids Begins to Emerge in Silicon Valley," *New York Times*, October 26, 2018, https://www.nytimes.com /2018/10/26/style/phones-children-silicon-valley.html.

19   Shannon Molloy, "We've raised Generation Hopeless: millennials who lack basic life and workplace skills. And it's a big issue," News.com.au, July 4, 2017, https://www.news.com.au/finance/business/weve-raised-generation-hopeless -millennials-who-lack-basic-life-and-workplace-skills-and-its-a-big-issue /news-story/f3256c05c19c356002103eb50e50cee1; Kate Davidson, "Employers Find 'Soft Skills' Like Critical Thinking in Short Supply," *Wall Street Journal*, August 30, 2016, https://www.wsj.com/articles/employers-find-soft-skills -like-critical-thinking-in-short-supply-1472549400?mod=djcm_OBV1_092216; Rurik Bradbury, "The digital lives of Millennials and Gen Z," Liveperson, September 2017, https://www.liveperson.com/resources/reports/digital-lives -of-millennials-genz/.

20   Kate Julian, "Why Are Young People Having So Little Sex?" *Atlantic*, December

2018, https://www.theatlantic.com/magazine/archive/2018/12/the-sex
-recession/573949/; Simon Denyer and Annie Gowen, "Too many men: China
and India battle with the consequences of gender imbalance," *South China
Morning Post*, https://www.scmp.com/magazines/post-magazine/long-reads
/article/2142658/too-many-men-china-and-india-battle-consequences; Anna
Louie Sussman, "The End of Babies," *New York Times*, November 16, 2019,
https://www.nytimes.com/interactive/2019/11/16/opinion/sunday/capitalism
-children.html.

21 Greg Wilford, "Young Japanese people are not having sex," *Independent*, July 8,
2017, http://www.independent.co.uk/news/world/asia/japan-sex-problem
-demographic-time-bomb-birth-rates-sex-robots-fertility-crisis-virgins
-romance-porn-a7831041.html; Eric Spitznagel, "You Can Sleep with the
Latest Sex Robots at This Brothel—But Only if They Say 'Yes,'" *Observer*,
November 27, 2018, https://observer.com/2018/11/sex-robots-hollywood
-brothel-requires-consent-real-doll/.

22 Michel Houllebecq, *Whatever*, trans. Paul Hammond (London: Serpent's Tale,
2011), 14.

23 Alvin Toffler, *Future Shock* (New York: Bantam, 1984), 452, 186; Brian
Merchant, "Fully automated luxury communism," *Guardian*, March 18, 2015,
https://www.theguardian.com/sustainable-business/2015/mar/18/fully
-automated-luxury-communism-robots-employment.

24 Glenn Harlan Reynolds, "When Digital Platforms Become Censors," *Wall
Street Journal*, August 18, 2018, https://www.wsj.com/articles/when-digital
-platforms-become-censors-1534514122.

25 Jacques Ellul, *The Technological Society*, trans. John Wilkinson (New York:
Knopf, 1964), 432–33; Amy Dockser Marcus, "Scientists Confront the Ghost of
Eugenics," *Wall Street Journal*, August 17, 2018, https://www.wsj.com/articles
/scientists-confront-the-ghost-of-eugenics-1534523929.

26 Yuval Noah Harari, *Homo Deus: A Brief History of Tomorrow* (New York:
HarperCollins, 2017), 67.

27 Ibid., 150.

CHAPTER 20—THE SHAPING OF NEO-FEUDAL SOCIETY

1 Marc Bloch, *Feudal Society*, trans. L. A. Manyon (Chicago: University of
Chicago Press, 1961), 246–47; R. R. Palmer, *The World of the French Revolution*
(New York: Harper & Row, 1971), 19.

2 Nicole S. Garnett, "Suburbs as Exit, Suburbs as Entrance," *Michigan Law
Review*, vol. 106 (2007–8), 277–304, https://scholarship.law.nd.edu/law
_faculty_scholarship/105.

3 Crystal Galyean, "Levittown," U.S. History Scene, April 10, 2015, http://
ushistoryscene.com/article/levittown/; National Association of Realtors, "Social
Benefits of Homeownership and Stable Housing," April 2012, https://www.nar.
realtor/sites/default/files/migration_files/social-benefits-of-stable-housing
-2012-04.pdf; Habitat for Humanity of York County, "Beneficial Impacts of
Homeownership: A Research Summary," http://yorkcountyhabitat.org
/~yorkco6/habitat/events/index.php?option=com_content&view=article&id
=100&Itemid=252.

4 Wendell Cox, "Suburban Nations: Canada, Australia, and the United States," *New Geography*, December 30, 2016, http://www.newgeography.com /content/005495-suburban-nations-canada-australia-and-united-states; At Home in Europe, "The ideal home of Europeans has five rooms," http://www .at-home-in-europe.eu/home-life/europe/the-ideal-home-of-europeans-has -five-rooms; Ben Weidmann and Jane-Frances Kelly, "What Matters Most: Housing Preferences Across the Australian Population," Grattan Institute, September 11, https://grattan.edu.au/wp-content/uploads/2014/04/109_what _matters_most.pdf; NAHB Economics and Housing Policy Group, "Housing preferences across generations," March 1, 2016, http://www.nahbclassic.org /generic.aspx?genericContentID=249797&channelID=311; Joel Kotkin, "The Progressives' War on Suburbia," *New Geography*, November 16, 2014, http:// www.newgeography.com/content/004773-the-progressives-war-suburbia.

5 Patrick Condon, "Government should supply housing for up to 40 percent of Vancouver wage earners," *Think Pol*, December 3, 2017, https://thinkpol .ca/2017/12/03/condon-govt-should-supply-housing-for-up-to-40-percent -of-vancouver-wage-earners/; Edward Ring, "The Density Delusion," California Policy Center, August 20, 2019, https://californiapolicycenter.org/the-density -delusion/.

6 "A home truth for the Tories: fix the housing crisis or lose power for ever," *Spectator*, April 21, 2018, https://www.spectator.co.uk/2018/04/a-home-truth -for-the-tories-fix-the-housing-crisis-or-lose-power-for-ever.

7 Joseph Chamie, "The Rise of One-Person Households," Inter Press Service News Agency, February 22, 2017, http://www.ipsnews.net/2017/02/the-rise-of -one-person-households/; Eric Klinenberg, *Going Solo: The Extraordinary Rise and Surprising Appeal of Living Alone* (New York: Penguin, 2013), 38–39; Council on Contemporary Families, "Reminder: Marriage Is No Longer the Mode," September 12, 2017, https://contemporaryfamilies.org/singles2017 factsheet/.

8 Jan Woronoff, *Japan: The Coming Social Crisis* (Tokyo: Lotus Press, 1984), 349–50.

9 Choe Sang-Hun, "A Writer Evokes Loss on South Korea's Path to Success," *New York Times*, September 8, 2012, https://www.nytimes.com/2012/09/08/world /asia/shin-kyung-sook-mines-south-koreas-sense-of-loss.html.

10 "All the Single Ladies: China Leads World in Unmarried People—Report," *Sputnik International*, December 21, 2016, https://sputniknews.com/art _living/201612211048842308-china-unmarried-people/; Chamie, "The Rise of One-Person Households."

11 Joel Kotkin, "The Rise of Post-Familialism: Humanity's Future," Chapman University and Civil Service College of Singapore, 2012, https://www.chapman .edu/wilkinson/_files/the-rise-of-post-familialism.pdf.

12 Mary Eberstadt, "'The Great Scattering': How Identity Panic Took Root in the Void Once Occupied by Family Life," *Quillette*, August 27, 2019, https:// quillette.com/2019/08/27/the-great-scattering-how-identity-panic-took-root -in-the-void-once-occupied-by-family-life/.

13 Klinenberg, *Going Solo*; Liz Greene, "Why Millennials Are Choosing to Be Child-Free," Role Reboot, February 6, 2019, http://www.rolereboot.org/culture

-and-politics/details/2019-02-why-millennials-are-choosing-to-be-child
-free/; Claire Cain Miller, "Americans Are Having Fewer Babies. They Told Us
Why," *New York Times*, July 5, 2018, https://www.nytimes.com/2018/07/05
/upshot/americans-are-having-fewer-babies-they-told-us-why.html; Pew
Research Center, "Parenting in America," December 17, 2015, http://www
.pewsocialtrends.org/2015/12/17/1-the-american-family-today/.

14 Morley Winograd and Michael D. Hais, "Millennials' Home Ownership
Dreams Delayed, Not Abandoned," *New Geography*, June 17, 2012, http://www
.newgeography.com/content/002919-millennials%E2%80%99-home-ownership
-dreams-delayed-not-abandoned.

15 Nina Bahadur, "Child-free by Choice: When You Don't Want Kids—but Your
Doctor Won't Listen," *Self*, March 1, 2018, https://www.self.com/story/childfree-
by-choice; Gladys Martinez et al., "Fertility of Men and Women Aged 15–44
Years in the United States: National Survey of Family Growth, 2006–2010,"
National Health Statistics Report, no. 51 (April 12, 2012), U.S. Department of
Health and Human Services, https://www.cdc.gov/nchs/data/nhsr/nhsr051.pdf.

16 John Fleming, "Gallup Analysis: Millennials, Marriage and Family," Gallup,
May 19, 2016, https://news.gallup.com/poll/191462/gallup-analysis-millennials
-marriage-family.aspx; Gretchen Livingston, "More than a million Millennials
are becoming moms each year," Pew Research Center, May 4, 2018, http://www.
pewresearch.org/fact-tank/2018/05/04/more-than-a-million-millennials
-are-becoming-moms-each-year/; Russell Heimlich, "Parenting a Priority," Pew
Research Center, March 24, 2010, http://www.pewresearch.org/fact-tank
/2010/03/24/parenting-a-priority/.

17 Greg Ip, "For Economy, Aging Population Poses Double Whammy," *Wall Street
Journal*, August 3, 2016, https://www.wsj.com/articles/for-economy-aging
-population-poses-double-whammy-1470249965.

18 James Pethokoukis, "On economic growth and the decline in US births,"
American Enterprise Institute, June 2, 2016, http://www.aei.org/publication
/on-economic-growth-and-the-decline-in-us-births/; Robin Harding, "Japan's
elderly care bill soaks up worker pay rises," *Financial Times*, May 29, 2018;
Bryan Harris, "Rise in Older Workers Challenges South Korea," *Financial
Times*, March 13, 2018; Eleanor Warnock, "Numbers of Japanese Elders in
Workforce Soar," *Wall Street Journal*, November 28, 2016, https://www.wsj.com
/articles/numbers-of-japanese-elders-in-workforce-soar-1480393642; Andrea
Thomas, "In Spite of Thrifty Image, Germany Races to Raise Pensions," *Wall
Street Journal*, November 25, 2016, https://www.wsj.com/articles/in-spite-of
-thrifty-image-germany-races-to-raise-pensions-1480084689; "Germany faces
huge shortage of skilled workers," Deutsche Welle, August 30, 2017, https://
www.dw.com/en/germany-faces-huge-shortage-of-skilled-workers/a-40294450.

19 Alejandro Macarrón Larumbe, *Demographic Suicide in the West and half the
world: Either more births or catastrophe?* (Scotts Valley, Calif.: CreateSpace,
2017), 33, 50, 60; "Winning: No Country For Old Men Or New Mothers,"
Strategy Page, November 13, 2018, https://strategypage.com/htmw/htwin
/articles/20181113.aspx.

20 Joe Myers, "China's working-age population will fall 23% by 2050," World
Economic Forum, July 25, 2018, https://www.weforum.org/agenda/2016/07
/china-working-ageing-population/.

21 U.S. House of Representatives, "Genocide: China's Missing Girls," Hearing Before the Congressional-Executive Commission on China, 114th Congress, February 3, 2016 (U.S. Government Publishing Office), https://www.govinfo .gov/content/pkg/CHRG-114hhrg99772/html/CHRG-114hhrg99772.htm.

22 John Dale Gover, "Xi's China Dreams Will Not Age Well," *Real Clear World*, November 9, 2017, https://www.realclearworld.com/articles/2017/11/09/xis _china_dreams_will_not_age_well_112625.html.

23 Robinson Meyer, "A Terrifying Sea-Level Prediction Now Looks Far Less Likely," *Atlantic*, January 4, 2019, https://www.theatlantic.com/science/archive /2019/01/sea-level-rise-may-not-become-catastrophic-until-after-2100 /579478/; Roger Pielke, Jr., "Some Good News—About Natural Disasters, of All Things," *Wall Street Journal*, August 3, 2018, https://www.wsj.com /articles/some-good-newsabout-natural-disasters-of-all-things-1533331596; Nicholas Fondacaro, "NYT Reporter Demands You Become 'Hysterical' About Climate Change," *NewsBusters*, November 25, 2018, https://www.newsbusters. org/blogs/nb/nicholas-fondacaro/2018/11/25/nyt-reporter-demands-you -become-hysterical-about-climate.

24 Steven E. Koonin, "Climate Science Is Not Settled," *Wall Street Journal*, September 19, 2014, https://www.wsj.com/articles/climate-science-is-not -settled-1411143565?mod=trending_now_1; Steven Koonin, "The Climate Won't Crash the Economy," *Wall Street Journal*, November 26, 2018, https://www.wsj .com/articles/the-climate-wont-crash-the-economy-1543276899?mod=?mod =itp&mod=djemITP_h.

25 Francis Menton, "What Is The Cost Of Getting To A 100% 'Renewable' Electric Grid?" Manhattan Contrarian, August 7, 2018, https://www .manhattancontrarian.com/blog/2018-8-6-what-is-the-cost-of-getting-to-a-100 -renewable-electric-grid; James Temple, "Wide-scale US wind power could cause significant warming," *MIT Technology Review*, October 4, 2018, https:// www.technologyreview.com/s/612238/wide-scale-us-wind-power-could-cause -significant-warming/; Leah Burrows, "The down side to wind power," *Harvard Gazette*, October 4, 2018, https://news.harvard.edu/gazette/story/2018/10 /large-scale-wind-power-has-its-down-side/; Niclas Rolander, Jesper Starn, and Elisabeth Behrmann, "The Dirt on Clean Electric Cars," Bloomberg, https:// www.bloomberg.com/news/articles/2018-10-16/the-dirt-on-clean-electric-cars; James Temple, "The $2.5 trillion reason we can't rely on batteries to clean up the grid," *MIT Technology Review*, July 27, 2018, https://www.technologyreview .com/s/611683/the-25-trillion-reason-we-cant-rely-on-batteries-to-clean-up- the-grid/.

26 Jack Dini, "Paris Accord Not Meeting Targets," *Canada Free Press*, August 30, 2018, https://canadafreepress.com/article/paris-accord-not-meeting-targets; Bjorn Lomborg, "Paris climate promises will reduce temperatures by just 0.05°C in 2100," Press Release, November 2015, https://www.lomborg.com /press-release-research-reveals-negligible-impact-of-paris-climate-promises.

27 David Friedman and Jennifer Hernandez, "California, Greenhouse Gas Regulation, and Climate Change," *New Geography*, June 25, 2018, http://www .newgeography.com/files/California%20GHG%20Regulation%20Final.pdf; Frank Dohmen et al., "German Failure on the Road to a Renewable Future," *Spiegel*, May 13, 2019, https://www.spiegel.de/international/germany/german

-failure-on-the-road-to-a-renewable-future-a-1266586.html; William Wilkes, Hayley Warren, and Brian Parkin, "Germany's Failed Climate Goals: A Wake-Up Call for Governments Everywhere," *Bloomberg*, August 15, 2018, https://www.bloomberg.com/graphics/2018-germany-emissions/.

28 Bjorn Lomborg, "Trade-Offs for Global Do-Gooders," *Wall Street Journal*, September 18, 2015, https://www.wsj.com/articles/trade-offs-for-global-do-gooders-1442589938; Bjorn Lomborg, "Pseudo Scientific Hysteria Is the Wrong Answer to Climate Change," *New York Post*, August 2, 2019, https://nypost.com/2019/08/02/pseudo-scientific-hysteria-is-the-wrong-answer-to-climate-change/.

29 Roger Pielke, Jr., "Book excerpt: The iron law of climate policy," *Financial Post*, October 4, 2010, https://sciencepolicy.colorado.edu/admin/publication_files/2010.47.pdf; Aaron Patrick and Bo Seo, "GetUp's aggressive, progressive tactics may have backfired," *Financial Review*, May 23, 2019, https://www.afr.com/politics/federal/getup-s-aggressive-progressive-tactics-may-have-backfired-20190522-p51pxs.

30 Ian Bailey, "Notley points to pipeline battle with B.C. as reason she won't attend Western Premiers' Conference," *Globe and Mail*, May 21, 2018, https://www.theglobeandmail.com/canada/article-notley-points-to-pipeline-battle-with-bc-as-reason-she-wont-attend/.

31 Alissa J. Rubin, "Macron Inspects Damage After 'Yellow Vest' Protests as France Weighs State of Emergency," *New York Times*, December 1, 2018, https://www.nytimes.com/2018/12/01/world/europe/france-yellow-vests-protests-macron.html.

32 Austin Williams, *The Enemies of Progress: The Dangers of Sustainability* (Exeter: Imprint Academic, 2008), 152.

33 Norman F. Cantor, *Medieval History: The Life and Death of a Civilization* (New York: Macmillan, 1963), 25.

34 Lyman Stone, "In a State of Migration," *Medium*, December 30, 2019, https://medium.com/migration-issues/more-thoughts-on-falling-fertility-366fd1a84d8; Rachel Lu, "The Problem with the 'Science' Behind Having Fewer Children for the Planet's Sake," *National Review*, July 15, 2017, https://www.nationalreview.com/2017/07/climate-change-study-population-reduction-childlessness-recommendation-preposterous-carbon-footprint/; Paul A. Murtaugh and Michael G. Schlax, "Reproduction and the carbon legacies of individuals," *Global Environment Change*, vol. 190 (2009), 14–20, https://www.biologicaldiversity.org/programs/population_and_sustainability/pdfs/OSUCarbonStudy.pdf.

35 Simon Evans and Rosamund Pearce, "Global coal power," *Carbon Brief*, March 25, 2019, https://www.carbonbrief.org/mapped-worlds-coal-power-plants; China Is a Highly Suspect Leader on Climate Change," *Wall Street Journal*, June 2, 2017, https://www.wsj.com/articles/china-is-a-highly-suspect-leader-on-climate-change-1496394151; Keith Bradsher and Lisa Friedman, "China's Emissions: More Than U.S. Plus Europe, and Still Rising," *New York Times*, January 25, 2018, https://www.nytimes.com/2018/01/25/business/china-davos-climate-change.html; Jia Hepeng, "Opinion: Why are there no climate sceptics in the Chinese media?" China Dialogue, December 28, 2017, https://www

.chinadialogue.net/article/show/single/en/10287-Opinion-Why-are-there
-no-climate-sceptics-in-the-Chinese-media-; Daniel K. Gardner, "Trump Is
Unwilling to Tackle Climate Change. China Must Step Up," *New York Times*,
December 10, 2018, https://www.nytimes.com/2018/12/10/opinion/china-trump
-climate-change.html.

36 Yu Shunkun et al., "China Wrestles with Power Shortages," *Power Magazine*,
May 1, 2013, https://www.powermag.com/china-wrestles-with-power
-shortages/; Rajesh Kumar Singh and Saket Sundria, "India Nears Power
Success, But Millions Still in the Dark," *T&D World*, May 2, 2018, https://www
.tdworld.com/utility-business/india-nears-power-success-millions-still-dark;
Project Partner, "China's Clean Water Shortage Intensifies the Poverty Crisis,"
https://projectpartner.org/clean-water/chinas-clean-water-shortage-intensifies
-the-poverty-crisis/; Rina Chandran, "163,000,000 People in India Don't Have
Clean Water. This Is Why," Global Citizen, April 25, 2018, https://www
.globalcitizen.org/en/content/india-day-zero-clean-water-access-shortage/;
Hannah Daly, "1.1 billion people still lack electricity. This could be the solution,"
World Economic Forum, June 20, 2018, https://www.weforum.org/agenda
/2018/06/1-billion-people-lack-electricity-solution-mini-grid-iea/.

37 Ted Nordhaus, "Impossible Environmentalism: Green groups promote utopian
fantasies," *USA Today*, September 7, 2017, https://www.usatoday.com/story/
opinion/2017/09/07/impossible-environmentalism-does-not-address
-sustainability-ted-nordhaus-column/570651001/.

38 Lewis Page, "Renewable energy 'simply won't work': Top google engineers,"
Register, November 21, 2014, https://www.theregister.co.uk/2014/11/21
/renewable_energy_simply_wont_work_google_renewables_engineers/; Lewis
Page, "Renewable energy can't do the job. Gov should switch green subsidies
into R&D," *Register*, June 26, 2015, https://www.theregister.co.uk/2015/06/26
/gates_renewable_energy_cant_do_the_job_gov_should_switch_green
_subsidies_into_rd/.

39 David R. Henderson and John H. Cochrane, "Climate Change Isn't the End of
the World," *Wall Street Journal*, July 30, 2017, https://www.wsj.com/articles
/climate-change-isnt-the-end-of-the-world-1501446277; Paul Mulshine, "The
'lukewarmers' show how environmentalists are in denial about denial," NJ.com,
March 12, 2017, https://www.nj.com/opinion/index.ssf/2017/03/the_radical
_environmentalists_are_in_denial_about.html.

40 Kristina Costa and Cathleen Kelly, "5 Ways the New Congress Should Support
Resilient Infrastructure," Center for American Progress, November 15, 2018,
https://www.americanprogress.org/issues/green/news/2018/11/15/461048/5
-ways-new-congress-support-resilient-infrastructure/; Bay Area News Group
and Paul Rogers, "Gov. Jerry Brown proposes easing logging rules to thin
forests," *Santa Cruz Sentinel*, November 20, 2018, https://www
.santacruzsentinel.com/2018/08/23/gov-jerry-brown-proposes-easing
-logging-rules-to-thin-forests/.

41 Jonathan Israel, *The Dutch Republic: Its Rise, Greatness, and Fall, 1477-1806*
(Oxford: Oxford University Press 1995), 9–11, 112.

42 Joseph Tainter, *The Collapse of Complex Societies* (Cambridge: Cambridge
University Press, 1988), 6–11.

43 Sara Grossman, "Gilbert F. White, National Medal of Science, Physical Sciences," National Science and Technology Medals Foundation, https://www.nationalmedals.org/laureates/gilbert-f-white.

44 Jeff Sluyter-Beltrão, "Iron law of oligarchy," *Britannica*, https://www.britannica.com/topic/iron-law-of-Oligarchy.

45 Shadi Hamid, "The Good Liberal," *American Interest*, March 2018, https://www.the-american-interest.com/2018/03/06/the-good-liberal/.

46 David Runciman, "Democracy Is the Planet's Biggest Enemy," *Foreign Policy*, July 20, 2019, https://foreignpolicy.com/2019/07/20/democracy-is-the-planets-biggest-enemy-climate-change/.

47 Venkatesh Rao, "Why Solving Climate Change Will Be Like Mobilizing for War," *Atlantic*, October 15, 2015, https://www.theatlantic.com/science/archive/2015/10/why-only-a-technocratic-revolution-can-win-the-climate-change-war/410377/; Bill McKibben, "A World at War," *New Republic*, August 15, 2016, https://newrepublic.com/article/135684/declare-war-climate-change-mobilize-wwii; David Wallace-Wells, "Can liberal democracy survive climate change?" *Economist*, March 29, 2019, https://www.economist.com/open-future/2019/03/29/can-liberal-democracy-survive-climate-change.

48 Joan Desmond, "California Gov. to Vatican: 'Brainwashing' Needed to Tackle Climate Change," *National Catholic Register*, November 12, 2017, http://www.ncregister.com/blog/joan-desmond/california-gov.-to-vatican-brain-washing-needed-to-tackle-climate-change; David Siders, "Jerry Brown: 'Never underestimate the coercive power of the central state,'" *Sacramento Bee*, December 7, 2015, https://www.sacbee.com/news/politics-government/capitol-alert/article48466200.html; "A Vital Partnership: California and China Collaborating on Clean Energy and Combating Climate Change," Asia Society, https://asiasociety.org/center-us-china-relations/vital-partnership-california-and-china-collaborating-clean-energy-and-comb; Alejandro Lazo, "Jerry Brown Allies with China to Fight Climate Change," *Wall Street Journal*, September 23, 2019, https://www.wsj.com/articles/jerry-brown-allies-with-china-to-fight-climate-change-11569273903; Li Jing, "Is China's 'city of the future' a replicable model?" China Dialogue, June 29, 2018, https://www.chinadialogue.net/article/show/single/en/10704-Is-China-s-city-of-the-future-a-replicable-model-; Matthew Stinson, "Salesman Xi," *National Review*, June 26, 2017, https://www.nationalreview.com/magazine/2017/06/26/xi-jinping-china-west-liberals/.

CHAPTER 21—CAN WE CHALLENGE NEO-FEUDALISM?

1 Martin Jacques, *When China Rules the World: The End of the Western World and the Birth of a New Global Order* (New York: Penguin, 2012), 149.

2 Larry Diamond, "The Global Crisis of Democracy," *Wall Street Journal*, May 17, 2019, https://www.wsj.com/articles/the-global-crisis-of-democracy-11558105463.

3 Hal Brands, "China's Master Plan: Exporting an Ideology," Bloomberg, June 11, 2018, https://www.bloomberg.com/opinion/articles/2018-06-11/china-s-master-plan-exporting-an-ideology; Yuen Yuen Ang, "How China's development story can be an alternative to the Western model," *South China Morning Post*,

February 3, 2017, https://www.scmp.com/comment/insight-opinion/article
/2067512/how-chinas-development-story-can-be-alternative-western.

4 Rachel Nuwer, "How Western civilization could collapse," BBC, April 18, 2017,
   http://www.bbc.com/future/story/20170418-how-western-civilisation-could
   -collapse.

5 Jonathan Tepper and Denise Hearn, *The Myth of Capitalism: Monopolies and
   the Death of Competition* (New York: John Wiley & Sons, 2019), 2.

6 Wolfgang Streeck, *How Will Capitalism End? Essays on a Failing System* (New
   York: Verso, 2016), 31–33; Danny Westneat, "Microsoft, Amazon, others excel at
   offshore tax dance," *Seattle Times*, April 6, 2016, https://www.seattletimes.com/
   seattle-news/microsoft-amazon-others-excel-at-offshore-tax-dance/; Sarah
   Fallon, "How Big Tech Companies Make Their Tax Bills Vanish," *Wired*, April
   15, 2015, https://www.wired.com/2015/04/big-tech-companies-make-tax-bills
   -vanish/; David Pring-Mill, "Are Tech Companies Avoiding Taxes?" *National
   Interest*, February 8, 2018, https://nationalinterest.org/feature/are-tech
   -companies-avoiding-taxes-2413; Jesse Ducker and Simon Bowers, "After a
   Tax Crackdown, Apple Found a New Shelter for Its Profits," *New York Times*,
   November 6, 2017, https://www.nytimes.com/2017/11/06/world/apple-taxes
   -jersey.html.

7 Darel E. Paul, "The European Center Weakens," *Real Clear Politics*, May 28,
   2019, https://www.realclearpolitics.com/2019/05/28/the_european_center
   _weakens_475904.html.

8 Barrington Moore, Jr., *Social Origins of Dictatorship and Democracy* (Boston:
   Beacon, 1966), 418.

9 Frederick Hayek, *The Road to Serfdom* (Chicago: University of Chicago Press,
   1972), 13.

10 Matthew Continetti, "Our Bankrupt Elite," *Washington Free Beacon*, March 15,
    2019, https://freebeacon.com/columns/our-bankrupt-elite/.

11 "Democrats: The Real Party of the Rich," *Investor's Business Daily*, April 2, 2014,
    https://www.investors.com/politics/editorials/democrat-political-donations
    -outstrip-republicans/; Rupert Durwall, "Behind the Green New Deal: An elite
    war on the working class," *New York Post*, March 26, 2019, https://nypost.com
    /2019/03/26/behind-the-green-new-deal-an-elite-war-on-the-working-class/.

12 Alexis de Tocqueville, *The Ancien Regime and the Revolution* (London:
    Penguin, 2008), 144.

13 John Hinderaker, "Exposing the Real Costs of 'Green' Energy," *Power Line*,
    March 12, 2019, https://www.powerlineblog.com/archives/2019/03/exposing
    -the-real-costs-of-green-energy.php.

14 Anastasia Lin, "The Cultural Revolution Comes to North America," *Wall Street
    Journal*, April 7, 2019, https://www.wsj.com/articles/the-cultural-revolution
    -comes-to-north-america-11554661623.

15 Rebecca Ratcliffe, "Record private jet flights into Davos as leaders arrive for
    climate talk," *Guardian*, January 22, 2019, https://www.theguardian.com/global
    -development/2019/jan/22/record-private-jet-flights-davos-leaders-climate
    -talk; Michael Shellenberger, "The Real Reason They Behave Hypocritically On
    Climate Change Is Because They Want To," *Forbes*, August 20, 2019, https://

www.forbes.com/sites/michaelshellenberger/2019/08/20/the-real-reason
-they-behave-hypocritically-on-climate-change-is-because-they-want-to
/#5e242363185a.

16 Eliza Relman, "Alexandria Ocasio-Cortez said billionaires shouldn't exist as
long as Americans live in abject poverty," *Business Insider*, January 22, 2019,
https://www.businessinsider.com/alexandria-ocasio-cortez-thinks-billionaires
-shouldnt-exist-2019-1; Walter E. Williams, "Our Planet Is Not Fragile," *Town
Hall*, March 6, 2019, https://townhall.com/columnists/walterewilliams/2019/03
/06/our-planet-is-not-fragile-n2542516.

17 Claire Malone, "The Young Left's Anti-Capitalist Manifesto," FiveThirtyEight,
January 22, 2019, https://fivethirtyeight.com/features/the-young-lefts-anti
-capitalist-manifesto/.

18 Keith A. Spencer and Nicole Karlis, "Silicon Valley, once a bastion of
libertarianism, sees a budding socialist movement," *Salon*, April 11, 2019,
https://www.salon.com/2019/04/11/silicon-valley-once-a-bastion-of
-libertarianism-sees-a-budding-socialist-movement/; Bryan Preston, "Is Gen
Z a Socialist Revolution in the Making?" *PJ Media*, August 22, 2019, https://
pjmedia.com/news-and-politics/is-gen-z-a-socialist-revolution-in-the-making;
Farhad Manjoo, "Why the Google Walkout Was a Watershed Moment in Tech,"
New York Times, November 7, 2018, https://www.nytimes.com/2018/11/07
/technology/google-walkout-watershed-tech.html.

19 Matthew Reitman, "A Guide to Doomsday Prep for the Super-Rich,"
InsideHook, February 2, 2017, https://www.insidehook.com/article/news
-opinion/guide-doomsday-prep-super-rich.

20 Claire Brockway and Carroll Doherty, "Growing share of Republicans say U.S.
risks losing its identity if it is too open to foreigners," Pew Research Center, July
17, 2019, https://www.pewresearch.org/fact-tank/2019/07/17/growing-share-of-
republicans-say-u-s-risks-losing-its-identity-if-it-is-too-open-to-foreigners/.

21 Edward Gibbon, *The History of the Decline and Fall of the Roman Empire* (New
York: Modern Library, 1931), vol. 1: 29–30, 33; Norman F. Cantor, *Medieval
History: The Life and Death of a Civilization* (New York: Macmillan, 1963), 25,
43.

22 Arthur Herman, *The Idea of Decline in Western History* (New York: Free Press,
1997), 66, 73; Clive Crook, "Why Citizenship Matters," Bloomberg, May 2, 2018,
https://www.bloomberg.com/view/articles/2018-05-02/citizenship-is-key-to
-liberal-democracy; Bradley A. Thayer and John M. Friend, "The dark side of
powerful China—its repression—can benefit US," *The Hill*, January 9, 2019,
https://thehill.com/opinion/international/424442-the-dark-side-of-powerful
-china-its-repression-can-benefit-us.

23 Carlos Echeverria-Estrada and Jeanne Batalova, "Chinese Immigrants in the
United States," Migration Policy Institute, January 15, 2020, https://www
.migrationpolicy.org/article/chinese-immigrants-united-states; Statistics
Canada, "Immigration and Ethnocultural Diversity in Canada," July 25, 2018,
https://www12.statcan.gc.ca/nhs-enm/2011/as-sa/99-010-x/99-010-x2011001-
eng.cfmary_Departments/Parliamentary_Library/pubs/rp/rp1819/Quick
_Guides/PopulationStatistics.

24 Robert D. Kaplan, "Was Democracy Just a Moment?" *Atlantic*, December

1997, https://www.theatlantic.com/magazine/archive/1997/12/was-democracy-just-a-moment/306022/.

25 Joseph A. Tainter, *The Collapse of Complex Societies* (Cambridge: Cambridge University Press, 1988), 1.

26 Gibbon, *The History of the Decline and Fall of the Roman Empire*, vol. 2: 92.

27 Samuel P. Huntington, *The Clash of Civilizations and the Remaking of World Order* (New York: Simon & Schuster, 2011), 305.

28 James Taranto, "The Politicization of Motherhood," *Wall Street Journal*, October 27, 2017, https://www.wsj.com/articles/the-politicization-of-motherhood-1509144044; Chad Day, "Americans Have Shifted Dramatically on What Values Matter Most," *Wall Street Journal*, August 25, 2019, https://www.wsj.com/articles/americans-have-shifted-dramatically-on-what-values-matter-most-11566738001.

29 David P. Goldman, "France Has Neither Nationalism nor Patriotism," *PJ Media*, November 11, 2018, https://pjmedia.com/spengler/france-has-neither-nationalism-nor-patriotism/; Tyler O' Neil, "German Headmaster Tells Christian Girl to Wear a Hijab to Avoid Beatings From Muslim Classmates," *PJ Media*, April 2, 2018, https://pjmedia.com/trending/german-headmaster-tells-christian-girl-to-wear-a-hijab-to-avoid-beatings-from-muslim-classmates/; Laura Backes et al., "Religious Symbols Take Center Stage," *Spiegel*, March 5, 2018, http://www.spiegel.de/international/germany/religious-symbols-at-heart-of-german-search-for-identity-a-1205572.html; Lee Roden, "Why Sweden doesn't keep stats on ethnicity and crime," *The Local*, May 8, 2018, https://www.thelocal.se/20180508/why-sweden-doesnt-keep-stats-on-ethnic-background-and-crime.

30 The Paris Statement, "A Europe We Can Believe In," October 7, 2017, https://thetrueeurope.eu/.

31 "Ben Franklin Who?" *Wall Street Journal*, October 3, 2018, https://www.wsj.com/articles/ben-franklin-who-1538608727; Colleen Flaherty, "The Vanishing History Major," *Inside Higher Ed*, November 27, 2018, https://www.insidehighered.com/news/2018/11/27/new-analysis-history-major-data-says-field-new-low-can-it-be-saved.

32 Henri Pirenne, *Mohammed and Charlemagne* (Cleveland: Meridian, 1957), 118; Roderick Seidenberg, *Post-historic Man: An Inquiry* (New York: Viking, 1974), 179.

33 Glenn Harlan Reynolds, "Robert Zubrin makes 'The Case for Space,'" *USA Today*, May 7, 2019, https://www.usatoday.com/story/opinion/2019/05/07/spacex-blue-origin-virgin-galactic-robert-zubrin-case-space-column/1119446001/.

34 David Pilling, *Bending Adversity: Japan and the Art of Survival* (New York: Penguin, 2014), 119, 177–79; Karel van Wolferen, *The Enigma of Japanese Power: People and Politics in a Stateless Nation* (New York: Knopf, 1989), 2–3.

35 Andy Kessler, "Zuckerberg's Opiate for the Masses," *Wall Street Journal*, June 18, 2017, https://www.wsj.com/articles/zuckerbergs-opiate-for-the-masses-1497821885.

36 Catherine Clifford, "About half of Americans support giving residents up

to $2000 a month when robots take their jobs," CNBC, December 19, 2016, https://www.cnbc.com/2016/12/19/about-half-of-americans-support-giving-residents-up-to-2000-a-month-when-robots-take-our-jobs.html.

37   Patrick Hoare, "European Social Survey (ESS) reveal findings about attitudes toward Universal Basic Income across Europe," Basic Income, January 20, 2018, https://basicincome.org/news/2018/01/europe-european-social-survey-ess-reveal-findings-attitudes-toward-universal-basic-income-across-europe/; Andrew Russell, "What Do Canadians think of basic income? It will reduce poverty but could raise taxes," *Global News*, June 7, 2017, https://globalnews.ca/news/3509763/what-do-canadians-think-of-basic-income-it-will-reduce-poverty-but-could-raise-taxes/.

38   Immanuel Wallerstein, *The Modern World System: Capitalist Agriculture and the Origins of the European World Economy in the 16th Century* (New York: Academic Press, 1974), 357.

INDEX